THE HAPPY DUST GANG

Dec '06

Dear Jonathan

Merry Christmas baby!

All my love
June
xxxx

David Leslie has worked for the *News of the World* since 1970. Since then, he has covered scores of major stories, including the tragedies of Zeebrugge, Piper Alpha, Lockerbie and Dunblane. He has been based in Glasgow since 1994, concentrating on crime and major investigations. He is also the author of *Crimelord: The Licensee*, about the elusive multimillionaire gangster Tam McGraw.

THE HAPPY DUST GANG

How Sex, Scandal and Deceit Founded a Drugs Empire

David Leslie

MAINSTREAM
PUBLISHING
EDINBURGH AND LONDON

First published in Great Britain in 2006 by
MAINSTREAM PUBLISHING COMPANY (EDINBURGH) LTD
7 Albany Street
Edinburgh EH1 3UG

ISBN 1 84596 182 X

Pictures reproduced by courtesy of the *News of the World*
unless stated otherwise

A catalogue record for this book is available
from the British Library

Typeset in Stone and Bookseller

Printed in Great Britain by
William Clowes Ltd, Beccles, Suffolk

ACKNOWLEDGEMENTS

Over morning tea at the delightful Mosspark Café in Glasgow, a valued friend asked, 'Why don't you write about the Happy Dust Gang?' In the past, I had heard the intriguing name but knew nothing more. My natural curiosity, however, made it a project impossible to ignore.

Researching the story has taken me to many parts of Scotland, to England, Ireland, Belgium, France, Holland and Spain. I have been truly lucky in making many new friends who have willingly given time and invaluable help with generosity and kindness. I can repay them only by respecting their private and genuine reasons for preferring anonymity. In addition to them, I wish to thank my colleagues at the *News of the World* – George Wright, Gary Jamieson and Kenny MacDonald; Deborah Warner, my patient and understanding editor at Mainstream; and Kim and Ove van Michels. While helping with work on this book, my fellow investigator, David Robb, died suddenly. As all who knew David will affirm, like the man himself, his advice, humour and friendship are irreplaceable.

CONTENTS

PROLOGUE

THE PARACHUTIST

'Do Ya Think I'm Sexy?' asked the man for whom a million women would longingly have turned down their bedsheets. The answer was, of course, 'Yes', although the owner of the gravelly voice posing the question was not around to hear it. He was in Las Vegas, or was it Rome or New York?

And this was Glasgow. Party time in Glasgow. Admittedly, in one of the better-off suburbs of the city that knew Rod Stewart so well, where his talent was envied and his singing admired. But had Rockin' Rod gatecrashed the gathering that night, his arrival would have been only a relative distraction compared with the main event: a visit from another man, one who had travelled far, keeping his movements and the names of his fellow journeymen secret. His gift would be a different form of music to the ears of the revellers: a new adrenalin called happy dust.

This was March 1980, and those who lived in Glasgow at the time did not know it but their city was on the verge of change. Young men and women were becoming more particular; they were more knowledgeable in the ways of the world, largely thanks to a new breed of television show centring on the high lives of the rich and famous. Soaps like *Dallas*, first broadcast two years previously, allowed ordinary people to imagine a lifestyle way beyond their reach. The Ewing family soon became a talking point in hairdressers' salons, doctors' surgeries and over back-garden fences. Provanmill, the home of Glasgow gangland figure Arthur 'The Godfather' Thompson would even be tagged 'Southfork' because it was said to bear a vague resemblance to the Ewings' home. The city where once thrills came from the rule of the razor and the boot of the mob now had a new panacea for monotony.

Those of the in-crowd wealthy enough to travel would boast of having visited Studio 54, the famed New York City nightspot, where celebrities, including Michael Jackson, Elton John, Cher, Calvin Klein and Liza Minnelli, would be happy to join fans in the queue for entry. In February that year, it had hosted one of the greatest parties ever seen in the city. Diana Ross, Andy Warhol and Richard Gere were among the guests. The bash was a farewell to its founders, Ian Schrager and Steve Rubell, before they were hauled off to jail for tax evasion.

Glasgow clubs would enviously try to emulate the free and easy format in which drugs featured as part of the entertainment in Studio 54 by turning a blind eye to this highly illicit activity, while keeping the other eye open for prowling police.

The party set were realising they had enough funds to afford to be more discerning. While the vast majority of the young and affluent used hash occasionally, moderately and quietly, only a very small minority sought in the drug more than a gentle lapse into serenity; they wanted a higher level of bliss, a means of escaping into fantasy. They had heard of cocaine, but learning of its existence was one thing and actually being able to experience it something entirely different. But a handful knew how. They had the money with which to buy it and, more importantly, the contacts that could provide it. Their circle was tiny, but influential. They were privy to a new form of entertainment available to those with sufficient money to buy into it: the world of hard drugs.

As partygoers sat about with drinks in hand, danced or simply listened to music, the air was filled not just with smoke but with anticipation. Because the little bags of powder the traveller would bring were the key to opening a Pandora's box packed with frills, excitement and, most of all, sex. At a party with booze, a girl might over-imbibe and briefly tease before falling over; at a party where cocaine was on the menu, it was another matter entirely: literally anything might happen. And invariably it did. They always had a sexual theme. Invitations to these gatherings were highly prized, the hosts admired and revered, guests who could bring along a line or two of snow much welcomed.

A new way of life was about to be born, although for many it would be a new way of death. Everyone had his or her own idea of pleasure – alcohol, hash and the thrill of fairly predictable textbook sex – but old habits were about to die. The Happy Dust Gang would see to that.

On the newly bought audio system playing a compilation of his hits, Rod had reached the end of a track and begun another, not knowing how apt it was for the occasion. 'Tonight's the Night' sailed out from the giant speakers. To some, the words brought a knowing smile. Tonight was the night. The night when fantasy came to supper. Until it did, this party might have been any other.

Tension was building, watches were being checked, telephone calls made and answered. No one had cocaine. It was difficult to get and expensive. Even a police raid and the most thorough search would have turned up not a grain.

Once more, the telephone rang. The visitor was on his way. Those in the know had a verse, a code akin to the deepest secrets of Freemasonry:

Everybody wants a share
of happy dust, but few dare
to buy, bring, sell or deal
in our new friend Charlie, even steal.
We're OK, we have a plan,
The Parachutist is our man.

The visitor was about to touch down.

1

CHARLIE

Some knew it as snow. Others tagged it white or Percy. Then there were those who whispered of Charlie, toot, coke. No-nonsense police simply called it what it was: cocaine.

Five thousand years ago, indigenous South Americans discovered that by chewing leaves from the Erythroxylon coca plant, and sniffing or sucking while they did so, not only did they feel happier but the leaves also kept their hunger at bay. That was good news when food was scarce and obtaining the raw materials for a meal could sometimes be a risky business. Then came the Peruvian Inca kings. They decreed that only royalty could enjoy the leaves, theorising that because the properties were so stimulating they must have come from the gods. Spanish treasure seekers initially made it off-limits to slave labourers but backtracked when they discovered how much the workforce relied on it. And the Catholic missionary priests who grew the Erythroxylon shrub and dished out its leaves three or four times a day to workers also quickly realised its benefits.

It was inevitable that, having such an impact in South America, the plant would at some stage make its way to Europe, along with other goodies found in the New World by the conquistadors. So, in the holds of treasure galleons, next to potatoes, pineapples, turkeys, sunflowers, maize and chocolate, the leaves made the tortuous 5,000-odd-mile journey back to Spain.

The plant had little influence in Europe until, in the late 1860s, scientists isolated its main ingredient: cocaine alkaloid. Its value as an anaesthetic was soon realised, as was the fact that it had many other properties. Users discovered that by sniffing or snorting cocaine, they could stay awake longer and feel livelier; it improved their concentration and work performance, allowing them to carry on working for longer, an attribute especially useful for writers or artists desperate to keep going when they hit a rich seam of inspiration; they felt happier, almost euphoric at times; and took on a sense of being masterful, confident and in control.

Over the years, cocaine has had many famous advocates. Robert Louis Stevenson was an Edinburgh schoolboy when the alkaloid was first separated, but by the time he was an adult he had become an occasional user. It was claimed he even wrote *The Strange Case of Dr Jekyll and Mr Hyde* while on a week-long cocaine trip. His wife, Fanny, was said to have admitted to friends, 'That an invalid in my husband's condition should have been able to perform the manual labour alone of putting 60,000 words on paper in six days seems almost incredible.'

Detective Sherlock Holmes, created by Sir Arthur Conan Doyle, would nowadays be more likely to be at the forefront of a dramatic investigation into the activities of a major international narcotics smuggling gang. However, in *The Sign of Four*, Holmes is seen by his great friend Dr Watson injecting himself:

> Three times a day for many months I had witnessed this performance, but custom had not reconciled my mind to it. On the contrary, from day to day I had become more irritable at the sight, and my

conscience swelled nightly within me at the thought that I had lacked the courage to protest. Again and again I had registered a vow that I should deliver my soul upon the subject; but there was that in the cool, nonchalant air of my companion which made him the last man with whom one would care to take anything approaching to a liberty . . .

Yet upon that afternoon, whether it was the Beaune which I had taken with my lunch or the additional exasperation produced by the extreme deliberation of his manner, I suddenly felt that I could hold out no longer.

'Which is it to-day,' I asked, 'morphine or cocaine?'

He raised his eyes languidly from the old black-letter volume which he had opened.

'It is cocaine,' he said, 'a seven-per-cent solution. Would you care to try it?'

At one point in history, coca leaves were openly moved about and cocaine itself was regarded as something halfway between a harmless plaything of the eccentric and a balm for illness. In 1886, Coca-Cola appeared for the first time, containing cocaine-laced syrup and caffeine. But, of course, there were drawbacks to the drug and, 15 years later, the cocaine element was removed.

Being careless and overdoing it could lead to confusion, irritability and the feeling that people close by were a potential physical danger. Heart and pulse rates went up. Over-indulgence could harm eyesight. And coming off cocaine frequently resulted in dizziness, fatigue, boredom and depression. To counter these unpleasant side effects, the user would take even more of the drug.

But there was one more side effect of the chemical that made the risks and the disadvantages worth it: it produced remarkable changes in the sex drive as a result of enhancing the imagination and encouraging the most outrageous fantasies. For women, it encouraged a lowering of defences and a craving for sex bordering on lust.

In merely sampling cocaine, the user was quickly led towards becoming instantly hooked on the drug, wanting everyone else to share the pleasure it brought and the great visions it created. The individual underwent a sense not just of having invented the wheel but also of needing everyone else to know that fact. Then regular users would undergo a bizarre character metamorphosis in which they would warn friends of its perils and seek to prevent them too becoming hooked. Addicts realised too late they had entered the carriages of a train taking them on a one-way journey to hell. The great doctor Sigmund Freud used patients' dreams to get to the root of their worries – he also used cocaine, reckoning it was a first-rate antidepressant. It was claimed he had snorted enough white powder to 'kill a horse'. Freud was convinced cocaine could cure a whole range of problems and encouraged his close family and friends to experiment. He also advocated it for its 'stimulative effect on the genitalia'.

Stephen King, whose work includes *Rita Hayworth and the Shawshank Redemption* and *The Green Mile*, was addicted to Charlie between 1979 and 1987, calling it his 'on switch'. He says it saved him from an addiction to drink that would have led to an early grave. It was while the horror writer was admitting his addiction that the Parachutist descended into Glasgow. For both, their involvement with cocaine meant taking risks.

By the beginning of the twentieth century, governments had realised the glamour of cocaine hid sinister consequences. Hundreds of people were dying worldwide each year through overdoses, while many more were being admitted to hospitals with brutal nose damage caused by snorting. Something needed to be done to check the spread and proliferation of cocaine, most of it produced in South America. And so gradually it was outlawed worldwide.

* * *

His customers called him the Parachutist because the ecstasy his bounty brought might have been made in heaven and dropped from the skies. Those deeply opposed to drugs – and there were plenty of them – would have said that what he brought was more likely to have been manufactured in hell. But wherever it came from, this was no manna, no free gift. It had to be bought and the asking price reflected the risks.

In the late '70s, the war on drugs was in its early stages and smuggling was mainly confined to hashish. It was relatively easy to get hold of at a price within the range of most wage earners. Harder drugs were expensive to buy and, as a result, their use was largely limited to the wealthy few who could afford to frivolously splash out, principally up-and-coming businessmen or a group of dealers who were making so much money from sales of hash they could afford to indulge and saw the logical next step as experimenting with cocaine. But soon governments realised they had a major problem. Police and Customs officers did not have the expertise, guile or resources of their counterparts in the twenty-first century.

Eighty per cent of the cocaine circulated in Europe came from Colombia, a country run by a series of cartels, each controlling the region in which it operated. They usually sailed the drug across the Atlantic hidden among cargoes in merchant and container ships, which would be met off the Iberian Peninsula by smaller boats that would land the smuggled consignment along the coastline of Galicia in north-west Spain or, more likely, in Portugal. From there, it would be driven overland to every country in Europe. Drug smuggling in general was becoming an art form. Smugglers used incredible ingenuity and always seemed to be one step ahead of any new measure the official gamekeepers could introduce.

The principal deterrent in the drug war was the dishing out of horrific jail sentences. But before a smuggler could be caged, he or she first had to be caught. Of course, it was no fun driving an ageing vehicle with the seat padding ripped out and replaced with stinking brown hash for up to 2,000 miles. But the rewards were high for anyone getting a load to its destination and supply could never match demand.

At every point of exchange, there were risks: the chance of being stopped by a police patrol and the discovery of the drugs in transit. Every mile brought its dangers – and there were usually more miles between the smugglers and their customers in Scotland than most. Couriers seeking higher wages could point to a series of disasters for others in their trade who had fallen foul of the law along the way.

And as every minute of every day ticked by, somewhere in the world an informer was saving his own skin by grassing the activities of fellow smugglers to sympathetic undercover detectives. That somewhere could be Scotland. No one knew for sure that theirs would not be the next collar to be felt or shoulder tapped by the men in soft shoes who policed the United Kingdom's drug routes. Even Paul McCartney had found himself in trouble back in 1972 when a local bobby stumbled on the greenhouse at his Mull farmhouse and found 12 marijuana plants growing inside. The Beatles superstar was fined £100.

So too had the man acknowledged as the world's greatest drug smuggler, former Oxford University graduate Howard Marks, come an expensive cropper because of a Scottish venture that went wrong. During New Year 1978, 15 tons of high-quality Colombian cannabis with a potential value of £20 million arrived in British waters in the oceangoing tug *Karob*. The drugs were landed on the island of Kerrera off Oban on the west coast of Scotland. But Customs investigators who had been tipped off were monitoring the movements of the smugglers, who panicked after overhearing by chance a radio message confirming they were under surveillance. They chucked the Kerrera batch into the sea with the result that 40 bales washed up on Mull, others landing at a spot known as Grass Point.

Marks, who had built up a bank of 43 aliases including 'Donald Nice', 'Albie Lane' and 'John Hughes' to run his dope-dealing empire, was arrested and, although making a mockery of any suggestion he was involved in the cannabis ring, would later be jailed at the Old Bailey for having false passports. In 1988, he received 25 years for racketeering in the United States. The warning was that nobody, whether the most adept or the most celebrated, was safe from the clutches of the catchers.

If these were the perils of hash, it was no wonder, then, that a harder, stronger drug such as Charlie was scarce. In Scotland at that time, it was almost unheard of and certainly very few could honestly boast of having experienced it. There were rumours of a family in the Partick area of Glasgow having managed to hide cocaine in a toy elephant brought back from a package holiday in Marbella, but they had paid £80 a gramme. Two young men from the East End of the city had also managed to conceal a small amount of cocaine amongst a consignment of hashish they had driven from southern Spain. They had been well paid by a group specialising in hash distribution to drive a packed car across Europe to Scotland. When their employer discovered their attempt at freelance work, he went ballistic, pointing out that if it became known hard drugs were about to invade Scotland security checks at border and ferry crossing points would be instantly stepped up, increasing the likelihood of capture.

So, cocaine was hard to come by and that meant a frustrating time for the rich young set who wanted to indulge, knowing the sexual rewards their pastime would bring and aware that having the ability to offer a line would elevate them to near-star status. They could set themselves apart from most of the other wannabe swing set in that they had money, and lots of it, but nothing on which to spend it. It was the equivalent of being stranded alone on a desert island and discovering a chest packed with treasure.

That is, until the Parachutist dropped in.

2

THE HAPPY DUST GANG

Charlie Parker's in Glasgow's Royal Exchange Square was the place to be and the spot at which to be seen. At some stage, anyone and everyone wanting to make an impression headed there filled with hopes of fun and laughs. It had the much-envied reputation as the city's trendiest watering hole. Young men eager to show off their wealth and score with a date did so at Charlie Parker's. Young women in low-cut tops and miniskirts anxious to please and attract by showing off breasts and long legs would head there in twos and threes, agreeing that in the event of a pull it was every girl for herself.

Opened in 1976 by up-and-coming restaurateur Ken McCulloch, Charlie Parker's gave Glasgow nightlife something it had never seen before: class. McCulloch would admit, 'Opening it was a gamble. At that time, it was virtually unheard of to even get ice with a drink. Publicans thought I was mad, but the public loved it.' The decor was, for that time, nothing short of sensational: avant-garde, art deco; full of black-and-white designs and big potted plants. Beer-swilling yobs out for a rowdy night would see the outside of the front door and nothing else because it was one of the first clubs in Glasgow to hire bouncers, big men in suits who vetted would-be entrants. It was their decision as to who was in and who was out. Their interest was in behaviour and dress. Look as if you drank beer by the bucket and it was 'Sorry, sir.' Look as though your clothing needed a dry-clean and it was a no go. Give the impression you might be short of a bob and you would be politely advised to try elsewhere. Be ugly, overweight, spotty or have your shoelaces loose and you would be on your bike. Few at that time believed it necessary to search guests. Hardly anyone was bothered about an occasional piece of hash hidden in a handbag or pocket. And as for anything stronger, well, it was so scarce the odds against finding something were astronomical. Doormen saw their job as reinforcing the unwritten code that Charlie Parker's was for slick, well-groomed people, the kind who wanted to show themselves as well-heeled and well-travelled by asking for exotic cocktails.

Lawyers, businessmen, footballers, anyone who mattered at sometime or other would be seen in Charlie Parker's. It was a meeting place for the young gods. There were golden girls with big rings hanging from their ears on the trail of riches, young uptown women wearing fur coats and no knickers. It was luxurious but to some clientele it was steeped in a cold, clinical atmosphere where customers watched one another fearful of being thought of as falling behind in their dress sense or not keeping up with the latest trend.

No one wanted to be left out of a secret. Anyone who thought of him or herself as beautiful headed for Charlie Parker's to stand in the aura of attraction. It was where good-looking people went to show off and to seek kicks. Charlie Parker's was for the beautiful people. People like an up-and-coming model named Carol Smillie, educated at the city's posh Hutchesons' Grammar School and the Glasgow School of Art. Or the beautiful, desired girls who stared out from the sides of cans of Tennent's lager. Even the waiters and waitresses had to be beautiful. One was a struggling young reporter named Lorraine Kelly from East Kilbride. She took a pay cut to work for the BBC and made up the difference by working at Charlie Parker's hoping for generous tips. 'I was probably the worst waitress in the world but had to stick it out. We wore shorts and high heels with a tight top tucked in, but I was always too fat and I used to wear my top hanging out so it was longer than my shorts.' Working there did no harm to lovely Lorraine; it taught her how to communicate with even the most awkward customers and she eventually moved into television journalism to become a celebrity in her own right.

Of course, there were other spots such as the Granary, Paul Joseph's Pzazz, the Warehouse, Douglas Timmins' Parallel Bars bistro. But Charlie Parker's was the favourite. To try to narrow the handicap, some of the rivals had a reputation for occasionally not quite playing the game. At one Glasgow nightspot, the owner was reputed to sometimes resort to entertaining female guests into whose suspender belts he would be hoping to entwine his fingers later by turning up at their table with a silver tray, glasses and an opened bottle of expensive Moët & Chandon champagne. It would not take an expert to realise the champers tasted remarkably like cheap Asti Spumante, but the girls were never heard to complain. In addition, the art of decanting was one practised in many drinking holes in Glasgow and elsewhere.

Visitors from London used to the sophistication of the Wellington Club, Chinawhite and L'Equipe felt at home in Charlie Parker's. And if it made history by offering ice, it was about to achieve infamy as the spot where snow first fell in Scotland.

Old Year 1979 was being celebrated in style at Charlie Parker's. It was packed, and each time a customer picked up a drink he or she would take a sly glance at their watch face as the hour of the bells approached. Familiar faces littered the tables and stools, but one person stood out: Brian Doran. Walking into any bar or nightclub in Glasgow at that time and seeing Doran was the modern-day equivalent of bumping into David Beckham. Doran might not have had his looks, or the international celebrity status of the most glorified footballer of his era, but in the pond that was Glasgow he was the biggest fish by far. Some would say the only fish.

Bespectacled, short and with receding hair, Doran had a charm and charisma that others envied. One of his contemporaries bemoaned, 'No one could understand how Brian nipped so many birds. Some gorgeous bird would be standing next to him, leaning all over him, shoving her tits in his ear and wiggling her bum against him and Brian wouldn't twitch an eyelash. It was as if it was expected. He would be like some Egyptian pharaoh surrounded by a bevy of slave girls every one desperate for his eyes to fall on them, for him to speak to them and to no one else. At that time, I was young, good looking, worked out and had a good body, and it was easy to pull a bird. But the birds I pulled weren't in the class of those that hung around Brian. Mine might be a shop girl or a pal's sister, a real looker, but the bird standing next to Brian with her arm around his neck would be a Miss Scotland finalist or a model who had made it onto the shortlist for the Tennent's cans. I was ten times better looking than him, but his birds were the ones you knew you'd never get near, at least while he was around.

'The trouble for everybody else was that it wasn't enough to be just good looking. You had to have a good motor, a good flat, lots of money in your pocket, a bit of clout and a wee bit of power. And the power thing kind of came first in the list of necessities. It meant you would never wait in queues anywhere. When you got near Charlie Parker's, the doormen would wave you forward past everybody else. In a restaurant, you were guaranteed the best table. They made a movie in 1990 called *Goodfellas* in which Ray Liotta played a guy who seemed to know everybody. He walked in while others waited. He knew all the short cuts and the side doors and everybody wanted him in their club. That was Brian. Everybody wanted to know him or to be able to go around saying they knew him. And everybody wanted to make sure Brian got what he wanted because if he did, then they would get a share. He handed out tips like confetti. Sharon Stone did it in *Casino*, tipped everybody from the head waiter to the guy who looked after her car. One of the scriptwriters must have visited Glasgow because that's what Brian Doran was doing 15 years earlier. When Brian went to Charlie Parker's, he didn't have to hang about waiting in a queue. Others did, but not him. It might be wet, but he didn't get wet. It might be cold, but he wouldn't get cold. While the others were waiting in the wet and cold, he was inside having fun.'

Doran had style and flair and an incredible gift for making money. Had he been an old-fashioned pirate, he would have been able to pick out a helpless treasure ship in the blackest of nights in the widest of oceans. He lived with his wife, Mary, and their six children in a huge mansion on Terregles Avenue in the Pollokshields area of the city. The house was worth £100,000 in 1980, an enormous sum then. It boasted four spacious reception rooms, five bedrooms, a billiards room and three bathrooms, and had a sought-after view overlooking Maxwell Park. In the grounds stood a double garage and a huge greenhouse, while on the drive up to the front entrance you were guided by lanterns. Strangers who had lost Brian's number and were searching for the house would be told, 'Just look for the Rolls-Royce or the Ferrari parked in the driveway.'

Brian was managing director of Caledonian Holiday Management Limited but best known for running the Glasgow office of Blue Sky Travel, which was registered in East Grinstead, Sussex. At a time when the package-holiday market was taking off, Doran had made sure he was at the heart of the lucrative boom. At Blue Sky, the tens of thousands of Scots who were finding themselves able, for the first time, to afford holidays abroad were guaranteed a good deal. Doran was a knowledgeable and helpful travel agent, and invariably his customers came back, after soaking up the sun in mainland Spain or Majorca, as brown as berries to start work again in factories and shipyards.

A one-time hairdresser, he had studied hard while a young man and graduated as a modern languages teacher. He spoke Spanish fluently, a skill that would be a massive asset when he chose a change of career.

A rival travel agent said of him, 'Brian was extrovert and larger than life. He looked like a man who had travelled the world. And when customers asked him for advice – probably nervous because they were thinking of going abroad for the first time in their lives – you could see them visibly relaxing, totally confident in everything Brian was telling them. He came across as a very nice, intelligent chap and an extremely good salesman. Of course, there were plenty in the trade, especially in Glasgow, who gossiped about his lifestyle and speculated as to how Brian could afford such a swish house and flash cars. But then he was running a very busy agency and the commissions would have been pouring in.'

An indication of his wealth was his ability to enjoy his hobby of football. Unlike most Glaswegians, it was not restricted to a weekly visit to a ground to watch the local team. Brian liked to participate and even his rivals would concede he was a pretty useful performer. Again, nothing especially unusual in that: over the decades, Glasgow has produced many of the world's great players. But his idea of playing football was a step above a kickabout on a council park. As a one-time teammate revealed, 'Brian was a footballing fanatic. He regularly arranged five-a-side games but not between any Tom, Dick and Harry. He ran his own team and the games were between ex-professional footballers. In the grounds of his home, he had his own private pitch, complete with floodlights, and just loved to play. He would buy brand new strips for his team and guys would go along there for a game knowing they would be getting free drinks, all the drinks they could handle, and sometimes free holidays into the bargain. But they were expected to remember where they were. Brian kicked one of the players out of the honey pot because he had gone in with a particularly tough tackle. Getting the red card could be expensive.

'He even took one of his teams out to Majorca for an all-expenses-paid break, staying in one of the hotels into which Blue Sky regularly booked a lot of holidaymakers. It meant the management there were very keen to make sure Brian's wishes were met. His party didn't just comprise himself and a few players; he brought a group of close buddies over as well, one of them a close friend of Alex Ferguson's. These were men who had largely come up the hard way, who had worked hard and taken chances but who now had money and knew how to enjoy it. When they entertained, they gave guests the best and expected the same in return. And Brian made sure they got just that. They were all big spenders bringing the sort of business any hotel would be glad to get. He spoke Spanish fluently which contributed to the very good relationship he had with the hotel owners and so when Brian suggested they get a little football team together for a challenge match against his party, they were more than happy to go along with that. The hotel, not taking the idea tremendously seriously, naturally assumed these were semi-out-of-condition guys over for a kickabout and produced a side made up of waiters, chefs and barmen. They had no idea what they were up against: men who had made their living from playing the game and who knew that Brian expected them to give their best. They did just that, winning something like 8–1 or 9–0. That would leave Brian feeling on top of the world because the reason he had done so well in business was by setting out to be a winner. And that philosophy applied to play as well as work.

'For the guests too, it was great because Brian looked on

them as his personal friends and he would foot the entire bill. "How are you doing, boys? You enjoying your holiday?" he would ask, genuinely concerned that everybody was having a top-class time. We were enjoying it all the more because it was the same hotel in which some air hostesses were staying and we made sure they joined in the fun.

'There were parties galore, courtesy of Brian, who was happy to pick up the tab. Attached to the hotel was a big, comfortable and very expensive restaurant, yet Brian never blinked an eyelid when we asked if we could bring our own "guests" along. "Of course," he told us. "You hit lucky with the air crew? Well, good luck. Make the most of it. Stick everything on the bill and make sure you have a good time. That's what we're here for. Everything is on me." Thanks to his kindness and generosity, we lived like playboys. Goodness knows how much it cost.'

The media would later claim Doran was tagged by associates as 'the Professor' because of his intellectual background. In fact, he was known as 'Whacko', the name coming from a popular black-and-white BBC television series screened in the late 1950s, starring the gruff, blustering comedian Jimmy Edwards as the cane-wielding headmaster of Chiselbury School.

One of Whacko's closest friends – they had been pals since their schooldays – was another successful businessman, Andrew 'Andy' Tait, who ran The Pantry, a thriving bakery on Byres Road in Glasgow. Big Andy was a hard worker who thought nothing of doing a 14- or 16-hour day. After work, he might even head off to one of Glasgow's exclusive nightspots in search of his buddy. Married with three children, he was one of the few in the city at the time who could afford to drive a prestigious BMW, a fact that would have significance later. He lived in a big stone-built £70,000 house in Cathcart. Some who knew Andy frowned on his occasional ventures into the high life but to the majority of his many customers, he was a respectable baker devoted to his family.

On the face of it, like many successful double acts, Brian and Andy appeared to have little in common. Doran was flash, brash, witty and sharp, while Andy was slower and sometimes naive. Their friendship was genuine. But much of the respect shown to Big Andy came from the fact that he was such a close confidant of Brian Doran. Like others, he benefited from Whacko's reputation, but the baker also envied his friend his renown as a womanising playboy and secretly harboured an ambition to become a Mr Big. He would get his way.

The circle of Doran's friends was wide and varied, though they might not exactly have come from all walks of life because keeping up with his dazzling social merry-go-round needed money, real money, not the sort earned by your average shipyard worker or labourer. And that was the thread spinning Brian and Andy together: what they did have in common was an ability to be big earners. On the periphery were the Bartletts, Alan and his brother Ronnie, seven years his junior. They had been born into wealth. The family ran an expanding and hugely successful fruit and vegetable business based in Airdrie in Lanarkshire.

No one can recall the Bartletts being among the celebrants in Charlie Parker's that night on 31 December 1979. Ronnie was just 16 years old then, much too young to be allowed in, and Alan was spending the evening with his family. But around 20 young people were in the Doran party, drinking, kissing and holding hands. Something, however, was missing. They had been hoping for a highly illegal New Year gift but the messenger had failed to materialise. He was to have brought cocaine, rarely seen in the city but highly prized. Only, before setting out from Spain, he had panicked after hearing of a German holidaymaker stopped at Málaga airport, a miserable five grammes hidden in a tin of pipe tobacco. He was now facing ten grim years of heat, stench, bad food and rampant homosexuals in the local jail. The Glaswegian had acted as a drug courier – a mule – in the past but reckoned he was nearing the end of his lucky run and that it was time to play safe. That meant letting down men who he knew relied on him and who would pay him enough to cover the cost of his holiday. The sickly prison meals and heat he could handle, but the constant terror of attacks by homosexuals scared him off.

Shortly after 10 p.m., the hour when the mule would have appeared, two men walked quietly into Charlie Parker's and found a place next to the Doran group. The newcomers were Robert Bruce, a dark-haired, likeable, happy-go-lucky young man who worked in the family butchering business, and his close friend, 23-year-old George Duncan, the older by a year, tall, well tanned and very evidently a man who took pride in his body and appearance. Duncan's friends had once been convinced he was marked out for a career as a professional footballer. Among his buddies was Thomas Sim. They had been friends as far back as they could remember, sharing the same boyhood fantasies, playing the same games and sitting together through tedious classes at Glasgow's Govan high school. Teachers would annually report to their parents that the boys had potential, but their minds seemed too far away from textbooks and homework, and that each needed to 'apply himself'. Thomas and George left clutching a handful of O level certificates. For a time, they worked in local shipyards, collecting a relatively comfortable £17 a week on a Friday. Years earlier, those same yards had inspired a wealth of fun for an apprentice welder named Billy Connolly, who had used his experiences to make audiences around the world laugh and at the same time build himself a fortune. Thomas and, in particular, George failed to see the funny side. George was fed up with finding himself virtually penniless on a Monday morning as a result of spending the weekend enjoying himself, then waiting until pay day on Friday, and after three years decided enough was enough. They watched the giant ships they'd helped build slide down slipways and head to exotic parts of the world and the pair wanted to discover for themselves what lay beyond the horizon. Warmth, they reckoned for certain. Therefore they handed in their notices and headed to the Spanish resort of Benidorm. They could have taken on building work, but the sight of scantily clad girls parading along beaches or shaking their bums and breasts to an Elton John duet with Kiki Dee, or a Dr Hook number or to the apparently invincible Sylvia as she belted out 'Y Viva España' convinced them they ought to be nearer to the action. As a result, they took on jobs distributing flyers advertising discotheques and clubs, hardly an onerous task, which had many advantages because it provided not only pay but also free entry to the same nightspots and the chance to chat up potential customers.

The pair stuck it out in Spain for almost three years but then decided it was time to move on. They had seen for themselves the thriving drug-smuggling trades and become aware of the risks. But it taught them a crucial lesson, one absolutely essential to the efficient smuggler: how to spot a dealer. It was knowledge they would not have long to wait before bringing into use. Meanwhile young, footloose and free, they headed for that most liberal of all European countries – Holland – where they were soon working as roof tilers and heading towards marrying Dutch girls. In the land made famous by windmills, Thomas found himself sucked into a flourishing drugs culture – and among those of his own age who enthused about the pleasures of hashish and cocaine in particular. Drugs, however, were a habit that held no virtues for George then, whose interest was in keeping fit.

Throughout their travels, Thomas and George had regularly returned to Glasgow for brief holidays or special events, such as an Old Firm game or New Year celebration. They had left as teenagers almost awed by the young businessmen who floated about the city in expensive cars. In Charlie Parker's that night George found it impossible not to compare the people he saw around him to those he had known when he lived in Glasgow. As a younger man, he had looked up to them. Now, sharing their company and joining their conversations, he noticed the conversation seemed obsessed with drugs – cocaine in particular. He heard partygoers grumbling because a supplier hadn't turned up and they had nothing. He realised these were the people for whom the friends he knew in Spain had been risking their necks by taking kit back. It had always seemed as if these people had been a social class above the likes of him, Robert and Thomas, entitled to respect and regard; now, they were moaning about a miserable missing few grammes of Charlie.

During one of his earlier visits to Glasgow, George had been introduced to a man who, it turned out, was a friend of Brian Doran's. This man had been interested to hear George lived and worked in Holland and they had talked about cocaine. 'I hear you get really good stuff over there?' the man said. It was more of a question than a statement. 'It's difficult to get it here and, even when you can, it's mostly rubbish.'

'I don't use it, but I'm told by people who do that it's top class,' said George. 'I gather you have to know the right people; you can't just turn up and expect to buy it on a street corner.'

'How much does it cost?'

'Don't know, but I'll find out for you. Next time I'm over, I'll make a point of meeting up and telling you.'

The man had been told George would be at Charlie Parker's that night and was waiting for him to appear, asking as they shook hands, 'Did you manage to get a price for Charlie?'

'Yes,' George told him, already knowing from Robert Bruce that the going rate in Glasgow was between £60 and £100 a gramme, and from Thomas Sim in Utrecht that good quality cocaine could be had for around £20 a gramme. 'But it depends on how much you want.'

Without waiting to be given a figure, the man said to George, 'Come on, there's somebody I'd like you to meet. Do you know Brian Doran?'

'We've met once before,' said George.

As he and Whacko shook hands, Doran asked him, 'How is Holland? I gather you might be able to help us out with something.'

'George can supply, but before he can give a price he needs to know the quantity needed,' said the friend.

'Well, how about 100 grammes, how much?' asked Doran.

'£45 a gramme. So 100 will cost you £4,500,' George told him.

'OK,' the travel agent said, 'I think we're on for this, but we'll need to talk it over and let you know. But will it be clean stuff, no shite? We wouldn't want people in hospital.'

'I would never do that. You're my own people and I wouldn't let you down.'

'When can you deliver?' Doran asked with some anxiety.

'Give me your telephone number and I'll let you know when I'm coming over. I'll just say when I'm arriving and won't mention what I'm bringing. I'll never do that, you never know who might accidentally overhear a telephone conversation.'

'OK.'

'Just one thing, I play it straight and I expect you to do the same. I don't want this talked about, I don't want my name mentioned, I don't want strangers coming on the telephone asking if I can help them out. I will deal with you and you only, and what you do with it is your business. As far as I'm concerned, the arrangement is between us and nobody else.'

'OK, that's fair.'

'One other thing.'

'What's that?'

'Cash on delivery.'

Three days later, George Duncan returned home to Holland and met up with Thomas Sim, who, as a cocaine user himself, knew the scene, what to look for, where to buy and how. The two were about to make a journey. In Glasgow, Brian Doran and Andrew Tait had lots to discuss. They took Alan Bartlett into their confidence.

The Happy Dust Gang had been born.

3

THE MONKEY

Six weeks after the New Year gathering at Charlie Parker's, George Duncan climbed from the roof of a building in Utrecht, 20 miles from Amsterdam, and was handed a message asking him to call a Glasgow telephone number. The conversation was short; the outcome that Duncan returned to Glasgow in late February 1980. From the city centre, he took a cab to a flat at 74 Highburgh Road, Hyndland – then a popular part of town for house-hunting young professionals, today, one of the most sought-after and expensive areas of Scotland. The flat was the home of Alan Bartlett, and he was there with Andrew Tait and Brian Doran. A young woman, a daughter of a wealthy Glasgow businessman, joined the three men. Tait and Doran did most of the talking.

'We're interested in what you were offering at New Year.'

'Right. I assumed you hadn't asked me to come all the way over to tell me you weren't.'

'Your offer is still on?'

'Of course.'

'What sort of amounts can you handle?'

'You tell me what you want.'

'The more we buy, the price goes down?'

'No, I've offered you a good rate at £45 a gramme. That's way down on what you're paying now. Maybe not even half. Further, I'll get you good gear and offer a reliable service. If I say I'll deliver, I'll deliver.'

'How much will you pay for it in Holland?'

'Who said I was getting it in Holland? Let me worry about where I buy it. All you have to do is place an order, then come up with the money.'

'How will you get it to us?'

'Again, that's my business. You don't need to know. Just make sure you keep this arrangement in-house. Don't go telling the whole world you can get good gear.'

'How soon can you deliver it?'

'A couple of weeks. I'll call and give you a day, then I'll ring again when I'm in Glasgow. You give me an address, and I'll drop in and deliver.'

'Drop in? You coming by parachute?'

'That's right. I'm the Parachutist.'

'OK, at New Year you said you could do 100 grammes, that still on?'

'Of course.'

'Right. A hundred it is. You know Byres Road?'

'Of course.'

'There's a shop there called The Pantry. It's Andy Tait's place. That will be the drop-off point. We'll wait to hear from you.'

One hundred grammes of cocaine was equivalent to around 3½ ounces.

George and Thomas had not been idle while they waited for their Glasgow customers to come to a decision. As soon as George returned to Utrecht from the New Year fun and the meeting in Charlie Parker's with Doran, he and Sim began making arrangements to ensure they had a regular supply available. The two men had done their homework thoroughly, with Sim especially enthusiastic at the prospect of making big money. They reasoned that if the first deal went well, it was odds on the Glasgow crew would want regular and ever bigger amounts. At the same time, they had no illusions. Doran and Tait in particular might be users, but they had an eye for business and would realise they could recoup their own costs by selling on the cocaine to their friends.

* * *

In comparison with the rest of central Europe, Holland is drug and pornography friendly. The Dutch are proud that from all over the world visitors come to watch live sex shows in Amsterdam's red-light district. Tourists wanting free thrills can wander about and gaze at the near-nude models who sit in windows displaying themselves, though this often leads to misunderstandings: enthusiastic punters failing to realise that what they see is for display purposes only and while sex is available inside at an inflated price it is invariably with an ancient crone who has seen better days.

As they are now, drugs in the 1980s were a slightly touchier subject. The authorities turned a blind eye to cannabis dealing, provided it was done discreetly, but trade in cocaine and heroin was frowned upon. Dealing had to be done undercover and the penalties when caught were as swingeing as, for example, in the United Kingdom.

The two Scots had taken a train from their homes in Utrecht to Amsterdam and begun to size up the possibilities of buying large amounts of cocaine. Sim already knew suppliers around Utrecht, but they did not want to attract attention locally by a sudden increase in demand. It would be obvious 100 grammes was far more than Sim would need for himself, so they had headed further afield where they were not known. Friends warned them to be cautious: strangers asking too many questions would get a polite shrug of the shoulders and, if they persisted, a swim in one of the city canals.

Amsterdam was a haven for men, and occasionally

women, on the run – frequently from drug-squad officers of the various European police forces. And journalists appeared obsessed with the pornography and narcotics trade. Reporters seeking interviews with police officers about this twentieth-century Sodom would be invited to headquarters, taken by lift to the first floor and introduced to the entire 'sex squad', consisting of two friendly English-speaking officers there to assure the world Holland was as much in control of the flourishing trade in the various constituents of sin as any other country. What was wholly innocent in Holland was often construed abroad as something sinister, they would say, pointing to a notice board on the wall of their office on which was pinned an article taken from a mass-circulation English newspaper specialising in sensational investigations. The cutting described how the paper had, in its own words, 'conducted a major investigation that uncovered a scandal of outrageous proportions'.

Two English journalists had 'infiltrated' a network of 'major drug runners', millionaires as a result of their vile trade in narcotics. These villains plotted from a base located in a bar in a dimly lit side street off the Oude Zijde Achterburgwal in the heart of the red-light zone. There they set up deals involving tons of cannabis. So open were they about the trade that the bar even displayed a sign advertising 'hash browns', a clear invitation, according to the journalists, of their contempt for authority. The article was duly published and caused a sensation – until a reader pointed out that hash browns were actually fried potatoes.

Duncan and Sim were wiser to the ways of the drug network. They had decided to contact a man Sim knew as 'the Monkey' initially, from whom he had occasionally bought cannabis during visits to the city. At the meeting, in a bar close to Dam Square, the three sipped beer as street entertainers maintained a cacophony that kept their conversation from prying ears.

The Monkey, a Colombian who had set up home in Holland ten years earlier after falling in love with a Dutch air hostess, had enough contacts in his head to fill a phone book. Although his homeland in South America was the centre of the world's cocaine trade, he made the most of a good living by arranging hash deliveries from colleagues in Spain; however, he was always happy to help out with clients seeking coke, knowing he could expect a reward later for setting up the contact. And while he already knew the Scots, he was a careful, shrewd man who wanted to be certain of their credentials. Should they turn out to be other than what they claimed, and the incredibly lucrative existing network be smashed as a result, the blame would fall upon him. The penalty for a foul-up was rumoured to be a one-way trip out to the North Sea.

Men in his line of business were constantly alert to the chance of betrayal. Four years earlier, Eric Jambert, a Frenchman sought by the Paris gendarmerie over a gangland killing and hiding out in Amsterdam, had passed to an acquaintance details of a syndicate smuggling cannabis through Spain. The acquaintance had given the information to Dutch police, who in turn gave it to counterparts in Spain. Many syndicates operated successfully and safely for the simple reason that they bribed police. This was an exception. Two members of the group were arrested and two tons of hash stored in a seaside villa ready to be hidden in a container lorry and driven to France was confiscated. The informer disappeared, almost certainly with police help, but Jambert was blamed. He was seized one night after leaving an Amsterdam bar and his body found three days later in Rotterdam, the major Dutch port from which ferries and giant cruise ships travel to destinations all over the world. His ears and nose had been cut off and his eyes burned out. Jambert had literally been shocked to death. The executioners deliberately dumped the corpse where it would be discovered so anyone letting the side down would hear their message.

The Monkey knew of the story and was constantly on his guard. But these men, he sensed, were genuine, an impression strengthened by the fact that they too were cautious, preferring to begin trading on a reasonably modest basis. As the meeting ended, he whispered a name and address to them, shook hands and headed off, promising to make a telephone call that would open yet another door.

The Scots took a leisurely stroll to the Jordan, Amsterdam's bohemian quarter, and sought out a brightly painted tailor's shop. They were expected, their drinking partner of a few minutes earlier having telephoned to announce they were on their way. He had told his associate the visitors were shopping for cocaine and could be trusted.

Heavily built, bespectacled and with a full head of grey hair, the shopkeeper, whom we are calling Joop, was initially wary, as he was of all new customers. His movements were quick, his eyes alert. The three spent some minutes in small talk, using a mixture of Dutch and English, until they were all comfortable, then Duncan and Sim were invited into a storeroom at the rear of the shop. This was clearly the tailor's workshop and from the unkempt appearance of the place it looked to be in the throes of redecoration. Paint-soiled trousers and overalls lay everywhere, but this, they were soon to discover, was merely a facade. Unrolling a pair of heavily marked dungarees, he uncovered from one of the pockets what looked like a yellowing tennis ball.

'Cocaine,' he claimed, holding it up.

'It's fucking yellow,' replied Duncan, a stranger to cocaine and therefore not to know that was the colour of high-grade cocaine in its natural state.

'Yes, we call it cat's piss. It's top gear.'

'Cat's piss? Is that what you've mixed it with?'

'No, no, this is very good gear. It's the natural colour.'

'But we'll never sell that. Nobody will believe this is the real thing. They'll think we've added something. What we want is the white stuff.'

'I can give you the white stuff, but you do realise, don't you, that it only becomes white because stuff has been added – chopped and re-rocked, we call that. Then it will turn white. But I don't keep the white here. Too risky.'

'But you have it.'

'I can get it, but it's not here.'

'OK, we have clients who are probably going to want stuff in 100-gramme batches. Can you do that amount?'

'Of course, no problem. When?'

'We are waiting to hear back from them. As soon as we get the go-ahead, we'll want to come back and trade with you.'

'That's no problem. I know who you are and I will do business with you. When you are ready, you must come here again to my shop.'

Now, six weeks after that initial meeting, the Scots were back at the shop asking Joop for cocaine. It was time to fulfil their first order from Doran and his friends. Joop explained the drugs were at his home and that they must wait until the shop was closed before going there together.

'The shop does not close for an hour,' he said, 'and to shut down early and walk off with yourselves would make the others think I was up to something. You are welcome to hang on in the shop till then.'

'Thank you for the offer, but why don't we nip out and have a coffee and a smoke, then come back when you lock up and you can take us to your house?'

'OK, then you can get a cab back into town.'

The buyers wandered about until they found a coffee house where they smoked a joint to calm their nerves before returning to the tailor, who drove them in a shining red Mercedes to a huge villa on the outskirts of Amsterdam. It was an astonishingly extravagant home for someone expected to exist on the profits from a fairly modest shop and a sign that he had a thriving income from some other source. In Glasgow, such a set-up would have attracted attention.

But if they were surprised by its outward appearance that was nothing compared with what they saw once through the front door. It was the sight of his wife that astonished the visitors.

Sim later admitted, 'The guy clearly had loads of money, but we expected he'd have a wife of about his own age, about 45. So we get inside and are shown into a big room he obviously used as a study. He asks us to take a seat while he gets his missus. George and I are on a settee and along much of the wall to our right is a huge fitted mirror. It seemed totally out of place. Against the wall opposite to where we were sitting was a roll-top desk.

'Suddenly, there's a rustling noise behind us and this cracking bird walks in. Actually, you could smell her getting near. Her perfume, whatever it was, was out of this world. And she is an absolute stunner: tall, jet-black hair down to her shoulders, with the most beautiful face, and lips covered in deep red that you just hoped would ask if it would be OK if they kissed you. She must have been about 30 but was wearing the shortest mini-dress we had ever seen. When she turned, you could see the bottom of her buttocks. After we'd shaken hands, Joop asks her to make coffee and chats about how he'll get the white when she comes back in and is asking what we're going to do with it once we have it. We tell him we want to get it to London, because there's no point in letting him in on the whole secret, and he's suggesting one or two possibilities, including an offer to introduce us to a girl who can do the business.

'It was hard trying to concentrate on what Joop was saying, knowing his wife was going to come back into the room any minute wearing that dress. When she does appear carrying a tray filled with cups, George and I almost have a heart attack. She goes down on her haunches facing us to put the tray on a little table. Her back is to the mirror and in it we can see her skirt ride up and show she's wearing a black G-string. Just a G-string! She must know what she's doing and so must her husband, but he just tells us to enjoy the coffee while he pops out to get the stuff for us.

'His wife then goes to the desk and starts putting stuff in

one of the bottom drawers. Again, her back is to the mirror and this time when she bends over the G-string gets pulled to one side. You can see everything. Everything. She is chatting away to George and me, but we don't take in a word of what she's saying. We don't know whether we're supposed to be embarrassed. I'm wondering if George has seen what I've seen, and later on I find he has been wondering the same to himself. She then moves to the other side of the desk and to keep our view George and I actually find ourselves moving the settee towards the mirror.

'Next thing, Joop comes back and starts talking to us. He shows us a pouch with the stuff in, asks us to take a finger dip to confirm it's good gear and from the desk brings out a tiny set of scales just to show there are 100 grammes. He's talking away and we're trying not to stare into the mirror. After all, this is his wife and we only met the guy for the very first time a couple of hours earlier. Does he know what we can see? That we will never find out, but we went back to Joop's house to do business many times and every time his wife was around she had on miniskirts and G-strings and always seemed to be looking for an excuse to bend down around the desk to dust or hunt for papers. I thought maybe she did it to turn her husband on. She was much younger than he was, but you could tell she was devoted to Joop. Lucky sod. One day she was there and had a top on cut so low that when she leaned over to put the coffee cups on the table, you could see her nipples. We were speechless.

'We had agreed a price with Joop – he'd sell for £10 a gramme. From the moment George told me about the conversation with Doran in Charlie Parker's, he had been saving like mad. The money we handed over to Joop that day was his. I never seemed to have spare cash. There was a huge bundle of guilders and he gave it to his wife to count.'

When she was satisfied, Joop shook hands, passed them his home telephone number and said he hoped it would be the first of many meetings. It was a sentiment they went along with – anything just to see his wife again. Relaxing in the back seat of the cab on the way back to the city centre, the pair let out huge sighs of relief.

'What did you make of that?' asked George.

'Hell, man, I've never seen anything like it. Was that deliberate?'

'Of course it was. She was laying it on for our benefit. If you had the choice of buying from some old tosspot or getting an eyeful of that every time you did business, who would you prefer to be counting your money?'

'I didn't see it that way.'

'Listen, Simmy, there are probably 50 guys in Amsterdam all doing the same as Joop. But why do you think he has the big house? How does he afford the expensive furniture? The flash Merc? And did you notice the paintings? I'm no expert but, brother, they were originals. Because punters go back to him, and half of them will do that to get an eyeful of his wife. It's like throwing in a free strip show with the goodies. He knows what he's doing.'

George was eager to recoup his outlay and bank the profits. The quicker he reached Glasgow, the sooner he would have his money. He had already decided to simply hire a car in Holland from one of the major rental companies and drive it and the Charlie over to Glasgow via a ferry route. After all, what could there be to attract attention in a Scot taking a trip back to his homeland?

In late February, he did just that, having telephoned ahead to warn Tait of his arrival. The journey went without incident and the money was waiting. In late April, he repeated the operation, staying on in Glasgow for a couple of nights to meet up with old friends. Once more there was nothing out of the ordinary to excite attention. It was, in fact, thought George as he drove back into Holland, all too quiet. It was unusual to make two crossings without being asked a single question by the authorities. Almost too good to be true.

On the law of averages, he was sure at some stage to

be stopped. And perhaps caught out. No point in taking unnecessary risks, he reasoned. Time for a re-think. Arriving back in Utrecht, he sought out Sim and told him of his concerns.

'Simmy, I've taken all the risks so far,' said George. 'You've done nothing apart from introduce me to the Monkey. Either you go next time or we come up with another method of transportation.'

Sim had no intention of putting his neck on the line. 'Let's ask Joop what he thinks,' he suggested.

During their previous meetings with the tailor, George and Thomas had implied their customers were in London. They called on him to say they would shortly be buying another batch, casually asking, as if it were hardly important, if he had any thoughts on safe methods of moving the cocaine into the United Kingdom. Joop said he knew a girl who did regular runs and asked if they would like her number. They took it and thanked him.

'Let's get a drink and look up this bird. I don't think we'll use her, but it might be interesting to find out what she has to say,' said George. Back in the centre of Amsterdam, the men rang the telephone number Joop had given them.

The girl answered. 'I've been expecting you,' she said. 'Anna called.'

'Who's Anna?'

'Joop's wife.'

'You know her?'

'Of course, she used to perform in one of the sex clubs.'

'Oh, you used to do that?'

'Yes, but now I work in a bar.'

'You're a barmaid, then? What's the bar like?'

'Why don't you visit me and find out?'

'OK, but we have to catch a train later.'

'I'm sure you'll think it worth the effort.'

'Does that mean we're in for a pleasant surprise?'

'You might say that. All I can promise is that you won't regret seeing me.'

'What's so special about the place where you work?'

'It's a topless bar.'

'And you are . . .?'

'A topless barmaid. That's my job. I'm told you're a couple of good-looking guys. You coming to see me? Anna said you might have a job for me.'

She gave them the address of a bar in the red-light district and just under a quarter of an hour later they were at a table having a drink with her.

Her dark ringlets were festooned with beads and her skin glistened with oil. She was completely unconcerned at being bare breasted and even performed a party trick, which, she explained, brought handsome tips from customers. It involved balancing peanuts on her lightly creamed nipples, then, due to some incredible and obviously practised muscle control, flicking her breasts to make the nuts fly off. Evidently, punters tried catching them in mid-air.

Her name was Sophie and she was French. She told them that from time to time she would act as a courier, taking drugs or pornography to London. 'Meet me at Schiphol airport with the stuff in a suitcase. You buy me return tickets and come over on the same flight, but do not sit near me. We meet up at Heathrow. The Customs people never check me. I just say I am a French student on my way to meet up with my parents in London. It works every time, and I am waved through while the single men are being stopped and their bags examined. I do this often.'

'Haven't you ever been stopped?'

'Never. Not once. I do not go through looking like this, you know. Jeans and a plain coat with my hair tied up. It's the down-at-heel student look. You guys would be sure to be stopped. You look like a pair of gangsters, and they'd think you were carrying dirty books and movies.'

'OK, the sixty-four-thousand-dollar question: how much, and how much notice do you need?'

'A couple of days and it will cost you £250 plus the price of my ticket.'

'When do we pay?'

'Once we're in London. I give you the suitcase, you give me the money. I hang around for a few hours and get a flight back. What is it you want taken over? Anna said it was drugs.'

Sim knew it was no use lying. 'Yes,' he told her. 'We're looking around at the moment.'

'Well, take my advice and don't go wandering around carrying drugs. Somebody might have seen you in Joop's shop and guessed you've bought from him.'

They finished their drinks, thanked her and said they would be in touch. Outside it was dark and the two decided it was time to get back to Utrecht. They wanted to be at work the next day, as if nothing had happened. On the journey home, they mulled over their situation. They had already made a profit of almost £7,000, so having got this far, the two Scots felt there was no sense in taking chances on what they did next.

They had established contact with what appeared to be a good source and one with the added attraction of a highly desirable woman happy to give them a free flash and, who knows, was there a possibility that if they wanted to buy more or in bigger quantities, Joop might throw in a session for them with his wife in front of the giant mirror as part of the deal? Things were looking good. Now they had to set up a foolproof method of getting the gear safely back to Glasgow.

Duncan saw that there were just two options for carrying the happy dust to Scotland: by air or by sea. There were advantages to each – but also potential snags. And George was a careful man. There were two possibilities, he reasoned, in using the air option. They could use a courier like Sophie or take it themselves. Familiarity was on their side: ever since they had left home to begin their teenage travels, the two had regularly gone back, so the sight of one or both at Glasgow airport or on the streets would not be looked on as unusual. And they were both clean:

no police force was looking for them; no Special Branch detective or immigration-control officer held an Interpol directive asking for information about their movements. So each could probably travel safely back carrying the stuff. However, airport checks were indiscriminate. They might look like innocent travellers returning for a Glasgow Rangers match, but lady luck could decide to intervene with the result that the little pouch containing their futures was revealed. It was pointless them taking risks when someone else was willing to do that for them, so if they were to opt for the sky route, Sophie would be the mule. If they flew in, they decided, it would be to collect the cocaine, which had already been carried there by another method.

The alternative was over the North Sea and that meant a boat. Using a fast yacht was instantly ruled out – it was too expensive and far too risky, with coastguard and Customs cutters continually on the alert. No, the sensible way would be to continue to cross by ferry, even though this involved a long drive from Amsterdam to one of the North Sea ports, a few hours at sea and then carrying on to Scotland. But they reasoned that once off the ferry and through Customs checks, barring an accident the odds against anything going wrong were so remote as to be discounted. George had twice sailed from Rotterdam to Hull. Now they decided that whatever mode of transport they eventually chose, they would vary the routes. Never would they use the same UK port consecutively. If someone became suspicious for whatever reason, they would at least make it difficult should a watch be placed on them at a particular landing point. They reasoned this was unlikely – and in the event would be proved right.

Sim left most of the thinking to his friend. Those close to George would say he was deep, an intelligent individual who worked out in his mind all the options and when he decided he wanted to, took his time before voicing an opinion. He had a prodigious memory and the ability to think on his feet, an asset that would prove priceless later on.

He thought long and hard about the safest way of ensuring their small but valuable packages would be carried safely, picturing himself on a ferry negotiating the various checks and looking for possible hazards, and came up with three possible solutions: hiding it in a lorry, secreting it in a car or travelling as foot passengers and carrying it themselves. They quickly dismissed the third option as being too risky. There were literally scores of hiding places in a vehicle but even a cursory search of a foot passenger was likely to uncover hidden secrets. If they opted to smuggle on the boat, then it had to be using a vehicle.

The most obvious and that favoured by most smugglers, whether the contraband was pornography, drugs, stolen goods or even the occasional human being, was by lorry, usually in one of the giant containers then favoured by haulage companies. The big advantage of this was saving time at entry: the containers would be checked by Customs officers at the point of exit, then the locks officially sealed. A seal that had been broken or showed signs of having been tampered with spelled deep and instant trouble for the driver; therefore, apart from an occasional chancer, who usually spent the rest of his days regretting his long-shot gamble, once closed and sealed the container was left untouched. At entry, Customs would, nine times out of ten, simply verify the seal number or code against a manifest and wave the vehicle on. There had to be exceptions, of course: no method of smuggling was wholly guaranteed not to be discovered but first Customs officers had to pick out a vehicle actually carrying contraband and then find it. When it came to be unloaded, the driver would make a brief, unscheduled stop, maybe in a lay-by or a hostel car park, to ensure his additional cargo was removed by him personally. He would then pass it to a waiting customer, who knew what secrets lay stored within the load.

Of course, this method wasn't always plain sailing. George had read of a container lorry packed with carpets destined for Scotland that had been stopped shortly after coming off a ferry at North Shields in Tyneside. During a previous trip, the Danish driver had been over-talkative, boasting how he could fool Customs officers whenever he wished. His bragging had been overheard in a Leith pub by the inevitable police informer. When he arrived with his next load from the Danish port of Esbjerg, he was stopped and the contents of his 32-ton container searched. Inside was a huge stash of pornography said to be worth more than £70,000. The driver lost both his freedom for six months and his lorry, which was confiscated. When he emerged from jail, he was forced to buy it back.

A week after their meeting with Joop, George and Sim travelled to Rotterdam. A colleague in the building trade had arranged a meeting with a driver regularly making deliveries to the United Kingdom. The two rendezvoused with the man at the main railway station, then headed for the docks, as he insisted on showing them how easy it was to smuggle. At that stage, he did not know what it was his visitors wanted carried over the North Sea and decided not to press the issue – if they wanted to let him in on their secret, they would. As evening turned to darkness, he led them to the port and told them to follow.

'You don't have passes or seamen's union cards, so there would be awkward questions at the security gates and you'd be turned back,' he said. 'But there's no problem. We only need to climb over a wire fence and we're in. Do what I do.'

He clambered over at a spot where the wires ran through concrete posts. George followed, but Sim, a few feet away, was about to pull himself up at a point midway between two posts when their guide stopped him.

'If you go there, it will vibrate the wires for some distance and somebody might hear. Climb near the posts where it's more taut.'

Inside, they wandered between rows of lorries, many with the rear doors of their containers open.

'The Customs examine one then go on to the next, leaving

colleagues to seal up,' explained the driver. 'All you do is nip in between the teams of examiners and sealers, hide whatever you have in the load and clear off. But you must make sure you get the correct lorry. One guy hid a box filled with dirty playing cards in a lorry, only it turned out to be the wrong one. Nobody knows where the stuff went or what happened to it.'

They thanked him for his trouble and said they would be in touch. A price had not been discussed and they preferred to keep him in the dark until and unless a deal was struck.

This raised the issue of trust. George was, by nature, a careful man. What might happen, he asked himself, if he gave the little bag to a stranger? What guarantee had he of getting it safely back when he met up with the courier in the United Kingdom? None, was the answer, and because he did not know any lorry driver well enough to trust him, a container was crossed off his list of potentials.

He and Sim were sure the answer lay with a motor car. There was nothing to stop them driving it over themselves, of course, but what if something went wrong? They remembered the story of the two Glaswegians who had been hired to act as mules. They had flown from Glasgow airport to Schiphol but, by chance, one had been recognised by an off-duty detective who recollected reading an intelligence circular naming the man as suspected of being part of a drug-smuggling ring. His concerns were passed to police in Holland, who agreed to watch him and his companion on their arrival. At Schiphol, the pair were met by a stranger, who led them to the airport car park, where he handed them the keys to a Peugeot car, telling them it had been fitted with a liquid petroleum gas tank. This actually held 32 kilos of Moroccan hashish and the vehicle ran on diesel. The Scots were handed enough money to cover the expense of taking the vehicle on a circuitous journey, which the businessman behind the racket was sure would guarantee a safe return. They drove through Holland, past border checks and into Germany, then north to Denmark, where they took a ferry to the Norwegian port of Kristiansand. The next leg would see them motor on to Stavanger, take another ferry to North Shields and then complete the final 170 miles to Glasgow. It was indeed a roundabout route, but the financier reckoned no one would expect drugs to come from Scandinavia.

All seemed to be going smoothly; however, the smugglers were unaware that their departure from Schiphol had been noted and passed on, and that police in Germany had monitored them arriving and leaving their country, at which point colleagues in Denmark took over. The Danes radioed Norwegian authorities telling them to expect the car after watching the ferry set sail over the Skagerrak. By now, the ultimate destination seemed obvious. It had been agreed in a series of telephone calls that the car would be allowed to pass unhindered until it crossed the border into Scotland. Continental police were happy with this idea; it avoided touchy issues that often arose from the arrest of foreign nationals and having to deal with over-fussy consular officials. But, as with all the best-laid schemes, the unforeseen wrecked all the careful planning and decision-making on both sides of the legal fence.

At Kristiansand, it had been decided to at least give the pair in the Peugeot the impression that they were not receiving special treatment by stopping the vehicle along with a handful of others for routine checks. The examination would be perfunctory and, in any case, at this stage, while it was generally accepted that drugs were stowed away somewhere, nobody knew for certain what they were or where they were hidden. So, as the Peugeot slowly made its way from the ferry ramp, it was waved down by a uniformed Customs official. There was nothing unusual about that, it was a common occurrence, but the driver had been tired and scared throughout the trip and now, after the long, worrying journey, his nerves were balanced on a razor's edge. Suddenly, he snapped.

'Fuck it!' he screamed and, despite frantic yells and curses from his companion, sped towards a sign reading

'Toll' and what he imagined to be the exit from the docks. Unfortunately, his sense of direction and knowledge of Norwegian were lacking and he found himself heading towards Customs, following a large arrow straight into a warehouse. Directly ahead was a party of mechanics dismantling a suspect lorry. Too late, he braked, but the car skidded, coming to a halt with the front wheels over an inspection pit. It was journey's end.

The Scots watched, in handcuffs, as the car was towed out. Demonstrating a courtesy their prisoners found remarkable but which is frequently typical, the Norwegian police and Customs officers carefully explained each step as the car was searched and stripped. The two had the impression they were regarded as VIPs. But it was a sensation that would not last. No one wanted the two smugglers to be able to accuse the Norwegian officers of planting evidence.

Almost the first point of examination was the fake tank: for the next few years, the two were guests of a Norwegian jail. What had been a well-thought-out plan had failed because of bad luck and a poor selection of driving team.

As far as George was concerned, the lesson from that disaster was to trust only those he knew, to keep the operation simple and to have control of it at all times. But, most important of all, not to be at the wheel or associated with the car during the dangerous periods: the minutes spent checking it on and off the ferry. George came up with the solution: he and Sim agreed to employ someone else to take that risk and would at the same time keep an eye on whoever they had chosen.

'We'll put the stuff in a car and get somebody to drive it over on a ferry,' said George.

'What if they decide to pull a fast one on the way across and switch some of the gear?' asked Sim.

'One of us will go on the same ferry as a foot passenger. He can keep an eye on whoever's driving, because you have to lock up and leave the car during the crossing.'

'What happens at the other end?'

'The car is driven off, then whichever of us has gone over gets the gear out of it and the driver just turns around and goes back with the next boat.'

'I assume I'm the one going on the ferry?'

'Right, and I'll meet you in Glasgow.'

'How do I get from the ferry to Glasgow?'

'Train or bus. Train will be quicker. Both are totally safe. Nobody checks what you're carrying.'

'How will you get there?'

'Probably fly in, although I might motor over now and again, but using a different route.'

Finding a reliable driver turned out to be easier than expected. Scouse Willie had a reputation for a cool head and safe driving hands. They had met him days after arriving in Holland from Spain, when his broad Liverpool accent led them to confuse him with the locals at first. He regularly drove over from Rotterdam to Hull and thus knew the ferry routine.

After work one evening, Duncan and Sim motored from Utrecht to Amsterdam and met Scouse Willie and his friend, 'the Stargazer', at a coffee house in Warmoesstraat close to the central railway station. The Stargazer was a middle-aged Dutchman whose nickname resulted from a genuine interest in astronomy.

'He used to be in the merchant navy, bringing white in from South America,' said Scouse Willie. 'Got away with it for years until they docked off New York and the coastguard came on board for a routine check. The skipper's manifest wasn't quite in order and the Yanks were becoming very officious, insisting they'd do a total sweep of his vessel. One of the coastguards was looking through the crew's quarters when he came across a toy the Stargazer had bought in Caracas for a nephew. It was a bear holding a telescope and when you wound it up the bear put the telescope to its eye and pointed a finger in the direction he was looking. It was really cute and the Yank was fascinated by it. He called in the others and was demonstrating how it worked. While they were preoccupied, the skipper suggested to Stargazer he might want to make a gift of the toy to the Americans. It was not so much a suggestion as an order and Stargazer had no alternative. There was the usual 'I can't', 'Yes you can' and the outcome was handshakes all round. The Yanks went off, giving the skipper a very friendly ticking off and a hint that next time a full search might be needed. The skipper was delighted with Stargazer, who couldn't tell him that the bear and telescope were stuffed with high-grade Colombian cocaine. It was the end of his sailing days with the merchant navy. There was no way he could risk going back across the Atlantic, so he switched to motoring in hash from Spain.'

Scouse Willie said he had brought his friend along simply to give advice on possible pitfalls.

'We want to take something over to England,' Sim told the Liverpudlian.

'You mean you want me to drive kit to Scotland?' was his response.

'No, oh no.'

'Look, don't try fooling me. The Monkey told me you'd met him – he wanted somebody to vouch for you and I was happy to do that. And the only reason anybody meets the Monkey is because they're looking for coke.'

'OK, but we don't want it taken to Scotland.'

'Where then?'

'England.'

'Where in England?'

'We want to vary the ports.'

'Good thinking. So what do you want me to do?'

'Drive the car on and off the ferry. One of us will be on the same boat but travelling separately as a foot passenger, and once you reach the other side you hand over the car keys and come back.'

'You don't trust me.'

'It's not that, but in case something goes wrong one of us will be around to help out if we can.'

Scouse Willie chuckled. 'You don't trust me but don't worry. I'm not offended. If it was the other way round, I'd do exactly the same.'

Duncan knew from friends in Glasgow how dangerous the word trust could be. Drug dealers had been given a warning as to what might happen should they be caught when four years earlier armed police had pounced on two Londoners, Matthew McHugh and Terence Goodship, minutes after they had arrived at the then plush Albany Hotel in Glasgow with cannabis. They worked for an international gang of smugglers who used expensive yachts to carry bales of hashish from the coast of Morocco to Britain. The two had been expecting to collect £6,000 in cash at the Albany but reckoned so without 'grass' of a different sort – police informer David Cussins.

His tip-off resulted in them appearing before Lord Allanbridge at the High Court in Edinburgh the following September. Following a lengthy trial, McHugh was found guilty of possessing a large quantity of the drug, while Goodship was cleared. Seeking to ease the sentence on McHugh, his defence advocate, one Malcolm Rifkind QC, who would go on to become Secretary of State for Scotland and later Foreign Secretary, had argued that cannabis was a soft drug. He said that, according to doctors, it did not cause major health problems to users. But his words cut little ice with the judge, who jailed McHugh for six years.

The case should have been included in a textbook for those selling and using drugs on the dangers of their profession and pastime. Cussins had led the cockneys to Glasgow with the lure of big money readily available, but while the unsuspecting pair was booking in to the Albany, he was actually feeding steak dinners to two police pals at his home. And if a relatively soft drug such as hash merited six years, what was the scale in years behind bars for cocaine, acknowledged as potentially lethal?

The lesson: informers lurked everywhere; nobody was to be trusted. And nobody was safe, especially the informer himself. There are exceptions to the rule, but as far as the criminal code of conduct is concerned, grasses and those who cooperate or collaborate with the police are the lowest of the low, a despised and vilified breed ranking lower than vermin. It was no wonder then that after details of his dastardly deed were leaked to the underworld, Cussins disappeared. He was found eight years later, shot dead in a ravine in Pennsylvania. But by then it was clear that the lesson had not been heeded – in Glasgow, at least. Nor would it ever be.

What too many concerned with making money from drugs overlooked was that while most who knew about their rackets would, through fear or friendship, keep their mouths shut, others would turn a blind eye only so long as their own lives were not affected. The most bizarre incident ever to involve the city drugs squad was the result of neighbourly tolerance being pushed too far.

Sitting at home in the lounge of his tenement block one night in the east of Glasgow, a man was disturbed by a rustling that appeared to come from his ceiling. He looked up and the hairs on the back of his neck stood on end as a small hole appeared in one of the corners. Gradually, it grew until first the tongue and then the head of a snake appeared and the creature began slithering down his wall, resting on the top of a painting. Terror and fury combined in the householder. He knew a neighbour kept reptiles, among numerous animals, a practice feared and abhorred by many living nearby. And he knew that in the same home in which they were kept was a den for drug dealing. As the snake rested, he bolted for the door and called the police, giving them the address where, he assured a detective at the other end of the line, drugs would be found. He also warned them that the place was the habitat of snakes and one cobra at least.

The report was put in the hands of the drug squad and in particular Detective Sergeant Ronnie Edgar and his colleague and friend Detective Constable Joe Corrigan.

They were used to raiding the homes of suspects and knew having a search warrant with them could usually save time – time frequently used by a suspect to make off through a rear window while police argued at the front door. Edgar was taking no chances here. He immediately applied for and was granted a warrant under the Dangerous Wild Animals Act, the first under this law ever to be sworn in Scotland. If while looking for creatures reckoned to be a risk to those living nearby the police discovered drugs, well, all to the good. And these men could sniff out drugs as a Bedouin could smell water in a handful of sand.

In the event, nobody hindered their entry, but inside, as they sat discussing the keeping of wild animals with the householder and his family, Edgar and Corrigan sensed something moving over their feet. Looking down, they started into the swaying face of a cobra.

'It's not dangerous,' they were assured, but they were taking no chances. An official was summoned from the then Glasgow Zoo, who took one look then vanished, returning in protective clothing to snare the cobra, then drop it into a sack. It was later taken to a zoo in England. Meanwhile Edgar and Corrigan began a search of the house. Corrigan lifted a floorboard and wafted his hand into the darkness beneath. He felt something soft and warm. It turned out to be a nest for rats, kept as food for the snake population. Elsewhere the officers discovered a boa constrictor, garter snakes, bats, cats and dogs. And heroin, resulting in a lengthy prison sentence for one member of the family.

Happily the drug squad had escaped injury. As time went by, members of the Happy Dust Gang would come to complain that they were bitten by snakes of a human variety.

4

SCALES OF SIN

While Duncan and Sim were hard at work organising the collection and delivery of the cocaine, they had called the Glasgow half of the Happy Dust Gang to assure Doran, Alan Bartlett and Tait that all was progressing well. In fact, there was an air of anxiety in Scotland. No one had Charlie and all over the newspapers headlines reported that a well-established smuggling route between Calais and Dover had been smashed when Dover Customs officers discovered a quarter of a ton of cannabis hidden in tins of tomatoes. The route had also been used to bring in cocaine, some of which occasionally filtered its way north of the border, and Charlie users now feared a huge price hike. The Scots need not have worried.

A week later, at the beginning of June 1980, a red Ford motor car left Amsterdam and made the short drive to Rotterdam. Scouse Willie was at the wheel and with him was Thomas Sim. The men had hired the vehicle from a garage owned by an acquaintance of the Liverpudlian. As they neared the ferry terminal, the vehicle stopped to allow Sim out. The car joined a line of vehicles waiting to board, while Sim purchased a single ticket as a foot passenger. He watched the Ford drive up the ramp and then walked on himself. Twenty minutes later, the doors were closed and the ferry set off on the eleven-hour overnight sail for Hull.

There was ample opportunity for the two to chat, have a meal together or share a drink – but they did neither, deliberately staying apart throughout the journey. The ferry berthed at breakfast time the next morning and Sim was waiting as the Ford was driven out of the terminal. He hopped inside, smiled and banged his fist on the dashboard. The trip over the North Sea had gone incredibly smoothly. As he had left the boat at Hull, Willie had been stopped by a Customs officer, a clipboard in his hand, who had asked him the registration number, checked his Dutch insurance details, briefly looked through the windows into the rear seat, queried where he was going and wished him a safe journey before waving him on. Willie knew, of course, not always to expect such an easy time of it. He pulled over outside a snack bar on the edge of Hull. The two looked like long-lost friends reunited by coincidence as they talked animatedly and headed inside, where they had coffee. Willie then waited while his friend took the Ford to a quiet corner of the car park. He spent 20 minutes alone in the car, then rejoined his companion for a second cup of coffee.

'Everything OK?' asked the Scouser.

'No problems. I've left things exactly as they were yesterday. Believe me, nobody will ever know and that means we can go back to your friend if we need the car again.'

'You need a lift to the railway station?'

'That would be great and it will fill in some time for you. You're going back the day after next, aren't you? What will you do?'

'I'm driving over to Liverpool to see some of the family. Stay overnight with them then come back over here late on tomorrow and hang about until it is time to go back on the boat.'

'Good thinking.'

'How long is your train trip?'

'I change at Leeds, then Edinburgh. It'll be late afternoon before I'm in Glasgow, but I just can't see anything going wrong now, touch wood.'

Ten minutes later, he was stepping from the car and buying a train ticket, then waving goodbye. Scouse Willie set off across country to Merseyside. That evening, he telephoned Glasgow to check everything had gone smoothly that end.

As Sim sipped British Rail coffee on the train, George Duncan was in the air. Earlier that morning, he had travelled by train to Schiphol, where he took a flight to Glasgow, arriving at the home of a friend near Govan shortly after lunch. An hour later, the telephone shrilled and Sim assured him everything was fine, ending with, 'See ya later.'

The two men were reunited that evening, by which time Tait had been contacted and had suggested a rendezvous in Bartlett's Hyndland flat.

'How was it?' asked the Parachutist.

'An absolute doddle,' Sim told him.

'It came off OK?'

'Yeah, the stuff was there safe and sound.'

It had been Duncan's idea to conceal the package of happy dust behind the dashboard. The hiding place had been well thought out. On a couple of occasions, they had driven back to Glasgow for brief reunions with their families and had taken careful note of the way in which Customs officers pulled cars over for searching. Undersides, seats and doors were given special attention and, in particular, screws were examined for any signs of tampering. Duncan had remembered that while once having a car radio fitted, a garage mechanic had loosened the dashboard panel by freeing screws underneath. He and Sim got to work one day and in just minutes discovered the perfect hiding place for their tiny package.

Doran was late for the meeting in the West End that night, but Tait and Bartlett clearly did not want to do business until he arrived. When he did, it was obvious to George, who had left Sim behind, that the three had been putting their heads together. They were evidently unsure whether the men from Holland could be trusted and wanted to give the impression that here, in Glasgow, they were no mugs to be taken for an expensive ride.

The trio produced a set of gold-coloured miniature scales complete with tiny weights and asked George if they could check out the contents of his pouch. He found it difficult not to burst out laughing, realising he was dealing with amateurs as far as the drugs business was concerned. Weighing out the sticky Charlie required extreme delicacy. Further, it was universally accepted that cocaine was sold in grammes – their weights were in ounces. This meant the trio had to make a telephone call to a pal to ask for the equivalent metric weight of an ounce. He gave them the answer: 28.3 grammes. They worked out by placing the 100 grammes on one side of the scales, they would need 3½ ounces balanced on the other, with a very marginal favour to the cocaine. Their friend called back to suggest that one gramme was very nearly the exact weight of a Marlboro cigarette; therefore Tait was despatched to buy a pack of the American-made filter tips.

When he returned, they tried balancing the cocaine against cigarettes but discovered with their first attempt that they had spooned too much of the drug and the result was that the scale plunged downwards, blowing powder over a table surface. It was at this point that George produced from his pocket a tiny set of Pesnet spring scales, used universally to weigh drugs. The scales consisted of a hollow cylinder with a spring down the centre. Replacing the cocaine into a polythene packet, he held the set by a finger, attached the bag to the foot of the scales and they watched as the spring was extended until a tiny marker showed the exact weight: 100 grammes.

'Where did you get that?' asked Doran.

'Try a shop supplying equipment for schoolkids,' George told the one-time teacher they called Whacko.

'How do we know it's accurate?'

'Try it with one of your Marlboros.'

They did, and were satisfied. Doran handed over the agreed £4,500.

'When can you get more?' the Parachutist was asked.

'Ring me and let me know when you're ready for the next consignment. I'll see what I can do.'

'Same price?'

'I'll let you know.'

As his taxi sped away from Hyndland, George Duncan could be allowed the smile that was emerging and spreading over his face. The £1,000 investment had produced a profit of £3,500 less expenses, but these would be no more than £500. That would leave him enough to buy 300 grammes. He realised Doran, Tait and Bartlett would hive off part of their supply to other users and recoup some of their outlay in the process. But just as that section of the fledgling Happy Dust Gang was expanding its business, he and Sim were about to do the same. The two men who had travelled over from Holland could be forgiven for spending the remainder of their stay in Glasgow having fun and relaxing. But others had been looking for George. He was contacted by telephone and sought out in clubs by more prospective customers hoping to persuade him to cater for their needs. Deals were struck, arrangements made. This was at the same time both a promising and a worrying development. Promising in that news he might be able to supply the needs of the middle-class cocaine circle had spread because that meant bigger turnover and bigger profits. Worrying in that his major concern from the very outset had been the indiscretion of those he dealt with. He remembered the careless manner in which the New Year partygoers had openly bemoaned the absence of their cocaine supplier. This was the crowd with which Doran, Tait and Bartlett mingled. The trio, he decided, might be free with their money but they were also a little too enthusiastic with their tongues. As time went by, he would discover just how talkative they could be.

Before leaving Glasgow, the Happy Dust Gang had expanded its customer list. Plenty of people wanted to buy, but there was no way Duncan or Sim would be telling their fellow conspirators about that. Had they done so, they were convinced their new partners would insist on sharing the proceeds and that was very much out of the question.

Four weeks later, George was back in Utrecht preparing for the next load when his telephone jangled and a Glaswegian voice asked if he had anything.

'How much do you want?'

'Same as last time.'

'See what I can do.'

'Same grade?'

'How was the last lot?'

'First rate.'

'Tell you what, I'll bring you a choice this time.'

'What about the price?'

'Same as before, £45 a unit.'

He called the number Joop had given him and Anna answered. He visualised her wearing only the tiny G-string, her nude breasts swaying as she picked up the telephone. They briefly exchanged pleasantries then Joop came on the line. He listened while the Scot explained he needed another batch. The Dutchman arranged a meeting near the shop.

'No offence, but I do not want you seen around too much,' he said. 'By the way, what did you do to Sophie?'

'How do you mean?'

'She hasn't stopped talking about you. Let me know if you are up for the idea and I'll arrange a little get-together at my place some evening, you and I, she and Anna. The girls would be happy to put on a little show for you.'

The idea might have been tempting, but there was no way George would take a bite at the bait. If something went wrong, Joop might decide to cut their connection and literally he could not afford for that to happen. Joop then took Duncan to his home. Anna had coffee waiting. 'Hope you enjoyed your visit last time,' she told her guest.

64

'I know Sophie enjoyed meeting you. Will you use her sometime?'

'Possibly, but I hope she won't be offended if I don't.'

'Not at all. Her offer is there, should you need it. She was only disappointed you didn't stay longer at the bar.'

George handed over £3,000.

'Your friends are still happy with what you gave them?' asked Joop.

'Yes, but they wanted to argue over the price,' George told him.

'Well, how much you asked from them is your business, but in London the price has gone up to £100 for a single gramme.'

'Are you saying you may ask more?'

'Not for the time being and not to you, my friend. Just give me a ring anytime and don't forget about Sophie.'

This time Duncan chose a ferry from the Hook of Holland to Harwich in Essex. It meant a much longer drive to Scotland, but with a profit of more than £10,000 at stake it was well worth the additional effort needed.

George had been amused by the efforts of Tait, Doran and Bartlett to give a good impression and so he decided to play a small deceit on them. After removing the pouch from behind the dashboard, he divided it into three identical polythene bags. That night in Bartlett's flat, he laid out the three on a shiny tabletop.

'You obviously know what's what, so I thought, as a special favour, I'd offer a choice.' Pointing to each package, he told them, 'This is Colombian, this Peruvian and this Bolivian. The Bolivian is more difficult to get hold of.'

They carefully took a tiny sample from each bag and, like wine tasters, each gave a different verdict as to their relative merits despite the contents being identical. Finally, after an argument, they opted for the Peruvian and paid £4,500.

'What will you do with the rest?' asked Doran, and George wondered if Whacko might then propose taking the residue

65

at a cut price to save him the risk of carrying it back to Holland.

'I might sell a little to a friend, but it will go back and I'll tell my supplier to stick to Peruvian in future,' George lied.

In fact, he had buyers waiting for the unsold bags. Word about the Parachutist had spread at an alarming rate: there was no doubt the Happy Dust Gang was well and truly in business on a grand scale. George had started out with the aim of making sufficient money to buy a new car; now his ambitions were heading in the direction of a new house.

5

THE GYNAECOLOGIST

For the likes of Doran, Tait and Alan Bartlett, cocaine was more than a key that opened the gateway to pleasure – it was a means of making money. Their customers would never be other than those they knew and, even then, there was never enough to go around. There was never any suggestion of the Happy Dust Gang dealing with strangers. But for the vast majority of those who bought it or were given it, the drug was merely a means to an end. Using white became the 'in' thing. Those lucky enough to have access to it, either because they were wealthy or were friends or associates of the Happy Dust Gang, looked on themselves as members of an elite, a sect dedicated to the pursuit of sex and pleasure, behaviour that others would see as shocking and scandalous. There had been other similar groups in Scotland in the past, but none with access to the ecstasy that was cocaine.

For a century from 1732, Anstruther in Fife was the seat of a club named Beggar's Benison and Merryland dedicated to the enjoyment of the idea of free sex. In his excellent book *The Beggar's Benison*, David Stevenson wrote how one of the club's sidelines was support for smuggling, a surprising fact considering the members came from differing social backgrounds, from farming to the Church, business to the law. Its members included a Presbyterian minister, a lieutenant colonel and lieutenant general, a bishop and a lord lieutenant. The same work discusses the story of the Wig Club, founded in Edinburgh in 1775, comprising largely of toffs who worshipped a wig said to have been made from the pubic hairs of the mistresses of Charles II. No doubt had the Happy Dust Gang been around at the time, its members would have been welcomed to both clubs with open arms.

However, as a result of the gang's groundbreaking deals, a scandal of proportions far greater than any other that had gone before was waiting in the wings, one that would set the agenda for the hard-drugs market. Of course, the nation's dirty-linen basket was not empty: Scotland's nouveau riche – comprising at their core the country's self-made businessmen and women – had already experienced more than their fair share of shame and disgrace about which to gossip over cocktails, canapés and cannabis. It seemed no sooner had one embarrassment been played out than more dynamite was delivered to blast wide open the one-time discreet social circles of the middle classes. For years, chatterboxes had dined on a juicy diet of sordid tales about murder, adultery and sexual perversion; soon, they would be able to look down their menus and see envy and greed had been added.

There were times when the party circuit had been littered with skeletons falling out of expensive cupboards. Nowhere was exempt, not even tiny Gigha, God's Island, off the Argyllshire coast. The island had close links to Sir James Horlick, of the famous bedtime drink family, whose exotic gardens at Achamore House are still a renowned visitor attraction. Gigha was then a haven of tranquillity, where violence was restricted to the taking of a fish or the shooting of vermin. But in 1961, the world of the 150 residents was turned topsy-turvy with the shooting dead of the island's £400-a-year ferryman, Nottingham-born Alan Flanders.

Together with their two children, the 27-year-old ex-Royal Navy sailor and his wife Tina, aged 30, had moved to Gigha in 1960. Alan Flanders' heavy drinking led to frequent arguments and it was a miserable marriage. In June 1961, a soldier who was waiting to make the journey, surprised that the usually punctual ferryman had not appeared to start up his motorboat *Danny Boy*, went to his cottage to knock him up only to discover his dead body. Flanders had been shot through the heart with a gun used to kill rabbits. Raven-haired Tina was arrested and charged with capital murder.

It was a shocking affair made all the more sensational by the fact that four years earlier Parliament had passed the 1957 Homicide Act, limiting the death sentence to five categories of murder – one of which was murder by shooting. So when Tina went on trial at the High Court in Glasgow in September 1961, it was for her life. She told the jury of a fight with her husband in which he told her, 'Sleep because it will be a long sleep. What I have to do, I will do later.'

Her version of the tragedy was that she had lain alone in bed but decided to creep downstairs for a cigarette. Alan was asleep on a settee with a gun beside him, which she tried to take from him, but in the struggle it went off. The prosecution tried to show the death in a different light, describing it as a 'cruel, cold deliberate act'. Sir James and Lady Horlick waited anxiously in a Glasgow hotel for the jury's verdict at the end of the three-day trial. The island had already lost one of its number; no one wished the death of a second. But their sleepless nights were soon over. Tina was acquitted by a majority verdict and that evening, with the Horlicks, could return home, to walk in the island sunshine with her children. 'No one can ever know how wonderful this moment is,' she said. 'There are no words to describe it.'

The Horlicks showed remarkable support for brave Tina, and their involvement in a murder case and their backing for a woman who had come so close to facing the hangman would become a talking point throughout Scotland's sherry set.

Memories of the story were recalled by a violent death in another remote part of the country in 1968. Only now a word that would become increasingly synonymous with murder and horror would be introduced into the equation, a relative newcomer to the vocabulary of those eager to throw themselves into Scotland's version of the swinging '60s: 'drugs'.

Maxwell Garvie had good looks, charm and lots of money. He was the catch scores of young women hoped to hook, and finally he fell to Sheila Watson, once a housekeeper at Balmoral, the Queen's fairy-tale castle in the Highlands in Aberdeenshire. The couple married and had three children, but then Sheila discovered her Dr Jekyll, the pillar of farming society, a man almost revered by his peers in the God-fearing community, was in reality a Mr Hyde. Maxwell had a vast appetite for sex and, fuelled by drugs and booze, it grew to terrifying proportions.

The luxury farmhouse he shared with Sheila and the children at Fordoun, Aberdeenshire, would see outrageous sex parties, outright orgies at which couples would flip coins to determine which wife would swap with which husband. Garvie started his own private nudist club, forcing his wife and others, including their children, to strip naked. To further degrade his wife, he began an affair with Trudi Birse, a policeman's wife. He would take her flying in his light aircraft, where, after putting the controls onto automatic, they would make love in the cockpit while the aircraft circled the fields above his farm. When Sheila told her husband that she had discovered the betrayal, his response was a perverse attempt to balance his own deceit by giving himself grounds to likewise accuse her of adultery.

Brian Tevendale, Trudi's brother, was a friend of Maxwell's. One night while he was staying with the Garvies, Brian was staggered to see the door of his bedroom being opened and Maxwell pushing a naked Sheila inside. The couple slept together and soon fell in love. The result was that when Maxwell became bored with Trudi and decided he would take his wife back, to his horror Sheila preferred her lover, 11 years younger than herself. An attempt to break the relationship cost him his life.

Early on 15 May 1968, he was shot in the head as he lay in his bed and his body dumped in a disused quarry. Detectives used the *Police Gazette* to appeal for news of the missing playboy, summing him up with these words:

> Spends freely, is a heavy drinker and often consumes tranquillisers when drinking. Is fond of female company. Deals in pornographic material and is an active member of nudist camps. May have gone abroad.

His body was discovered three months later after conscience-racked Sheila confessed the murder to her mother who informed the authorities.

Crowds queued for seats at the trial in December 1968 at the High Court in Aberdeen. During one session an insurance salesman gave evidence that Sheila would be paid more than £55,000 in life insurance on her husband's death plus their home, three cars and the farm income. Ten days after the trial began, the jury found wife and lover guilty of murder and both were jailed for life. Twelve years later, both had served their time and were released to renewed talk about the goings-on that had attracted worldwide media interest. Sheila went on to run a bed and breakfast on the north-east coast of Scotland and Tevendale to pull pints in a Perthshire pub before dying of a heart attack in 2003.

Scandals in which high living, sex and nudity featured were inevitably favourite topics at get-togethers of the well off, who could afford to indulge in trips to nudist colonies and flights in private aircraft. And descriptions of wife-swapping antics would put ideas into the heads of others elsewhere in

Scotland, their inhibitions loosened by soft drugs. Among the hard up, there was a feeling of resentment and disgust at the indulgences of the wicked wealthy set. But for many what was to follow was worse.

In 1976, the *News of the World* published photographs of Princess Margaret in a swimsuit on the island of Mustique with Roddy Llewellyn, a man 17 years her junior. At the time, the princess was married to magazine photographer Antony Armstrong-Jones, the Earl of Snowdon. It later emerged that she and Llewellyn, son of a well-known equestrian, had been close since 1973. Strongly royalist Scotland was outraged and shocked, not least because at just about every party one or another of the guests could claim some sort of knowledge of Mustique's owner, millionaire brewing heir Colin Tennant, whose ancestral home, The Glen, was in Peeblesshire in the Borders. It was at The Glen that Roddy had first been introduced to the princess and five months later she invited him to Les Jolies-Eaux, her villa in Mustique, given to her as a honeymoon present by Tennant. The island was a refuge for the famous and celebrated, a playground for the international jet set. Raquel Welch had bathed nude there. Visitors included Rolling Stone Mick Jagger, Jerry Hall, Raine and Johnny Spencer, Lord Lichfield, Prince Andrew, Koo Stark and pop singer David Bowie. Two days after the *News of the World* article was published, the Snowdons announced they were to separate and eventually went on to divorce. There was speculation galore about the extent of the relationship between the Queen's sister and the younger man. Party gossips thrived on it, especially as the friendship continued until 1980, the scandal ironically ending just as another was getting under way.

The same year that Mustique became the centre of the world's attention a Glasgow sheriff's courtroom was the focus of a sexual shocker that had people roaring in the aisles. Flamboyant Maurice 'Jimmy' Cochrane, a 51-year-old former managing director of city firm Rotary Tools, was jailed for a year and fined £800 after being convicted of eight corruption charges. Cochrane ran the business from a fur-lined office. And, it was claimed during a trial stretching over ten laughter-packed weeks, that from there he organised gifts and girls for customers to improve his chances of winning orders.

The one-time deep-sea fisherman, boxing-booth boss, dance-hall attendant and vacuum-cleaner salesman had bizarre ideas for boosting business and testing staff. An attractive brunette applying for a job as a clerk was persuaded to sit on a giant inflatable toy elephant in his office and told it was a lie detector. If she told a porky, its eyes would shine. When she answered a question, Cochrane turned on spotlights, which gave the appearance of the elephant's eyes lighting up.

He ordered salesmen to kneel down in front of a life-sized Chinese idol he named Bung Ho and to pray for new orders. Once, he stripped stark naked in front of a trio of astonished businessmen and began pedalling his office exercise bicycle to shock them. Prospective sales-team members might find themselves interviewed by a giant teddy bear. During a business trip to Paris, he horrified the boss of his parent company by taking off his wig and placing it on the hotel floor. Expensively dressed women carefully stepped over it.

On another extraordinary occasion, as he and his secretary Carolyn Schultz, whom he married five months before going to prison, climbed into bed at their home, he shouted to a visiting salesman, 'Donald, in you come.'

During the first night Carolyn slept with Cochrane, she woke up to discover his wig lying on the pillow. 'I had no idea what it was. I just screamed and jumped out of bed. I did not know he was bald, though I wondered why he never let me run my fingers through his hair. After that, if I ever caught him dancing at a party with one of those awful escort agency girls, I would creep up and tug his wig off. It was hilarious to watch the bird's face. She would be horrified to find herself dancing with a man who one minute had a luxurious thatch of hair and the next was as bald as a coot.'

73

One of the escort agency girls was an attractive blonde called Anna Grunt who had the court in stitches describing being hired with two colleagues to join a dinner party laid on by Rotary Tools at the Crazy Daisy Restaurant in Glasgow. After dinner, she was paid £35 to go off to the Excelsior Hotel at Glasgow airport to have sex with John Sim, a National Coal Board official. He commented, 'It became obvious we were going to the room together. She said she would come up with me and I accepted the offer. I spent the night with her in the same bed. I looked on the evening as one of the best chances I had ever had of going to bed with an attractive girl.'

Cochrane's lawyer, Ross Harper, told Sim that the 'beautiful but skinny blonde had been provided as an omelette surprise – crumpet in the Excelsior'. The case summed up Cochrane's business philosophy, as he had once explained it to a salesman: 'All men are bent and we will exploit that. You will find the man's weakness whatever it is. Money, pornography, 5 per cent or women.' Like the Four Horsemen of the Apocalypse, those same vices would be unleashed once again on a society desperate for a new buzz.

Throughout the latter part of the 1970s, posh society had been shocked by a mystery that remains to this day: the disappearance of a married woman and her three-year-old son. In May 1963, Renee MacDonald married her childhood sweetheart, Gordon MacRae, and the couple settled down to life together in a luxury bungalow in Inverness, and had a son, Gordon. But the marriage collapsed, although husband and wife stayed good friends. Renee began an affair with her husband's company secretary, Bill McDowell, a married father of two, and became pregnant. Andrew was born in 1973, after which she and the children moved into a house given to her by her forgiving husband. Gordon MacRae also provided a BMW for his wife.

The affair was meant to be a closely guarded secret, known only to a handful of Renee's closest friends. She was certain

McDowell would be leaving his own wife and marrying her, and confided he had asked her to join him for a weekend in Perthshire and wanted her to take Andrew along.

On Friday, 12 November 1976, Renee headed south with Andrew in the BMW, a pushchair in the boot. About 10 p.m., a passing train driver spotted the blazing car and alerted the police. Officers raced to the scene but found no trace of mother or son, while the undamaged boot was empty. Initially, it was thought Renee had simply disappeared with her son to a new life elsewhere. But doting mothers do not abandon children, and Gordon Jnr remained behind. Police launched a murder hunt, one that continues to this day. That someone could apparently slaughter an innocent child and a young woman guilty only of falling in love horrified Scotland. This was a couple from a well-off background, one in which scandal and violence was generally kept discreetly undercover.

But society was changing. Old values were disappearing. No one was immune. There had been a time when to discuss the ruling classes was simply not done. However, there were many in the higher echelons of society who appeared oblivious to shooting themselves in the foot. Their actions brought discredit not only on themselves but also on others around them. Once they had been respected; now, more and more, they were becoming figures of fun and ridicule. Those who had been accustomed to looking up to them now found themselves witnesses to what happened between the bedsheets: hitherto closed doors were being left open.

A well-kept secret among the upper crust was also soon leaked out about rich landowner David Liddell-Granger, resident at Ayton Castle near Eyemouth in Berwickshire. The bizarre situation caused hilarity, even incredulity. The ten-bedroom castle had played host to Prince Michael of Kent, Prince Alexander of Yugoslavia and the actor Christopher Lee. Eleven miles away at Duns, also in Berwickshire, was the mansion where Sir Eric de la Rue, a member of the family who ran the world's biggest and best-known banknote printing company, lived with his American-born wife, Lady Christine. At the age of 19, she had wed a Greek lawyer only for the marriage to be annulled on the grounds it was never consummated.

David and Sir Eric were friends. So, too, it emerged, were David and Lady Christine. They had met soon after she'd married Eric in 1964, when he was aged 57 and she 22. 'I joined the same hunt as David and he used to catch my horse when it ran loose,' she said. 'He was my knight in shining armour.' Friendship became love. David's marriage to a cousin of the Queen broke up and in 1979, Christine left Sir Eric and moved into the castle, sleeping there but during daytime heading back to cook lunch for her husband.

'I'm not interested in babies. They grow up and cause too much damage, breaking furniture,' said Sir Eric. 'None of my family has been divorced and I don't like the idea of it. I'm prepared to let things carry on as they are.' Later, he would become too ill to look after himself and followed his wife to Ayton Castle, where she and David cared for him until his death in 1989.

Across the country in Ayrshire another scandal was about to feed the voracious appetites of the party faithful. At Maybole lived the young Archibald Angus Charles Kennedy, Earl of Cassilis and his attractive wife, Lady Dawn. A teenage milkman named Stephen Brown lived nearby in a council house he shared with his parents. Two families worlds apart, but when the earl and countess's marriage broke up the blame landed on the milkman.

He told of bathing with Lady Dawn in champagne and covering one another with trifles after he cycled over to her lavish home one day to hang wallpaper. Stephen's revelations were a sensation, to put it mildly. Once, he said, they had fled to a friend's flat. 'There was a mattress on the floor in the living room and we knelt on it and kissed passionately. Dawn helped me remove her sweater. I unfastened her white bra while she unbuttoned my shirt. We then took off the rest of our clothes and embraced, slowly exploring one another's bodies. This was the first time we'd been in bed together for over a week and so much had happened that we made slow, passionate love. Then we kissed each other all over before making love again.' Inevitably, in 1989, the marriage ended in divorce.

The earl became the 8th Marquess of Ailsa, entitling him to a seat in the House of Lords. Lady Dawn moved to London where, in 1992, she was arrested after failing to appear for a court hearing to look into allegations she had been raped. The prosecutor told magistrates, 'She has been living off prostitution and is a heroin addict.' The lady of class had been sucked in by drugs; others were about to follow.

In Glasgow in particular, and central Scotland in general, cocaine sparked a million fantasies. An outsider peering in might have thought he or she was being given an insight into goings-on at the making of a soft-porn movie – and, frequently, its hard-core version. For Thomas Sim, it was entry to a Garden of Eden of which he had previously only dreamed.

'The women all seemed to go for tiny miniskirts or really short hot pants and the sort of boots Julia Roberts would make famous in the movie *Pretty Woman* ten years later in 1990. We called them "Fuck Me Boots" because they were a sort of code from the wearer that given a couple of drinks and a line of Charlie, she'd be up for anything. White stiletto heels, another favourite, were "Shagging Shoes".

'One guy took a married woman home in his car from a party one night and they detoured to Strathclyde Country Park to the south of Glasgow to do the business on the back seat. When they'd finished and the woman was rearranging her clothing, she couldn't find one of her white stilettos. They hunted high and low and then she started panicking about being home late. The guy thought that was hilarious because it was almost morning by this time. In the end, he just dropped her off and she walked up to the front door carrying the remaining shoe. Later on, his own wife wanted to go shopping, and she was a few yards from the car when he saw the stiletto, the heel stuck in the roof lining. He grabbed it just in time.

'At one party in the Rock Garden, a popular club in the city, a crowd of women all turned up wearing flying suits made of a yellow silk material with zips down the front. They were see-through and skintight and you could see who was and who was not wearing knickers and brassieres. And most weren't. They had a competition in which guys were blindfolded and held paper clips fashioned into hooks between their lips. The idea was they had to hook the zips and pull, but a couple of the women got tired of waiting and gave the men a hand. One of them just took her suit off and stood there being admired. She was as high as a kite.'

Sometimes hosts would offer a line of coke to guests with the same lack of ceremony as a martini or a glass of Scotch. Hosts would try to outdo one another in their inventiveness. At a party in Shawlands, couples were encouraged to bid clothing for lines and when they ran out of garments, performed sex acts with their wives, or the wives of other guests, while the rest of the merrymakers cheered them on.

'At house parties, you'd find lines of cocaine set out in the kitchen on the table, a fridge top or even on the washing machine,' said Sim. 'If you didn't take a line, then you were looked on with suspicion and someone would ask if there was something wrong with you – were you ill, perhaps?

'Brian Doran was a sought-after celebrity. When he walked in, people would sing the Electric Light Orchestra hit tune "Mr Blue Sky". If they'd made a new Carry On series and called one of the films *Carry On Cocaine*, then Brian would have taken Sid James's starring role. Everything revolved around him.'

The success of a party was frequently reckoned by the amount of happy dust available, with Andrew Tait a well-known supplier. Hosts would encourage the best-looking young women in the city to join in the fun. The girls had heard of cocaine but because of the difficulty in obtaining the drug to most it was a mystery. It was the rich man's drug circulating in a social scene beyond the means of all but a select few in Scotland. The ambitious social climbers all hoped to be gathered in and become members of the club. Enviously, they eyed those to whom the door had already been opened. All had one thing in common: they exuded an aura of attraction. For some, that attraction was wealth – possessions, like a big house or expensive cars. For others, it was good looks. For a lucky few, it was both. Being rich meant you could attract the good-lookers, young men and women – but mainly women. Among them were those who saw the happy dust circle as a means of improving their lot. There were wannabe models who nurtured faint dreams of stardom, wives who were happy to use their bodies if it meant furthering the careers of their husbands, and then those who sought simply the security of netting a rich, handsome husband. In Glasgow, cocaine was the equivalent of the infamous Hollywood casting couch.

Until they were invited into the select but expanding group, few of these luvvies had experienced cocaine. One, now a successful west of Scotland businesswoman, recalls, 'You might go to a friend's home, just for a chat, and they'd give you a drink and then say "How about a livener?" and offer you a line of cocaine. And you would be expected to shoot the line.

'For me, this wasn't quite the surprise it was for many others. I had friends in the south of Spain who regularly smoked joints and when I'd been over there visiting them, it was commonplace for them to offer hash to all their guests. The difference was that hash was ridiculously cheap, while cocaine was hideously expensive and very few people knew how to get hold of it. Just as hash was socially acceptable over there, cocaine became almost a magnet that drew you to parties where it was available.

'I first snorted coke at a house in Pollokshields around about mid-1980. At that time, it was a rarity. My initial reaction, I remember, was "Wow, where did that feeling come from?" I felt so good I couldn't believe it. I was suddenly a star, somebody important and powerful who had the right to mix with celebrities, somebody who everyone around would want to be with. I had heard the expression "walking on air" in the past and now that is what I believed I could do. And I felt incredibly randy, not in the sense of being forward or dirty, just exhilarated, happy, willing for sex. Of course, this did not last, but at that time I was sure this mood of such joy could go on forever. And I wanted it to. I'd have done anything just to have it continue because this was a sensation I had never ever experienced.'

Depending upon the strength of the powder, the effects of cocaine generally mean euphoria is reached in around 15 minutes and gradually fade until after about an hour the sensation has disappeared. It is at this point that a user wants more. This caused a problem for party hosts encouraging their guests to enjoy the drug. Having proffered one line, they would be badgered for more. From the point of view of the Happy Dust Gang, this was excellent news. Their customers simply wanted more and more. And hosts able to afford cocaine soon learned they were rewarded for their outlay in many different ways.

That cocaine loosened inhibitions was beyond doubt, but then the majority of users were already in a mood to be wanton. What was remarkable was the sight of a couple whose neighbours would have sworn to be the epitome of respectability seemingly abandoning themselves to the search for sexual bliss. Cocaine made no distinction between sexes or attitudes. You took it because you wanted to feel different and be different.

A classic example was that of an infamous party held in a large house in Pollokshields in the spring of 1981, as ever-increasing demands were being made of the Parachutist. The house, not that occupied by the Doran family, boasted a games room (estate-agent-speak for a room big enough to hold a full-size snooker table). As an excuse for a celebration, the owners quoted a wedding anniversary and shunted their children off for the night to relatives living elsewhere in the city. They had friends who dealt with the Happy Dust Gang and ample income to afford a healthy supply of white. Some weeks after the event, a major fallout over a business arrangement meant one of the guests was ostracised and, piqued by effectively being thrown out of the inner circle of Glasgow's rich, decided to sell his story to a national newspaper. It was effectively an exposé of the birthday party.

'Lines of coke were laid out in the dining room and there was even a bundle of crisp banknotes at the side to be rolled up and used for snorting. It was the height of one-upmanship. Most of those present were businessmen, but there were at least two lawyers with their wives and a very senior middle-aged banker, who was obviously adept at rolling the note and for that reason you knew he was a regular cocaine user. You had to wonder whether his investors would have given him such a free hand with their money had they known of his habit.

'Normally, a party would take an hour or so for the booze to take effect and for things to warm up, but when there was Charlie around, within 20 minutes things would be buzzing. This was no exception, but most of the action was in the games room. Somebody had come up with the idea of four couples playing a sort of strip snooker. If the women potted a red, then they could nominate a guy who had to remove an item of clothing. The men had to pot a red followed by a colour to point to one of the females and get her to take something off. All the men were out to get the owner's wife starkers and he was shouting them on. She was a beautiful woman, at least 40 years old with red hair, heavily built but not fat. There was a rumour that she had been a fashion model when she was younger. Her skirt was knee-length, but each time she bent over to play a shot it rode up and there was no doubt she even gave it a little hitch to make sure it did. Hard as they tried, the men could hardly pot a ball, while she must presumably have spent a bit of time practising and as a result it was the guys who were losing their clothes. She would pot a ball, point the tip of the cue at something they were wearing, give her victim the most demure smile and simply tell him, "Off."

'The other women thought this hilarious until a couple of the men had a lucky streak and she had to unbutton her blouse and slip off her skirt. It was amazing to see an outwardly prim mum strutting about in pants and a bra and acting as though it was what she'd wanted to do all her life. That was the effect of cocaine. She told the other women, "Let's all strip," and they did. The redhead took off her bra and said the next man who potted a red and a colour could do whatever he wanted with her. When one did, she grabbed him and his wife and the three headed upstairs. "Come on," she was shouting. "I have some gear in the bedroom. We know the Parachutist."

'There were younger, unattached girls at the party, two in particular, very very good looking. One had stripped to just her hot pants and boots and was dancing surrounded by men. It made you wonder if this was her first time with Charlie.

'What was surreal about the whole scene was that nobody was being sick, nobody was shouting, nobody wanted to fight, nobody was falling about or acting the fool. Most of the couples appeared to have brought their own happy dust and were offering little polythene packets of white powder around as if they were peanuts or crisps at a pub bar on a night out. The wife of one of the lawyers wore a wraparound blue dress and was sitting on an armchair cradling a drink. Friends would wander up, undo the dress and pull it back to show she was bare breasted, fondle her and tie it back in place as if nothing had happened. She just smiled and nodded, out of her head. Throughout the house there was more naked flesh on display than at a nudist convention, but everything gave the impression of being highly civilised and normal, as if this was the way in which everyone was expected to behave.'

There was never any chance of the newspaper publishing the man's account, particularly when senior executives were told the identities of some of those present. These were men with bulging bank balances, easily capable of funding a major libel action. For the whistleblower and his family, the welcome mat would never again be rolled out.

Meanwhile this was the era when the party scene in Glasgow was at its zenith. The advent of cocaine, thanks to the Happy Dust Gang, sparked a million laughs and pleasures. It might have been the key ingredient in the recipe for fun, but this was the time too when the city was home to personalities who not only *believed* in enjoying themselves but set about doing just that.

Frank McAvennie was in 1981 a young footballer with St Mirren, being talked of as a future Scotland international. Frank was quick on the field and a swift mover off it. He loved to party and as a professional athlete was much sought after by women, in the way the wives of rich Romans would pay well for a night with a gladiator before he faced death in the arena. McAvennie would later become caught up in sensational revelations about taking cocaine, but for now he needed no stimulant to aid his enjoyment. Drugs were for others.

'It was a great time for parties. I had a set of twins for my 21st in November the previous year. Those were among the happiest days of my life and I enjoyed every moment. One of my friends owned a big house and had installed his own sauna, which was a real novelty. Until then, we had only seen naked Swedes sitting in them on television thrashing themselves with branches. And that was enough to convince my friend a sauna would be a very good idea. When word got around about his sauna, everyone wanted to try it, especially guys who thought you only had to open the door to see a bevy of naked girls sitting around. Of course it wasn't like that at all, well not at first anyway. So my pal hit on an idea to liven things up. He'd persuade the girls to leave their clothes at the door and go in naked, promising them there were towels waiting for them as they came out. And there were towels. The teeniest you ever saw. The smallest bath towels in the world. Once one girl showed she wasn't over-shy it wasn't long before others were showing off. Some would simply come out of the sauna and wander about stark naked. This was a time when all over the world women were burning their bras. So they'd go to a party bra-less.

'There were all sorts of games going on, strip poker and the like. You got hold of a willing girl, asked her if she fancied a good time and lots of fun, and took her along. When she asked, "What should I wear?" you would reply, "A G-string." In addition, if it was your lucky night, she would do as she was told. As things got lively, off would come their dresses and they would be wandering about in G-strings, high heels and nothing else.

'There was a lot of talk about drugs, but not so many around because not many people could afford them and the drugs scene was much more underground then, much more discreet. Drugs were a middle-class thing, something for the wealthy. Struggling young footballers couldn't afford them and they weren't part of our scene. But I'd heard about the effects drugs could have. I knew if I took drugs, I wouldn't be able to train and that would be the end of my career in football. But all the talk about them made me curious. And maybe all that curiosity would lead to what was to happen to me later on.

'In Glasgow, we'd go to Maxwell Plums on the Quayside just around the corner from the Warehouse. My nights were Saturday, Sunday and Wednesday, with Sunday the favourite. Paisley was a great party spot in the '80s, with one of the hottest spots the Cotton Club where Richard Park of Radio Clyde, later to become head of music at Capital Radio, was the DJ. Colin Barr was resident at Toledo Junction on a Monday night. These were the places to be and to be seen. It was such a brilliant time. The style was for girls to wear as little as possible, to show as much of themselves as possible without being indecent, although sometimes even that went out of the window. Most of the birds I met seemed to be blonde with very long legs. As a footballer, you were something of a celebrity and all the girls wanted to be with you. In those days, we were lucky. Now, celebrities and footballers can't go anywhere without having to look over their shoulders for kiss-and-tell girls. They make eyes, offer you everything and then run off to the newspapers. It wasn't like that then. If you scored with a girl, it was between her and you, and most of the girls I scored with didn't want anyone to know it was with me.

'We were so lucky. You could score with a girl and know you'd get away with it. Your name wouldn't be in a newspaper a few days later and, in the same way, if you were into drugs you could rely on the girl not telling. That's why the drugs scene was a close circle, a small circle, a close-kept secret.

'I loved the parties. They would generally end up with about ten people and that's when the real fun would start. One night at a pal's house, he confided he had bought a baby monitor. It was one of those very useful pieces of equipment that you plugged in beside the baby in the cot upstairs and listened to a microphone downstairs for all the reassuring noises. He set it up in a bedroom and persuaded some couples to take their turn having sex not knowing we were sitting in his kitchen downstairs listening in and roaring with laughter.'

In 1985, Frank, still one of the most popular and likeable Scots players of all time, was transferred to London club West Ham, where he became caught up in the champagne and cocaine lifestyle. Much later, he admitted to the *News of the World*, 'Just hours after my transfer on a celebration trip to the West End of London, I spotted another footballer, an international, sitting glazed, helpless and alone after taking cocaine in a crowded nightspot. It was pretty awful. It shocked me.' Ironically, as he was beginning his happy dust experiences, the members of the gang who had introduced the drug to so many in Glasgow would also be starting out afresh.

Another highly skilled young player making his rounds of the nightspots while the Happy Dust Gang was thriving and who would become linked to cocaine was Maurice Johnston, born in Glasgow in April 1963. Like Frank, Mo would become a household name, scoring 14 times for his country and causing a sensation in 1989 when the ex-Celtic star signed for bitter city rivals Rangers.

Maurice built a reputation with Partick Thistle as one of the most dangerous goal-scorers in the country before being snapped up by English club Watford, then moving to Celtic in 1985. His home was once raided by police and he has denied ever using drugs, but in 1986 teenage model Diane Edgar made lurid allegations in the *News of the World* about drug-taking and wild sex parties during a six-month affair with him. During the interview, she gave her version of what happened at the beginning of the 1985–86 season when Mo was about to fly overseas with Celtic:

> He'd driven me and a friend in his Porsche to Glasgow airport. He parked outside the airport hotel. He got into the back seat with his mate. I could hear them arguing and I could hear Maurice say, 'Give me some,' and the friend say, 'For God's sake, don't be so stupid. You're about to get on a plane!' I turned around to see what was happening and I saw Maurice take a tin foil packet from the friend and open it. Inside I could see some white powder. Maurice put it to his nose and had a big sniff.

This allegation was made just weeks after Frank McAvennie's bitter encounter with the effects of cocaine on the international footballer in London. Friends of both men would later blame these off-pitch problems on having been acquainted with cocaine during their formative years. There was no suggestion either had taken it while they were establishing themselves in Scotland. But both were lovers of the club scene, knew how and where to party, and could not have failed to have been present when others were snorting.

As the cocaine habit spread, users became bolder. Some might say more daring, others careless and indiscreet. The Parachutist was paranoid about security, constantly stressing to Doran and Tait, in particular, the need to be vigilant and not to boast that they had access to apparently limitless supplies. But once he handed over his polythene-wrapped packages, control of what then happened was out of his hands.

As an example of how quickly problems could develop, take a party in a leading Glasgow massage parlour, now no longer in existence. The sauna was, of course, merely a front for prostitution, but a small group of couples regularly involved in the thriving wife-swapping scene would meet there monthly with the knowledge of the owners. It meant, with the kids tucked up in their beds under the care of a babysitter, that they could indulge without the worry of curious neighbours.

All would take along toot. One of their favourite games involved the wives or girlfriends hiding the drug and the men trying to discover it, which usually meant an excuse to congregate in the changing area and strip the women. Naturally, no man would be expected to search his own partner. It was relatively harmless fun and snorting would be limited to the cubicles normally used by prostitutes to offer massages – and the inevitable 'extras' – to clients. The atmosphere was generally convivial, the swappers keeping to themselves. All had gone well until one of the members, a man we will call 'John', who had connections to the offshore oil industry, decided to spice up proceedings. He invited two of the sauna prostitutes to join in the fun by taking part in the search of the wives. The professionals were happy to do so. To them, this was business and they had been assured they would be paid. There was much groping, fondling and afterwards most of the group adjourned in twos and threes to the cubicles. The evening ended with mutual good wishes; however, this departure from tradition would later become a talking point among the prostitutes, a topic for laughs as they waited for clients in what was advertised, somewhat tongue-in-cheek, as the VIP Lounge.

One of the women mentioned the incident of the search to a regular but despised visitor, a police officer who would occasionally even appear with an overcoat hiding his uniform and who insisted upon free services in exchange for his turning a blind eye to the running of what was obviously an illegal brothel.

'Bet you'd love to search all your women suspects like that,' she teased.

'Oh, who are they?' the policeman asked, feigning indifference.

'A crowd who come in every month. They bring along some Charlie and screw each other's wives.'

'Yes, but who?'

'Don't know the names, but you can tell from what the women wear they're loaded.'

'And they come every month?'

'Roughly every month, yes.'

'So they'll be back when?'

The prostitute realised her mistake and began to back-pedal, using her hands to try distracting her inquisitor. 'Leave me your number and I'll give you a shout next time they're here,' she lied.

When the policeman, now retired, had gone, the woman spoke to the owner. 'That bastard was asking me about the swappers. He wanted to know if they were into cocaine and when they'd be coming back,' she said.

Contrary to popular misconceptions, those running saunas have a high regard for the welfare of patrons. In this case, a call was made to one of the swappers warning about the discussion with the cop. Discretion would have advised postponing further gatherings for several months;

instead, the swappers merely switched venues and by a miracle were able to continue their activities unmolested for a number of years.

No one could dispute that the cocaine supplied by the Happy Dust Gang triggered memorable parties. It certainly excited the imagination. A gramme would normally provide up to ten lines, ten snorts, with three snorts enough to see the average user on a high throughout the evening. At one mid-1981 bash in the West End of Glasgow, the hosts offered a full gramme to the winners of a bizarre contest. The idea was for a wife or girlfriend to slowly remove her clothing and gently hang the garments on a coat-hanger suspended from the penis of her chosen partner. Clearly for this to work the male had to be stimulated, a task for which anyone could offer assistance. Each woman took it in turn to remove a garment. Those who had arrived in stockings and suspender belts were clearly at an advantage, the almost total weightlessness of the nylon having little or no effect on the hanger. The event was filmed with the intention of mass-producing the result and selling copies, until it was pointed out that this would clearly identify all those present should it ever be discovered cocaine had been circulating at the party. It was agreed the celluloid would be destroyed, which was a pity, as those attending would later claim the winner managed to hold the entire outfit worn by his wife, with the exception of her shoes!

Despite the concerns of George Duncan, the taking of cocaine was not restricted to private functions. Sometimes it was used openly, too openly, causing frictions that could spill out into open confrontation and attract unnecessary attention. A close friend of his and Sim's had become heavily involved with a remarkably attractive Glasgow model who, unable to exist solely on bookings, worked part time in one of the bars frequented by the gang. One night as she was serving drinks on one side of the bar, he, on the other, began a conversation with one of her friends seated on a high stool. Before arriving, he had snorted a solitary line, admirably refusing his girlfriend the same privilege, sensibly arguing that she was working. He could not help noticing that the girl on the stool was wearing a short skirt held together on her thigh with a large pin and he wondered what the effect would be if the pin were released. He reasoned it was worth finding out and politely enquired if she might care to enjoy a line.

'What about your girlfriend? Won't she mind?' he was asked.

'Absolutely not. She's already sampled,' he lied, handing her a tiny phial and suggesting while powdering her nose she might care to inhale deeply.

She emerged and within 15 minutes was evidently feeling the effects, noticing his gaze upon her thighs and adjourning once more, briefly, to the ladies' room. When she resumed her seat, he discovered to his astonishment she had removed her knickers and there were traces of happy dust at the top of her thighs.

Dropping to his knees, he was about to sample what was on offer when a familiar face peered over the counter and he heard a voice he knew so well. 'Changing jobs, are we? You training to be a fucking gynaecologist?' It was the end of a beautiful friendship.

6

BOMB PUSHER

George Duncan and Thomas Sim began arranging regular cocaine-smuggling journeys to Glasgow always using a hire car rented from a different company and never taking the same route twice, varying between Rotterdam or Zeebrugge to Hull, the Hook of Holland to Harwich or Dover, and even Dunkirk in France to Dover. With Sim as his willing assistant, Duncan was the mastermind: the solver of problems and inventor of ideas. However, while the group called themselves the Happy Dust Gang, Duncan was rarely happy with what he saw or heard. And there were times when he was appalled.

Sim would later admit: 'Tait, Doran and Alan Bartlett seemed only interested in being able to say to their pals, "Do you want some Charlie?" to give the impression they were big-time. George was continually warning them to be more discreet, but the longer it went on the more indiscreet they became. It was he and I and Scouse Willie who were taking all the risks. We knew our end of the operation was secure but couldn't get rid of the thought that it would be they who would let us down at the end of the day. They thought they were the top of the tree and would mouth off to all and sundry. One of the problems about cocaine is that the first thing you do once you've taken it is want everybody else to do the same. It turns you on and you want to turn someone else on in the same way – especially a good-looking girl – because it has such an aphrodisiac effect and you cannot resist the feeling that once she takes a line she'll do anything you ask. This is why the use of cocaine has spread through the universe and by the best possible method of advertising, word of mouth.

'When we left Glasgow for Spain, Doran, Big Andy Tait in particular, and other up-and-coming businessmen, such as Bartlett, were the sort of men we looked up to. We were picking up something like £17 a week, but they drove flash cars and had lifestyles so many envied. Clearly, at some stage, someone had said to them, "Try this," and given them some Charlie. It would probably be a friend who had been holidaying in Spain or North Africa and had come across the drug and thought it might be fun to take some back to Scotland. These were the type of people who would try new ideas in business, take risks to improve themselves and would experiment with something like cocaine, even if at first only for laughs, to see what the effect was.

'When we came back and found they were into Charlie and sticking £150 a time up their noses, we knew they were only playing at it, getting a few grammes here and there, using it, running out, then going through hell until they could get more. And the way they were using it was all wrong. Here were successful young guys with a few quid in their pockets and not appreciating just what they were playing around with. The night all this really began, George and I had walked into Charlie Parker's and could not believe what we saw. The bar was doing well, but the toilets were even busier. There were more transactions going on in them than there were on a busy day at the London Stock Exchange. So many people were disappearing into the toilets, I thought somebody had sold them dodgy gear and they were suffering from diarrhoea.

'People were flocking around Brian Doran like bees around a honey pot. Smartly dressed guys kept patting the breast pockets of their suits and we found out later they had bought biro pens and removed the nib and ink reservoir to create a tube for snorting. They believed they were very clever lightly touching the pocket as if to say, "I'm a member of a very secret club restricted to the wealthy who can afford to do cocaine." It was absolutely pathetic.

'George pulled out a soft leather pouch to show them how it was really done. Inside were a little mirror for putting the cocaine on, a tiny gold spoon for lifting it from your packet or container, a gold-plated razor blade for chopping and sorting it into lines, and a gold-plated cylinder, trumpet-shaped at one end to act as a sort of coke vacuum while you inhaled through the other. Most people in Holland who were into cocaine had a pouch; they were a form of status symbol strung around the neck on a gold chain. When the Glasgow people saw what George showed them, they crowded around. "Gonnae get me one of those, big man?" they would ask.

'After we got things going with that first delivery, they came to think they were the experts, not us; that what they were doing was the right way and we were the amateurs. There were times they would look at us as though we were telling them the world was round. The incident over the Peruvian, Colombian and Bolivian showed how little they really knew. We persistently tried warning them to be careful, but they were getting too much kudos through being able to supply in Glasgow.

'They'd be asked, "Hey, this is good stuff, where did you get it?" Somebody would want to show how clever he was by saying, "From the Continent." And if Spain was suggested, they wouldn't be able to resist coming back with "No, Holland." And it didn't take a genius to work out that George and I had originally been from Glasgow, were now living in Holland and regularly came back over on visits. They had no inkling that, as a result of their indiscretion, others in Scotland had approached us and asked if we'd supply them also.

'We chose our customers carefully and had a hiding place in Glasgow where we could leave packets of coke for weeks, knowing they would never be discovered. Once, we brought a batch of 100 grammes for Tait and Doran but before we left for Holland they were on the telephone saying, "That stuff's no good," so we apologised and promised to replace it. We said we'd arrange for more to be sent over while we were still in town, but all we did was hang around for a couple of days then hand them the original stuff back only wrapped differently. When we rang up to check that this time it was OK, they told us, "That's much better," even though it was the same gear. Sometimes we wondered how it was these people were so successful in their businesses.'

When word got round of Doran's role in controlling the cocaine market in Glasgow, he was approached by an Irishman who was said to be heavily connected to an Ulster-based loyalist terrorist organisation. This man had a serious drink problem and was known to be a braggart – he had actually been told to leave Northern Ireland because he couldn't keep his mouth shut. It was probably only the fact that he was such a fool that saved him from being shot by the opposition. He approached the Happy Dust Gang, wanting to buy Charlie from them and saying that if they agreed, it would put them in the good books with his organisation. They were actually thinking it over when somebody pointed out that one of his squad had been driving a car packed with explosives en route to Belfast city centre one night when it ran out of petrol. They got out and were pushing the car bomb when an army patrol came on them and they ran off. That was the calibre of brainless idiot some of those in Glasgow would have done deals with.

'George especially could not understand behaviour like this,' Sim continued. 'It was second-class behaviour from folk who strutted around as though they were in the top league. Yet here were the so-called elite acting in a way we associated with the working classes. The great thing about cocaine at that time was that it was a class divider because it cost money – it was way beyond the pocket of the average working man. Some might have thought it a form of divine intervention that ordinary people could not afford it; it was the prerogative of the stars and celebrities, of the rich and famous. To have cocaine was to look like them. It was to say, "Look at me, I am so rich I can afford to take coke." However, putting coke up your nose was also God's way of saying, "You have too much money."

'We had this constant dread that because things had gone so well, that so many people had begun talking about the Parachutist – the man who landed regularly with supplies – that it was inevitable the day would come when someone would have their collar felt, that there would be an end to it. Not just have your collar felt but put in the pokey. And if it happened to one, then all would suffer. Maybe we should have told ourselves warning bells were ringing. The problem is that when you have come from the bottom of the Fourth Division and you find yourself playing for a spot in the Champions League, then to continue having the means of staying in the top flight is a risk you are willing to take.

'We had left Glasgow at a time when you looked up to these men, they were made people with good jobs. In Holland, there is a saying: "Your bed is made for you." It implies that the bed looks beautiful and comfortable, sweet-smelling with soft pillows and clean sheets. It is there, waiting for you to lie down, relax and feel good. In other words, everything is in place for you. There's nothing for you to do but enjoy what is there. That was how it was for them. On the other hand, in Govan, where I was brought up, everything was hard. It wasn't a case of made beds rather that you didn't even have a bed. If you wanted one, then you had to go out and get yourself one and then make it up. You had to work for something before you could reap the benefits from it. And in Govan there were certain rules of the street, one of them being that you were taught to keep your mouth shut and not to grass when anything went wrong. George had learned that lesson well but felt there were others who would collapse under pressure from the police.

'These were people who, in many cases, had been sheltered from the realities of life such as the value of having a secret and keeping it. They ought to have kept the existence of the Happy Dust Gang to themselves or at least to their very immediate circle, but vanity got the better of them. It's like the 14-year-old schoolboy who rushes into class on Monday mornings bursting to tell everybody, "I had sex at the weekend with this cracker from over the road." What do his pals say? They want to know what it was like, how it felt, who the girl was, and if they can have a go with her themselves. Everyone else wants to try and it's odds on the girl won't want anything more to do with the boy. Someone older and wiser would have kept it to himself but by shouting it to the rooftops suddenly the boy's a minor celebrity.'

And that was how it was with Doran and Tait, only they did not want to stop there.

7

THE IBROX CONNECTION

Ibrox Stadium in Glasgow, home to the Gers, Rangers Football Club, is one of the world's great soccer grounds. The club motto, 'Aye Ready', might appropriately have been Andy Tait's cry on Saturdays during the football season when the Gers were playing at home because the big, likeable baker had one of the most prized contracts in the game: he supplied the pies nearly 50,000 fans devoured on match days. That meant preparing hundreds of extra delicacies and making sure they were baked in time and ready to be hurried across the city and through the thronging crowds. It was just as well his cooking was on the ball because during the heyday of the Happy Dust Gang his grub was virtually all the faithful had on which to salve their hunger for success. The side was going through a lean spell, with Aberdeen clinching the league title in 1980, Rangers' bitter city rivals Celtic taking it the following two seasons, then unexpected champions Dundee United grabbing it in 1983. Andy's pies were an off-field distraction from upsets on the park. If fans left Ibrox feeling as sick as parrots, it was not because of anything they had eaten.

So successful was the pie run that the club itself would

later decide it would do its own cooking and at the same time pocket all the profits. No one could or would say whether this change was the result of Andy's involvement with the Gang becoming public knowledge. But back then in catering circles being baker to the Blues was, if not a Royal appointment, one regarded as being highly prestigious. There would have been many who looked longingly at the arrangement and who would have been satisfied to have a fortnightly moment of glory as the supporters handed over their money and tucked in. But that regular 90 minutes of fame was not enough for Tait. He wanted to be a bigger fish in an exotic pool.

Andy had quit school in 1959 at the age of 14 during an era when the main headache for leavers was not whether they would find a job but which career to choose. For a willing and reasonably intelligent teenager, jobs were abundant, although that situation would soon alter for the worse. However, for the young Andy, catering was his chosen trade and he set to the task of learning with gusto. It was hard, dusty work and he would frequently head home with the wind blowing flour from his hair and eyes.

Thirteen years after handing in his school books, Tait got the chance to work for himself and he took it with both hands, becoming the new owner of The Pantry. It meant working hours that few would have endured. Frequently, he was in the bakery at 3.30 in the morning, ironically sometimes listening as he opened up to the sound of happy revellers on their way home after whooping it up in one of Glasgow's many popular nightspots. It would be six in the evening before he left with the rest of his staff. The city might have rested on the Sabbath, but it did not cease eating and that meant a seven-day week for Andy and the other bakers.

In 1975, three years after taking over ownership of the bakery, he decided it was time to expand and bought into a partnership in a city centre restaurant on Sauchiehall Street. It turned out to be a move he would regret. The spot needed investment, lots of it, and was soon in financial difficulties. His partner threatened to pull the plug, leaving Andy, who had pledged his home and The Pantry as security against buying into the development, to face losing everything for which he had worked so hard. He earned £15,000 a year, a princely sum back then, but even that was not enough. He found himself in a nightmare scenario that would eventually destroy him; however, when a possible solution leapt out, he thought his worst fears were over. His wife, Geraldine, worked for Brian Doran at Blue Sky Travel on Berkeley Street in the city. Whacko had a good relationship with his employees, treating them as equals, friends rather than mere workers, and it was by no means extraordinary for Geraldine to mention during a casual conversation that her husband had money troubles. Her boss did not hesitate. 'What can I do to help?' he asked.

It was a straw to be clutched and the baker grabbed it. The two men arranged for lawyers to draw up an agreement under which the travel agent would loan £10,000 and Tait offer his home as security. That should have been the end of his woes; however, as time passed, another bug would arrive to eat at the foundations of his world: fatigue. This was the excuse he would later give for becoming a founder member of the Happy Dust Gang at any rate.

Andy and Whacko became close friends after the former schoolteacher bailed him out of his financial mess. The two men got on well together and enjoyed each other's company. Through Doran, Tait discovered there was more to life than work and home. There existed a world of fun and music, and a white powder he had been told would act as the perfect stimulant to counter the tiredness caused by working horrendously long hours. In fact, he was assured by those in the know that it would do more: it would give him a stamina, drive and verve he had never known. It was called cocaine.

But there was one problem: getting it.

Supplies were limited and consequently it was expensive.

Even Brian Doran, a man with the uncanny knack of seemingly finding a way around any hurdle, had to at times admit defeat; in fact, the two were discussing the very scarcity of cocaine the night George Duncan and Thomas Sim arrived in Charlie Parker's from Holland.

In the weeks that followed that first meeting, Doran, along with Tait and Alan Bartlett – some would later describe Ronnie Bartlett as a member of the Happy Dust Gang but in reality all would accept he was very much on the fringe of the racket – realised the advantages of throwing in his lot with the exiled Scots. Before that, those with Charlie to sell, seeing a flash car or well-dressed customer, simply thought they could afford to pay more and so pushed up the price. Doran could almost lip-read their conversations each time he drove to meet them. 'Look at this fucker. See that car. Bet his suit cost a fortune. Fuckers like him are loaded. He's wealthy. Filthy rich, make the fucker pay through the nose. He can afford it.' Now, there would be a set rate. And a further advantage was that Duncan and Sim were men prepared to operate on trust. They did not ask for money up front; it was to be cash on delivery.

Having established contact with a regular source that could supply enough for his medicinal needs, Andy Tait might have been expected to stop there. Any regular user of cocaine will admit that one fix is never enough. As the effect wears off and life returns to its old, depressing self, another is needed, and then another. And on it goes. So it was with Tait and the rest of the gang.

And it was not enough just to satisfy themselves. They saw an opportunity to serve the needs of others by becoming dealers themselves and, in doing so, score doubly: first by making money, and second by giving them a bizarre power. They had agreed to pay £45 a gramme, so asking members of the circle in which they mixed for £50 or £55 would certainly keep their own customers happy, as they would make a huge saving compared with the price they had been accustomed to paying. And having the ability to decide

100

who could and could not have happy dust would make them men to be sought out, shown recognition, treated with respect and flattered: men to be courted. And the deeper the drug took hold on their customers, the greater would become their renown. Tait had watched the near adoration afforded to Doran; now he could join the elite.

Most drug dealers have the problem of finding suitable cover for their activities. Many sell from their homes and, in doing so, attract attention from neighbours disturbed by strangers arriving at all hours. Others must simply settle for operating on street corners or from vehicles, thus risking being spotted by a passing policeman. And Andy Tait had the ideal outlet. Strangers popped in and out of his shop constantly, and there was nothing unusual about a sales representative being invited into the back of the shop to discuss business. Selling cocaine with the cookies might sound corny, but it had a ring of security.

The fact that much of the business became centred around The Pantry had the effect of making Andy Tait feel he was the linchpin of the racket, the leader of the Happy Dust Gang. No one contradicted this impression, but it left the baker under the illusion that he was something of a cocaine expert, a misapprehension of which Duncan and Sim would take cruel advantage. In his naivety, Andy failed to realise all drug dealers are unscrupulous. They may set out with the intention of acting honourably but virtue soon disappears. Their business is one of risk and the intention is to make money, money to buy more drugs, whether for their own use or to sell to others. The more drugs they possess, the more money they make. Of course, if a gramme of cocaine can somehow be turned into two grammes, then its worth doubles. Mixing additives to any drug is, though if at times dangerous, an accepted swindle. Glucose powder is a favourite cocaine additive. If the over-exuberance of an additive leaves the mixture weak, then the remedy is to drop in cheap amphetamines. Mannitol was Duncan and Sim's favourite, a substance sometimes sold as a mild laxative for children. Sim later confessed, 'When we first got to know this crowd, we noticed how much of their drug-taking activity involved running to the loo, so we thought there was no reason to change that. All we did was give a helping hand.'

In reality, this was not such a wicked deception. Mannitol, a white, odourless, sweet-tasting powder, has the effect of keeping the nose running after snorting, the fluidity acting as protection against users losing their septum – the cartilage that separates the nasal passages – and their looks. It is a miserable condition that requires a painful and complex rebuilding operation. Celebrities to have fallen victim to this in recent times include *EastEnders* actress Daniella Westbrook and *Baywatch* star Yasmine Bleeth. If anyone travelling to The Pantry and emerging moments later with a tiny packet of cocaine suspected it was other than the complete and genuine article, then they said nothing. Nor did Doran, Tait or Bartlett at the Glasgow end of the gang. But then no one wanted to disrupt an operation that was proving hugely successful.

Before 1980 was out, cocaine was almost taking over the Glasgow social scene. The more that appeared, the more that was wanted. But then that was the effect of cocaine. Users discovered their appetite for the drug was never satisfied. Initially, it made them into sex-mad extroverts but once the drug gripped they went into a shell, became almost reclusive, deceitful and distrustful, not wanting anyone near for fear a visitor might have designs on their precious supply of cocaine. 'Cocaine isn't a problem,' they would say. 'It's not having money with which to buy more that is the problem.'

For the Happy Dust Gang, money was not a problem. The difficulty, discovered Duncan and Sim, was keeping up with the increasing demands on their services and those of Scouse Willie. They were making increasingly frequent visits to the home of Joop, always taking deliberate care to treat Anna with courtesy and respect. The Scots did not want to jeopardise their friendship, but it was at times difficult not to blatantly stare at her. During one visit in the summer of 1981, she emerged from a sunbathing session in the garden wearing only the bottom half of her bikini and a white muslin blouse through which her golden breasts jutted.

'Your friends are happy with the stuff?' Joop said.

'Can't get enough,' the Parachutist told him.

'You cutting?'

'Yes.'

'Then cut more. The people you are supplying clearly do not appreciate quality.'

'Good idea.'

'And play hard to get.'

'Hard to get?'

'Tell them you don't have any and will have to make extra trips to get more. Then you can push up the price.'

'Right.' George didn't mention that the suggestion had sounded even better when he had thought it up weeks earlier.

Later that summer, after making a delivery in Glasgow, Robert Bruce told Duncan that Big Andy was desperately trying to get hold of him.

'What's he want?' asked George.

'I think they are looking for more gear,' replied Robert.

'I've just left them 300 grammes!'

'Yes, and that's gone already. Business must be booming and they want some more.'

George phoned The Pantry and arranged to meet the baker that afternoon.

'Brian's looking for more kit,' said Tait.

'I haven't any.'

'Look, we'll pay more.'

'I've told you, there's nothing here. I'll need to go back to Holland.'

'Surely you can get some somewhere?'

'I'll make some phone calls, but I'm promising nothing.'

A cocaine supplier knows he has a captive audience. Those

he supplies are under his control for the simple reason that if he is not there, they cannot enjoy themselves. They fall into the grip of the fear that the strung-out feeling left after taking cocaine on a regular basis will persist. It is at this stage experts use the word 'dependency' to describe their condition. In that state, a user will pay anything, literally, for more. What then determines price is not how much is in a wallet or pocket, but how much the supplier insists must be paid. Whatever is demanded they will pay. Somehow. Even if they must beg, borrow or steal in the process. If their nearest and dearest, their wives and children, must go without so they can buy, then so be it. So it was when Doran and Tait, like Oliver Twist, asked for more.

Of course, George Duncan had more. Safely secreted with a friend of a friend in Glasgow. He called Tait.

'I can get some, but it means getting it brought over. One of my people will fly in, but he wants a good bung because it's so risky.'

'How much?'

'£90 a gramme. He'll bring 100 grammes.'

'Fucking hell! That's £9,000.'

'Take it or leave it. That's what you were paying before anyway.'

'Yes, but we weren't buying anything like that amount.'

'Look, Andy, don't fuck me around.'

'Let me speak to Brian. Ring me back in ten minutes.'

Duncan knew he had his man hooked. Two hours later, he was clutching a pile of banknotes.

Duncan was at home in Utrecht a fortnight later when the telephone rang. He answered and heard the voice of Brian Doran.

'How are you, George?'

'Fine, and you?'

'Great. But I need to see you. Something's come up.'

'What's happened?'

'Well, I have a party arranged.'

There was no need for Doran to say more. George knew

without the words actually being spoken that he needed cocaine: the name of the drug or anything remotely close to it would never be used down a telephone line.

'I was there two weeks ago,' George replied.

'Yes, I know, and it was much appreciated.'

'And I'm coming back over in four weeks.'

'Four weeks. That's no use, George, I need to see you immediately.'

'Sorry, it's the best I can do.'

'George, I can't wait four weeks. The party is this weekend and there are some people coming who I really want to make sure have a good time.'

'Brian, I can't come. I've been promising and promising my wife Rosa we'll have a holiday and we're off to Benidorm for a fortnight.'

'Benidorm. Where?'

In seconds, Duncan remembered a hotel in the resort outside of which he and Sim had dished out free disco tickets. 'The Madeira Palace.'

'I know it.'

'I can't let Rosa down. I'm booked up and I'd have to change all my plans to come to Glasgow.'

'Look, George, tell you what, if you can come to Glasgow, I will get Robert Torrance from Blue Sky Travel to arrange a connecting flight for you that same day to Benidorm and there'll be a little extra for you.'

'Let me talk it over with Rosa. I'll call back.'

The couple duly flew to Glasgow and stayed overnight at Doran's expense. He imagined his friend had arranged a ferry trip at short notice; however, in light of the previous scenario, Duncan had organised an extra delivery to the man holding his supply in Glasgow. Now he needed only to retrieve part of the stash, take it to Doran and collect the cash. When the deal was done, he and Rosa flew to Benidorm, where they soaked up the Spanish sun for two weeks. It had been a lucrative deceit. And it would not be the only one.

In early 1982, the Parachutist received another frantic call from one of his friends in Glasgow.

'Big Andy's looking for you.'

'What's he want?'

'He says he's been trying to get hold of you in Utrecht but can't get an answer. Nobody's answering the telephone.'

'Yes, I told Rosa to ignore incoming calls if I wasn't there. What's up with him anyway?'

'You know Andy. He's panicking in case something's wrong.'

'So, what did you tell him?'

'I had to put him out of his misery. I told him you'd been working in Nijmegen for a couple of weeks and not to worry.'

'And what did he say?'

'He wants you to ring. Says it's urgent.'

In fact, George Duncan was nowhere near Nijmegen or even in Holland. He was in Glasgow, having travelled there a couple of days earlier for a family celebration. There was nothing sinister behind his decision not to tell the other gang members he was in town, he simply wanted to be left alone to enjoy what was a private party. But he could guess why the baker wanted him and realised that here would be an opportunity to have his expenses paid once again.

'Ring Andy and ask what he wants, although I reckon you know as well as I do what he's after. Say it's awkward for me to get to the telephone, but you can pass on a message to me.'

'He'll be wanting Charlie in a hurry.'

'Of course he will and he'll want me to come over with it.'

'You fly bastard, I know what you're up to.'

'Just make the call, then meet me at the Old Toll Bar on Paisley Road West.'

Minutes later, the friends were chatting over a beer. Sure enough, Tait and Doran were on the lookout for happy dust.

'I told him you'd be over sometime the day after tomorrow.'

'What did he say to that?'

'He wanted to know if you'd bring gear, another 100 grammes.'

'What did you say?'

'That you'd help them out, but it would cost an extra £5 a gramme to cover expenses. He grumbled you were making enough already but then agreed.'

'They're desperate.'

'You should have told them it would be a tenner extra.'

For two more days, George enjoyed a relaxing time with his family, venturing out of town only once to collect from the man holding the cache he kept for emergencies. Then he rang Tait at The Pantry.

'Hi, Andy. I gather you've been looking for me.'

'Thank fuck. You in town?'

'Just got here. I've had to make a lot of arrangements and it has cost me. I want this stuff off my hands quick.'

Within the hour, he had visited the bakery and the switch was made. George rejoined his family and the following day was back at his Utrecht home. His first caller was Thomas Sim.

'How was the trip?'

'Great, everybody is asking for you.'

'See any of the gang?'

'Big Andy. Sold him some stuff.'

'How was he?'

'He looked awful. Stressed out. Andy is becoming a worry.'

107

8

SLEEPLESS NIGHT

If a list of commandments was to be handed down to criminals, the first would surely read 'Thou Shall Not Underestimate the Police'. All too often crooks discover to their cost that a well-run enterprise, the secret of which is restricted to a trusted few, has been monitored by the law for a considerable time. Often this is simply down to police officers passing on a number of seemingly unrelated pieces of observation or intelligence that individually mean nothing but when added together by a highly trained collator point to there being some illegal racket on the go. And so it was with the Happy Dust Gang.

As the 1970s had drawn to a close, police knew smatterings of cocaine had been reaching Scotland, but the amounts were so small it was almost impossible to trace either the couriers or their customers. In fact, there were basically no customers. What cocaine was smuggled past Hadrian's Wall was for the personal use of the smugglers. However, as 1980 progressed, an increasing number of informants began telling of increasing amounts of Charlie. Time after time, their handlers would ask the same questions: who was selling and who was buying? Invariably, they could not supply answers. An occasional name would be passed over – X is having a lot of company these days, Y seems to be suddenly well off, Z has bought a new car but nobody knows where the money has come from. Much of the time, police had to take these tips with a heavy pinch of salt. Informants were notoriously unreliable, often motivated by greed or envy. A long-time rival might be seen driving about in a new car but it was actually being paid for by his wife's part-time job or a successful flutter on the horses. The name Brian Doran often cropped up in the same sentence as cocaine, but no one could be certain that he was involved.

There was one overriding reason why police informants – 'snouts' – were never able to root out the Happy Dust Gang: tip-offs about drugs came almost exclusively from hash dealers shopping rivals in an effort to put them out of business and thereby improve their own illicit profits. Snouts lived among poorer, working-class folk in the giant sprawling housing schemes that littered Glasgow, where by tradition the idea of telling tales to the police was looked on as abhorrent. But drugs were different, eating away at lives and pockets, so with few exceptions these calls, invariably anonymous, came from the working classes. The cocaine circle, at that time, comprised young, wealthy go-getters – the relatively low-paid working classes were not invited to parties where lines were snorted – so grasses missed out. Both they and their police bosses were sure a cocaine line had been established. But who was behind it?

George Duncan knew the class gap acted as protection. He understood the difference between just surviving on the breadline and having money to squander. He knew that so long as users maintained discretion there was little likelihood of discovery. However, as time went on, he began to fear that this was just a pipe dream. Too many people were making jokes about what was coming out of The Pantry. And through friends and family in Glasgow, word was reaching him in Holland about police suspicions on the increase. Suddenly, flats were being raided. Known hash dealers, whose activities had been tolerated to a degree because they were on such a tiny scale and who were effectively blackmailed into collaborating with the police, found themselves answering the door to be greeted by a posse of stern-faced detectives holding up a search warrant. The purpose of many of these raids might have appeared to be a crackdown on cannabis, while in fact the police surmised that if a man dealt in one drug, then he might graduate to another or know who was handling a different substance. The police actions were tinged with an air of desperation.

George's friend Robert Bruce became a target even though he was not known to be involved in any drug trade. He joined the list of suspects solely because of his relationship with Duncan: it had been rumoured cocaine was arriving from Holland, and George lived in Holland, travelled over fairly regularly, usually to watch Rangers, and when in Glasgow generally called on his long-time friend. As time went by, detectives would beat a well-worn path to the door of Robert's first-floor flat. That they never discovered drugs there was simply due to George knowing his friend could come under the spotlight. He didn't wish to get him into trouble, so stored his reserves elsewhere. And Robert had a 'no drugs kept here' rule, although others would break this from time to time.

On one memorable occasion, an evening party was in full swing with a few friends sharing a joint or two. Among them was Duncan, who had arrived a few hours earlier from Holland and had called in after visiting another friend. Music played, but it became evident that something was happening in the street outside. There were raised voices and the partygoers heard a woman cry out, cars screeching to a stop and doors slamming. Stepping to the window and peering outside, one of the little group suddenly burst out, 'Fucking hell! Cops! They're all over the place.'

'Quit worrying,' Robert told him. 'We're only having a joint. If you have anything, flush it down the toilet.'

Then he became aware of George and knew something was wrong. 'Fuck me, Robert, I've got £22,000 worth of Charlie in my holdall. I was on my way to drop it off and popped in for a beer.'

'George, you've got to lose it. Fuck off into the bog and flush it away. If they find that lot here, we're all for it.'

George was horrified at the thought of a fortune disappearing down Sir Thomas Crapper's invention and finding its way into the sewers of Glasgow. Likewise what might follow: cocaine was a well-known stimulant and the effect on the rat population might be positively explosive.

He hesitated.

'Come on, George, they'll be busting in here any second.'

He headed into the bathroom with his holdall and bolted the door. Delving into clothing and cigarette packets, he produced a number of sachets stuffed with white powder and was sitting on the seat, trousers around his ankles, ready to stuff the contents into the pan.

'What's happening?'

'Cops are all over. Get rid of it! Get rid of it!'

'Not until I hear them battering on your door.'

'You'll get us all in jail. Lose it. If they hear the bog being flushed, they'll know something's up.'

At that moment, the sound of approaching footsteps caused the occupants of the flat to freeze. He heard the flat door being pushed open and prepared for the worst. Instead of a angry shout telling them, 'Don't fucking move anybody,' it was a friendly voice. 'Bloody hell, haven't you been outside? Cops are swarming all over.'

'We thought we were being raided,' Robert told him. 'What's up?'

'Fucking mugger. Snatched an old woman's handbag and a taxi driver chased him up the street and phoned the cops. Somebody grabbed the sod and pushed him against the door of your close until the cops showed.'

There was a rush to the window in time to see police

disappearing. From inside the toilet came the sounds of someone being sick.

It would not be the only drama the flat witnessed. A year later, police arrived as a party was in full swing. They showed up on the pretence of a neighbour complaining he was unable to sleep due to the noise level. In fact, it was purely an excuse for Strathclyde's finest to take a look around.

'Might as well have a look around while we're here,' one of the gatecrashers told Robert, adding courteously, 'Don't mind, do you?'

'You're wasting your time,' the host replied, knowing he was wasting *his* time trying to convince the police of this.

A sniff resulted in the accusation, 'Somebody's been smoking hash.'

'A couple of guys were here earlier, but they've left,' Robert answered them.

The police clearly disbelieved the excuse, but a cursory look around produced nothing. After the officers left, one of the party rushed to a bedroom window, heaved it open, then cursed loudly. 'Bastards!'

'What's up?'

'I had a wee lump and when I heard the cops, I stuck it on the window ledge so they wouldn't smell it. When I went to get it, there was a seagull sitting on the fucking sill with the stuff in its beak. The bugger's vamoosed with it.'

'What did it look like?'

'Well, kind of grey and white . . .' For a second, the penny failed to drop. 'Ah, fuck off.'

There were times when unexpected visitors to the homes of Happy Dust Gang customers would be other than the police. One man, whom we shall call Billy to avoid embarrassing him, as he is now a happily married and successful Glasgow property entrepreneur, lived in a flat three floors up in a pleasant tenement block in the Ibrox area back in 1982. At the time, workmen were repairing the roof of the tenement. It was a big job necessitating scaffolding, which covered the entire front of the building. This is Billy's version of the story.

'I was in bed having a smoke after doing the business with this gorgeous, black-haired girl who used to come around from time to time for a joint. She was at college in Glasgow and when she stayed out late used to tell her parents she was at some student union meeting or on a course trip to Edinburgh or Stirling. It was a bit of a job persuading her to visit because she was paranoid about her folks finding out. Once she even got it into her head that her dad had hired a private eye to have her followed.

'It was summer and that lovely time late at night when dusk has just fallen and you can hear the birds chattering as they get ready to settle down. The girl had a wonderful imagination when it came to sex; I think she'd picked up ideas at school and we were discussing what we would shortly be doing to one another when I heard my name shouted.

'"Billy, Billy, Billy," and right away I recognised the voice of a pal who used gear from time to time.

'"Fuck it," I thought. "Bollocks."

'He was a good mate who often called on me, but I could never get it into his head that at no time did I keep anything in the house. The police knew where I stayed, that I sometimes had visitors who were into hash, or even the occasional line of Charlie, and had made unexpected calls from time to time to sniff around. They never found anything because there was nothing for them to discover. I decided to stay silent and hope he'd go away.

'"Billy, Billy," came the shout again. He was on the pavement outside and I knew if his voice was carrying to me, then the people living in the downstairs flats were bound to hear it as well. And now the girl was asking who was there.

'"Just a pal. Keep your voice down and he'll go away."

'There was no way I was getting out of bed, even for a bosom buddy, especially with the promises she was making.

The door was locked and we'd turned the lights out because having sex with the curtains pulled back and the window open seemed to add to the fun. I could hardly get up and close them in case he saw me. It all went quiet for a couple of minutes, then somebody tried my door handle and was shouting, "Billy, Billy." The girl started giggling and I pulled a sheet over her head. Another rattle at the knob, then the visitor headed back down the stairs.

'"Brilliant," thinks I to myself and the girl sat up to pull back her hair, showing her breasts in profile. Her nipples were rock hard. She knew what she was doing and the effect it was having and began a smile. I was about to make a grab for her when there came the sound of the scaffolding shaking and banging. Next second, a figure was climbing through the window.

'"You got any Charlie, Billy?" a voice was asking.

'"For fuck sake," I started and was about to point out my place was clean when there was a scream from the girl.

'"Who is it, what's happening?" She was shaking and shivering. I knew if the lights had been on, her face would have been pale with terror.

'My pal was in the room, looking like something out of the Cadbury's Milk Tray adverts.

'"Fuck off! Fuck off, I've got nothing. I've got somebody else here," I was hissing at him.

'He got the message and apologised but forgot to ask for the door to be unlocked and instead clambered back through the window and started off down the scaffolding. '"Sorry, hen. Now come here."

'She was stiff with fright and not at all keen to get going again, and when I rolled over to her half of the bed, I found out why. During the excitement, she had peed herself. But I never found out whether it was through ecstasy or fear.'

When George got wind of the incident, he gave a rueful smile because it was an indication of how sought after the product the gang supplied had become. Maybe he ought to have been upset because had a passing policeman spotted the caller, awkward questions would surely have followed. But then he knew of other occasions when the use of happy dust caused problems of a different nature altogether.

A well-known member of Brian Doran's circle, whom we are calling Donald – he was married at the time and still is – had been introduced to cocaine at a party where Whacko was among the guests. As a result, Donald had discovered a reawakening of his interest in the opposite sex. His wife had no idea at the time that he was into cocaine – she would later discover his secret and help him beat an addiction that came close to destroying the family and which led to appalling financial disasters. One night shortly before Christmas 1981, Donald had explained to her he needed to be in England on business and would not be home that evening. This was, of course, untrue; in fact, Donald had begun an affair with the daughter of a leading business family who owned a considerable number of properties in the East End of Glasgow. This woman, whom we will call Jessica, had first taken cocaine during a visit to Spain, where her good looks had brought her an invitation to share the supply of an older, swarthy, charming hotelier. She had awoken the following morning surprised to find she was sharing his bed, a situation that displeased and embarrassed neither. Her paramour once invited himself to meet up with Jessica in Glasgow, where in a hotel room both realised there was something missing from their glut of passion – cocaine. She telephoned the Happy Dust Gang and by chance Thomas Sim was in Glasgow. He knew her and agreed to come to her hotel room.

'We'll probably be in the bar, so I'll leave the door open. Just let yourself in. I'll put the money under the bathmat,' she'd requested.

And Sim did so, only to walk in on a naked Jessica straddling an equally nude Spaniard.

'Hi, Simmy,' she said. 'Leave it on the table, please. The

money's still in the bathroom.' And continued with her labour of love. Her beau had been appalled at this evident sign the woman was less chaste than he had imagined and the affair ended the following morning.

Sometime later, Jessica related the story to Donald after being introduced to him by Doran. She was reminded of it when George happened to appear. Donald was unaware that the Charlie crowd had a private name for his mistress. They called her Dirty Jess because frankly she was without limits when it came to sex and indifferent to shame. Her sexual wiles and inventions fascinated Donald and on the night his wife believed him to be in England, he had booked into the Sherbrooke Castle Hotel in Pollokshields with Jessica. Neither knew, nor cared, that the following evening thousands of soccer fans would be flocking to a special challenge match at Ibrox to celebrate the opening of a new stand. The visitors were Liverpool Football Club and a number of leading players were staying at city hotels, including the Sherbrooke Castle.

After a pleasant meal in town and a couple of drinks in the hotel lounge, the lovers headed for bed. As they were about to climb the stairs, they met a mutual friend of Donald's. For a second, both men froze, then laughed with relief at each seeing the other with a girlfriend. Jessica and Donald had each brought a supply of happy dust, which they laid out in neatly cut lines on a bedside table, promising that they would reward themselves with a line after each successful bout of lovemaking. Hours later, they heard a commotion outside the door followed by a rap. Donald opened it to discover his friend looking flushed.

'Fuck sake, Donald, you need to chill it. You're waking everybody up. People are threatening to leave the hotel because of the racket and if it gets into the papers that you're here, you'll be in real trouble.'

'What time is it?'

'Eight.'

'In the morning?'

'What else?'

'Hell, we've been at it all night. Jessica gets very loud when she's excited. Sorry.'

She giggled when he told her of the conversation, but when they stared at the table it was clean.

'I have to go,' Donald told her. 'I have a meeting at ten.'

'Me too. Donald, you were sensational.'

Under an hour later, they were at reception checking out. In front of them, a big man in a wide-brimmed hat and Crocodile Dundee-style overcoat was complaining and even warning a couple who were about to book in having evidently travelled north for the match that night.

'I don't know why you are checking in here,' he said. 'I couldn't get a wink of sleep all night for some bird screaming and yelling. Dunno who she was with but each time she shouted out it was a different guy's name.'

He turned to collect his bag and Donald looked into the tired eyes of the legendary goalkeeper Bruce Grobbelaar.

9

POWDERED BOUQUET

Liverpool won the challenge that night in Glasgow, but during the after-match chat between players, journalists and club officials, the story of the night of ecstasy became a topic for hilarity. Who the girl was and what had inspired her performance was the subject of considerable speculation. In addition, inevitably, someone threw the subject of drugs into the pot. And there was a drug known to trigger extreme sexual pleasure. Cocaine. The incident only fuelled gossip that the happy dust was now coming into Scotland on a regular basis.

From the start of the enterprise, George Duncan had tried to stress the need for as few people as possible to be in the know. At the Dutch end, only he and Thomas Sim knew the identities of the other members of the gang, and Scouse Willie's involvement ended at whichever ferry terminal was chosen as a landing point. But in Glasgow, Bartlett, Doran and Tait were acting with alarming indiscretion. Incidents involving cocaine sparked the occasional funny story but the fallout from the laughs that drifted on the wind could easily float in through the window of a police station.

* * *

Haggs Castle is one of the more desirable areas of Glasgow. Behind its wide streets are large stone-built detached residences that are now and were in the heyday of the Happy Dust Gang home to young businessmen and well-educated professionals – the culture well able to afford cocaine. In late 1981, the ancient patriarch of one of these families, an avid gardener, had fallen and died from a heart attack while out walking. On the day of his funeral, he had been laid at home in his coffin for friends and relatives to pay their last respects.

The family was well connected throughout Scotland and two of its younger members had travelled a considerable distance to be present. They had many friends in Glasgow with whom they frequently spent weekends watching a soccer match and going on to a club and party. At one get-together, they had been introduced to Brian Doran and, through him, to Andrew Tait, who made little effort to cover up the fact that he could supply happy dust. Indeed, there was a feeling among insiders that Big Andy revelled in his role as a man of stature in the drugs field. Before the funeral, the two men had called in at The Pantry and when they left a short while later to seek their car parked in Byres Road, one had in his pocket a tiny packet of white powder.

Moving through the various rooms and mingling with the other mourners, one of the pair was startled to see a police car pull up in the street outside and two uniformed officers climb out. The police appeared to take a special interest in the men's car – the reason was simply a new form of security lock holding the gear lever in neutral – before heading towards the house. It was a routine call. The police were just returning some of the old man's effects retrieved at the scene of his fall. But for the young men inside, it was a different scenario: they had taken possession of cocaine and driven off, a police car had pulled up shortly afterwards, their own vehicle had been scrutinised and now the police were about to call. The one holding the happy dust, convinced he was about to be hauled off and searched, decided he had to get

119

rid of it immediately and dumped the packet in the nearest hiding place.

Five minutes later, after watching the police leave, he returned to retrieve his treasure only to see the extravagant bouquet of white roses disappearing through the doorway in the arms of the undertaker, who was following the coffin, resting on the shoulders of the bearers. The flowers were carefully placed in the hearse, sat on the coffin throughout the solemn church service and remained there as the bouquet was carried to the family tomb.

The dead man had made an unusual request to close family. On his demise, he wished flowers to be scattered in his grave. And so the bouquet, along with a dozen others, disappeared under tons of earth, and with them the tiny sachet of happy dust. The owners recounted the story that night in Charlie Parker's much to the amusement of the other drinkers.

When George Duncan got wind of it, he was not amused. 'They should have shut up about this,' he told Thomas Sim. 'Too many people are talking about what Andy sells. I have a horrible feeling about this.' Indeed, the ability of the Happy Dust Gang to provide ever-increasing deliveries of cocaine was triggering ever more bizarre episodes in social circles. Often they were the result of the relaxation of sexual defences that the powder brought.

A friend of the gang members was squiring a young woman from Newton Mearns whose friend was an occasional dining partner of Brian Doran's. The consensus, even among grudging rivals of the women, was that both had the looks and figures of film stars. Wherever they went, heads turned. Following an especially wild party in Shawlands, at which lines of cocaine had proliferated like goosepimples in an Alaskan naturist camp, both women left with this friend. At his home, he and his girlfriend, who had satisfied herself with alcohol, ignoring the offered cocaine, climbed into bed. She immediately fell into a deep sleep, at which point her coke-soaked companion left the settee on which she had announced she would stay for the night and hopped in the other side. It was clear she wanted not just sex but sex to music.

The man, finding it difficult to come to terms with his good fortune, placed on the turntable the first record that came to hand, then returned to bed. The number happened to be 'Do Ya Think I'm Sexy?' As Rod croaked out the words, the couple entwined with an enthusiasm and fervour he had rarely before experienced.

When their passion was sated, they fell asleep and in the morning the girls awoke to find themselves either side of their consort. The man's girlfriend had slept through both the sexual torrent and the admirable efforts of Rod. Both women were normally restrained, even demure, and would never have countenanced what had gone on. Alcohol, they admitted freely, stimulated them and made them horny. Cocaine, of course, took this not a step but a mile further.

This was demonstrated a few evenings later when the man met up with both women at Maestro's nightclub on Glasgow's Scott Street. Unknown to the management, cocaine was being used and at the end of the evening both ladies had snorted at least a couple of lines each. Now seated in the back of his Jaguar and about to be driven home, they felt absolved of sexual constraint. So much so that when business associates of the driver approached and told him, 'You'll get nowhere with that pair,' he turned to his passengers and suggested they give each other a kiss, then proceeded to watch the pair mutually groping, fondling, unhooking, undressing and French kissing in a style that would have sent the director of any lesbian pornographic movie into raptures.

'You're the bees knees, man,' he was told with considerable envy. Next day, the women would surely regret their surprising public display of affection. But what happened would be a talking point, just one more cocaine-inspired scandal to set tongues wagging.

The same women were present, although not participants,

when cocaine had been taken at the man's home. They agreed to accompany him in his Jaguar to Barrhead Dams, a noted and at times notorious courting spot for lovers. On the way, they passed a Mercedes parked off the road in the entrance to an industrial estate. He instantly recognised it as belonging to a friend, a leading Glasgow businessman at the time and even more prominent in the city now. It was known to all except his apparently devoted wife that he had been having an affair with one of his employees, a well-made brunette who slavishly went along with his insistence that she wore the lowest of low-cut garments, revealing her generous cleavage. Halting the Jaguar, he decided to have fun at his friend's expense and quietly creeping up to the Mercedes was just able to make out through heavily steamed-up windows what appeared to be the bare back of a woman. He banged on the rear nearside window and was horrified to see the face and much of the naked chest of the Mercedes owner's wife, while the face of a stranger loomed in the background gloom.

Another bizarre episode in 1981 could have proved fatal in more than one sense. Peter, not his real name, was the close relative of a leading Scots show-business celebrity. A man of international stature, he had been helped along the way by Peter, much talented in different but significant ways. Where the two differed was in their attitude to drugs. While the star found them abhorrent, Peter was a devotee of happy dust. In it he found a freedom from the pressures of constantly having to maintain the spotlight on those who looked to him to keep them at the top. Few understood his worries or the hideously long hours he was forced to work, sometimes weeks on end without a break and occasionally around the clock. The result was that he packed into his free time generations of high living.

David, a successful businessman, was one of his closest friends, whom he trusted implicitly. Together they had a reputation for snorting their way through enough cocaine to satisfy an army of addicts. One night, David received a call from his wife to say Peter was looking for him and was in a room at the Albany Hotel in Glasgow, then favoured with the show-business fraternity. David rang his friend, who told him he had booked a room for each of them, urging him, 'Come on up. I've got loads of good stuff and there's a girl here desperate to meet you. She's right up for it.'

David did so, finding Peter utterly spaced out on a bed, while on the floor on her back, wearing only tiny pink panties, lay the girl. She appeared motionless. David was alarmed that when he shook her, he got no reaction. He slapped the girl's cheeks, gently at first, then more firmly, and eventually rushed to the bathroom to fetch a glass of chilled water that he poured over her. There was still no movement.

'She's dead!' he gasped.

'Dead! No way.'

'Dead. I'm telling you. Dead. What has she had?'

'A line, maybe two, nothing more. She was fine. You sure she's not sleeping?'

'No. Dead! Come on, we're out of here. Come on, come on, we're in deep trouble.' Pulling out his handkerchief, David began carefully wiping the glass he had handled, the knob of the door he had gripped on his way into the room, and even the girl's cheeks.

It was at this point that she groaned and sat up. 'Who are you? Got a drink?' she asked him, making no effort to hide her quivering breasts.

'I thought you were dead. You were out, hardly breathing.'

'Oh, I go like this sometimes when I have a line. It's something to do with asthma. The doctor says I should leave off. It knocks me right out.'

Later, when the girl had gone, David told Peter, 'Did you realise the shite you might have been in if she'd been really dead? Her body would have been found in your room and the cops would have been swarming all over you.'

'No, they wouldn't.'

'Why do you say that?'

'Because I booked the rooms in your name and paid in cash! The one we were using was yours. I used the telephone in your room to call your home.'

'Fuck sake, that was me right in it. Why?'

'I didn't think you'd mind. I didn't want my wife to find out I was here.'

'Bastard. I was sure she'd snuffed it.'

'Oh, I knew she was OK. She often does that. It was hilarious watching your reaction.'

'Bastard!'

In pleading with the fellow members of the Happy Dust Gang to keep a low profile and avoid bringing themselves to the notice of the police, George was fighting a losing battle.

Brian Doran was one of the worst offenders. When supplies ran short and George was unable to arrange quick deliveries from Holland, Doran had driven his Rolls-Royce to the homes of others reputed to be in the drugs business. One of these men lived in Castlemilk, a sprawling housing scheme to the south of Glasgow where the residents had been abandoned to make the best of pitiable amenities. Many of the city's poorest families lived there. And so did low-life criminals. It was an area in which the appearance of a new car would attract attention; his gleaming Rolls-Royce a positive buzz – one that reached the ears of the police. What, they wondered, was there in such a run-down spot that could attract a wealthy travel agent? One of the potential answers was drugs.

The last thing the gang wanted was attention. There was no need to openly publicise themselves or their wares. Yet one of their most frequent customers, publican Jacob Kinsell, would do precisely that.

At 32, Kinsell was popular with the glitzy crowd who frequented discos such as Manhattan and the Warehouse in the city centre. Likeable and bright, he was a man going places, jointly owning a public house in Paisley and a clothes shop in Queen Street. And both were doing well – so well, in fact, he could afford to drive about in a swanky gold-coloured Porsche. It was the type of car that begged to be noticed. And it was. Friends of George Duncan had spotted the Porsche near The Pantry. Jacob had gone calling on his friend Andy to buy cocaine, the crafty cookery expert unable to resist his businessman's nose for profit by adding £15 to the £45 a gramme he was paying.

Sometimes Jacob was merely collecting happy dust for his customers, but there was a side to his activity that would later lead to more sinister suggestions. Jacob, from time to time, dished out tiny free samples to young people. It would later be argued that, along with the scores of people spreading the gospel about the pleasures to be derived from snorting coke, his largesse wetted their appetites. What was concerning police was the growing number of gullible young people who were becoming hooked to the extent that they needed only to be shown white powder to believe it was the real thing. That made drug-squad detectives all the more determined to catch those who dealt.

They were convinced George was involved and once more decided on snap raids at the home of his friends. One such raid targeted the Shawlands home of a Glasgow drug dealer. Among those being entertained was George, who was wary of coming face to face with the police. He had just clinched a cocaine deal and had a few hours to kill before his flight home. In his pocket was a cheque for £27,000, a passport and a plane ticket.

'I'm not coming in if you've any gear here,' he told his host when he arrived.

'Don't worry, there's nothing here, George,' he was assured.

Within five minutes of sitting down with a drink, drug-squad police began rushing the door, shouting, battering and ordering it to be opened.

'I thought you had nothing here,' complained George above the racket.

125

'Honest, George, there's nothing. Stop worrying,' said the homeowner, anxious that unless he could reach his door in time the entire wall would cave in with it. In the house, police made a beeline for George but seemed uninterested even in the highly incriminating contents of his pockets once they had searched him and discovered, to their apparent disappointment, he was clean. A search of the building produced a similarly blank outcome. 'Nothing here, boss,' the detectives reported to the inspector.

'Look again,' they were ordered. 'You can't have searched properly. I know there's something.'

'We've looked everywhere, honest.'

'Then you've missed it.'

He began wrinkling his nose. 'There, can you smell that?'

Four other noses twitched in unison.

'What's the smell?'

'Dunno. It's familiar, but I can't place it.'

'Well, fucking find it.'

The search was repeated to no avail until the senior officer, bloodhound fashion, went on hands and knees and began crawling about the floor sniffing. His nose took him in the direction of an electric fire attached to the wall, which he ripped from its mounting. On a hot plate at the rear was a tiny lump of cannabis. It had been pushed through a ventilation panel, but unfortunately for the partygoers fell onto a hot plate at the rear of the fire where, warming up, it had begun to give off a sweet, sickly odour. By the time it was recovered, the lump was a pinprick. A lucky escape. But the message had gone home. No one was safe.

And no one was exempt from the occasional paucity of happy dust. One night as he was about to enter Charlie Parker's, Thomas Sim literally bumped into Brian Doran. He later related to Duncan how Whacko was racing outside, holding a handkerchief to his mouth. In the street, he was violently sick, much to the consternation of his friends.

Eventually, he recovered and Sim asked him what had caused the problem.

'I hadn't any coke, so I tried hash,' he said.

Sim burst out laughing.

'What's the joke?'

'Sorry, Brian, no joke and I'm not laughing at you. Just at the thought of somebody who snorts as much coke as you being ill on hash.'

'What's funny about that?'

'Hash is harmless.'

10

CHINESE FLUSH

Police, meanwhile, were becoming ever more certain that local gossip was based on fact. The frequency of their raids increased. Once more, Robert Bruce found himself in their sights and this time it was his enjoyment of early 1980s music that made him a target.

Robert had a much-admired Alfa Romeo parked outside his flat. It was a car that attracted considerable attention from envious neighbours. One cold, crisp day in February 1982, he had been to Glasgow city centre with a friend to buy a huge stereo player and giant speakers. The two had, with difficulty, squeezed the boxes containing the expensive equipment into the Alfa Romeo and set off back to his flat on Paisley Road West.

It would later transpire that, by this stage, the police had been tipped off that Duncan and Sim might be involved in the importation of cocaine. And knowing George regularly appeared at Robert's home, the forces of law and order had decided to put the flat under observation. Watching from a lay-by further along the street, the surveillance team saw the car pull up at the house and the driver and his passenger begin to unload the huge cardboard cases, then struggle inside the building. It was an innocent scene but, under the circumstances, the watchers wondered if they had struck gold. What, they wondered, did the boxes hold? They could see they clearly had Bang & Olufsen marked on them, the name of the renowned audio specialist, but was that a cover?

The police had already convinced a sheriff that they had enough evidence to suggest Robert Bruce hid a guilty secret in his flat – although, in fact, the evidence was based on his friendship with George Duncan alone; there was nothing substantial to incriminate him. Nevertheless, the sheriff had authorised a search warrant. By the time the police arrived at the flat, Robert was scratching his head over how to follow the instructions for wiring up the new equipment. His friend was in the toilet, having the previous night sampled a meal from one of Glasgow's growing number of Chinese takeaways, some of which had a reputation that could best be described as highly dodgy.

'What's going on in there?' the officers demanded to know, shouting through the bolted door, convinced the man behind it was about to send something more than the remains of a meal speeding to the sewers.

'What do you think?'

'What are you doing?'

'What would you be doing if you were in here, ya bams?'

'Well, just don't flush it.'

'Whit?'

'Don't flush the toilet.'

'Ya kiddin?'

'If you flush, you'll be arrested and done for obstruction.'

'You don't want me to flush away what's in the pan, is that it?'

'That's it.'

'Then it's your funeral.'

Privately at least one policemen was desperately hoping to hear the sound of the cistern emptying and filling up. He dreaded the command to lift the contents into a polythene evidence bag to be taken away for forensic testing to see whether there had been an attempt to get rid of drugs, in particular cocaine.

As the conversation continued, officers announced they would begin searching and threatened to leave no stone unturned. Their search warrant said they had reason to suspect illegal substances were being hidden in the flat and they were determined that wherever they were, they would be found.

'In that case,' they were told, 'you won't object to us searching you before you start.'

'You can't do that.'

'Why not, you got something to hide? Or is it something to plant?'

'What are you accusing us of?'

'Nothing, but some nasty people say the police mysteriously find things that had not been there before. Show us you've brought nothing with you.'

The police agreed but then began a systematic hunt for evidence. Pots containing plants were turned upside down, and the plants themselves removed and the soil around the roots checked and sniffed. A hot water bottle was emptied, the contents tasted and a torch shone into the interior. It was like a scene from a Keystone Cops movie. In the well-kept kitchen, every packet, box, tin and jar was opened. Sitting bemused in his front room, Robert Bruce heard a startled cry of triumph and was summoned into the cooking area. The doors of his wall cupboards stood open and a police officer was clutching a light-coloured tin.

'What's this?'

'Andrews Liver Salts.'

'Andrews Liver Salts?'

'Andrews Liver Salts.'

'But what's inside?'

'Andrews Liver Salts.'

'Are you saying this contains Andrews Liver Salts?'

'Yes.'

'What is it used for?'

'For your liver, that's why it's called Andrews Liver Salts.'

'It looks like something else to me.'

'Such as?'

'An illegal substance.'

'Well, why not find out?'

'How.'

'Put the powder in a glass of water and drink it.'

'Oh, yes, and destroy the evidence.'

'No, it will make you feel better.'

'Look, I have reason to believe that what is in here is not what you make it out to be.'

'Not Andrews Liver Salts?'

'No. I'm taking it away for forensic examination. You'll be given a receipt.'

'Why not just send one of your boys to the shop over the road and buy me another tin?'

'Now, now, don't be wide.'

The police produced a tiny spatula and removed a miniscule amount of the chalky powder, which was scooped into a polythene evidence bag, carefully labelled and stored in a briefcase. Convinced they had struck gold – or white – the police turned their attention to the stereo equipment. It was still in the protective cellophane it had been wrapped in before leaving the factory and was quite obviously untouched. The cardboard cases too were empty.

That left the car and the toilet. Robert's friend had emerged from the latter, conforming to the instruction not to wash away what he had left behind. There was a muttered discussion among the police team, culminating in one officer being detailed to enter, take a brief look and if all seemed innocent to pull the chain. He did so with alacrity. The Alfa Romeo was a different matter. A search warrant must specify the area under suspicion and theirs did not include the car.

'We'll just take a peek in your car,' announced the police team.

Robert asked to look once more at the warrant. 'It's not mentioned on here. Does that mean you can't touch it?'

'Yes. But we can hang on here while one of our people goes off and gets a further warrant.'

'No, you can't.'

'Well, we haven't completed our search of the flat and want you to remain here. While we're finishing off, well, somebody could just turn up with a warrant covering your car.'

'Look, I'm not under arrest. You have no authority to search my car. There is nothing to stop me walking out of here and driving it away. If you argue, we'll call my solicitor right now.'

'That would indicate you had something to hide.'

'No, it wouldn't. It would indicate I knew my rights. As it is, I have nothing to hide. You could call here every day with a search warrant and find nothing because there is never anything here to hide. All you have is a tin of Andrews Liver Salts. You want to go over the car, go ahead. But you've embarrassed me enough with the neighbours already. All I ask is that if anybody asks what you're doing, you say you're thinking of buying it and just want to look it over.'

It was a sensible compromise. Of course, if Robert had decided to drive away, the police could have used their own vehicles to block him in. But that would risk the sort of noisy confrontation in which neighbours and friends might decide to lend a hand. And the whole investigation was supposed to be based on discretion. Police were searching for drugs that could have been anywhere in Glasgow and if word about their suspicions spread, then every dealer within a five-mile radius of the Strathclyde Police headquarters in Pitt Street would be heading for the nearest hiding place.

Robert knew they would find nothing. The vehicle had never been used to carry drugs. Had it been taken apart and the seat covers ripped out, nothing would have been discovered. So, as police inspected it, helpful passers-by believing he had found two potential buyers passed the pair helpful comments on the merits of the car. In fact, it later transpired that the locals had been suspicious that they were a couple of drug dealers looking for a getaway vehicle.

Nothing more would be heard of the tin of Andrews Liver Salts, but the incident had a major knock-on effect. Robert telephoned his friend George to warn him the police were on his trail. But George was already too steeped in overconfidence to alter the way he operated and vowed to carry on regardless. Robert also contacted others, suggesting they stay away from his home that weekend, telling them, 'There's too much heat. Wait till things cool.'

Most of them thought he was simply making up an excuse so they didn't come round to visit, that he had a hot date lined up and wanted privacy. He would later admit, 'It was as if I had cried wolf to everybody, even though it was the truth. It was impossible to convince people I was telling the truth. I tried to even mark Brian Doran's card at the time but then began wondering to myself if Doran had started the whole police action off.'

Robert's guesses would turn out to be shrewd. The reason why police had mounted an operation aimed at looking into Duncan's associates was because he had been set up himself. Precisely by whom no one could be sure, but this treachery would prove to be the final nail in the coffin of the Happy Dust Gang. Some had already made a fatal mistake by opening their mouths. This was the final error. But by the time of the Alfa Romeo raid, Brian Doran, Andrew Tait and Alan Bartlett were already in the bag.

No one should have been surprised. The writing had been on the wall. Customs officers in Scotland had been watching airports for weeks, noting details of travellers flying regularly between Glasgow and Edinburgh and Schiphol. On the grapevine came news of the capture of three people from Auld Reekie. Undercover drug-squad officers had been tipped off about a drug ring operating in the city and had even been provided with the name of the ringleader. And there was an even juicier bonus. Their informant was able to tell them, almost to the day, when the next load would be smuggled in through Edinburgh airport. On the day in question, police tracked the suspect, aged 46, from his home to a travel agency in the city, where he bought tickets to Amsterdam, giving two to a waiting man and woman. The enterprise was doomed, not least because using an airport hugely limited the number of places in which a smuggler could hide contraband on baggage and body. And the further disadvantage was that the courier could not distance him or herself from forbidden fruit.

Police watched as the travellers boarded a flight for the 441-mile hop to Holland. They had already alerted Dutch colleagues to the probability of Schiphol being used; now they passed on the flight number. When the jet landed, plain-clothes politie were waiting. They saw the trio head for the airport lockers and, using a key thought to have been mailed earlier to the leader, take out a suitcase, then wait for the next flight back to Scotland. Customs investigators were waiting at Turnhouse. Inside the suitcase, they found £20,000 worth of cannabis resin in cunningly sealed coffee packs.

The bust was a warning that the authorities might pounce anytime, anywhere, and that informants were at work. Not everyone heeded the inferences that were to be drawn from this bad news, even when the following year all three were jailed, the ringleader for four years, the woman for one year and her companion for six months.

11

THE CALLER

The arrests at Turnhouse had a far-reaching significance few realised. What might have appeared a routine police operation had exposed a link to Holland. A major source of the increasing amounts of drugs coming into Scotland was now placed under the spotlight. Memos flew around the desks of senior Scots officers suggesting additional attention be paid to intelligence with a Dutch connection.

As far as the dozen or so members of the Strathclyde Police drug squad were concerned that information was old hat. What mattered was that officers of the politie were jolted into action. Politically, the Netherlands could not afford a reputation as the drugs colander of Europe. As the unchallenged diamond-clearing centre of the Western world, it needed to demonstrate its security services could handle any major criminal enterprise. So, at a conference in Amsterdam in late 1981, senior police commanders agreed to make infiltration of the drugs network a priority.

But like secrets the world over, within days news of the decision had been passed to the principal smugglers. They, of course, expected to be kept up to date with any developments that could affect their lucrative trade. After all, they had enough police officers on their payrolls.

* * *

Joop depended for his supplies on a Colombian family with whom he had first come into contact in the mid-1970s, a time when he had been dealing in Moroccan motored from Spain. They had introduced him to cocaine, far less bulky and much more profitable, and pointed in his direction a handful of small-scale dealers in Holland. The Monkey was a family friend and agreed to their suggestion to put business Joop's way, so he became a major player. As his links with the family deepened, so his fortune grew.

One night during a meeting in Amsterdam's red-light area, he had watched a statuesque brunette, her nude, oiled body glistening in the spotlights as she performed sexual aerobics on stage with a heavily muscled young man at the Casa Rosso theatre. He sent her a note, asking if she would join him for a drink in an adjoining bar. The girl received dozens of similar invitations but was intrigued by his promise of a 'business proposition' and took up his offer. Immediately, she was attracted by his old-fashioned courtesy.

'My name is Anna,' she said. 'What's your proposition?'

'Marriage,' said Joop.

'You've never met me,' she said. 'You're mad!' But she was entranced by this crazy stranger.

'No, I'm not mad. I'm rich, successful, healthy and ambitious. But not mad. In that very first tick of time in which I saw you, I knew I wanted you with me. Crazy? A little maybe. But not mad.'

A drink was followed by dinner.

'I also want you to buy me a house,' said Joop. 'A big one.'

Two months later, they were married.

Anna gave up the stage to perform with her husband

and sometimes, for his pleasure, with others of both sexes. It had been her idea to install the giant mirror. From time to time, Joop would invite police acquaintances to his home and always found an excuse to disappear, leaving Anna to suck out the latest intelligence relating to the drugs trade. It was after one of these sessions in early 1982 that Anna told her husband the heat was about to fall on drug gangs and that police were aware of a link with Scotland, although what precisely the connection was they did not know. This was worrying news.

Joop liked George and valued him as a friend and customer. He was one of dozens of people with whom he did business, but George was reliable, straightforward and treated Anna with respect, although he knew the Scot and his friend enjoyed the little private shows she gave them during their visits. And he loved the name George told him their customers in Scotland gave them, the Happy Dust Gang.

'You must be extra careful, my friend,' he told George. 'I know the police both here and in Scotland believe cocaine is coming in through airports. How you get the stuff to Scotland is your business, but I thought you should know if you don't already.'

'Thank you for the warning,' replied the Scot, deciding that much as he trusted Joop there was no way he would impart any details about what was close to a foolproof arrangement with Scouse Willie. 'We'll bear in mind what you say.'

The cartel to which the Colombian family belonged was not stupid. It survived by always being one step ahead both of the law and of rivals. That was achieved by knowing everything possible about those with whom it dealt. Intelligence was safety and the cartel invested fortunes in investigating the backgrounds of customers. Joop had been stringently vetted. So were his major customers, including Sim and Duncan, and both had passed with flying colours. For more than two years, the Happy Dust Gang had enjoyed a freedom to buy, deal, sniff and snort at leisure, a freedom George had continually urged the others to jealously guard. Now, as he left Joop's home, a nagging voice told him the gravy train was in danger of coming off the rails. Too much loose talk, too much arrogance, too many in the know: the avalanche was spiralling dangerously out of control.

The issue of cocaine, meanwhile, was taking on a national significance. No longer was this a lucrative little trading arrangement confined to a select wealthy band based in the west of Scotland; cocaine trafficking was becoming very big business. The IRA, ever needy of funds to buy bombs and arms, was casting an eye at the trade. It had huge support in Scotland but was wary of offending those high-principled old diehards who saw entry into the drugs market as a betrayal of the very working classes it represented. In the end, greed and dwindling funds would triumph. Already there were rumours of meetings in North America with Mafia leaders.

Margaret Thatcher's government was toying with the idea of taking away the assets of the traffickers by imposing fines equal to the amount of money estimated to have been made illegally. As time went by, the principle cast in stone that a man was innocent until proved guilty would be reversed as asset-seizure legislation became more prolific. In the not-so-distant future, an individual found with cash would be assumed to have made it illegally and to avoid having it confiscated had to prove otherwise. And now there were other reasons why the government was alarmed by cocaine. Rumours were surfacing about sailors attached to Royal Navy submarines based at Faslane on the Gare Loch taking drugs to relieve their boredom while on long patrols. In 1980, the US Navy, which had a base at nearby Holy Loch, had introduced random urine sampling as part of an anti-drugs drive. Now, it was claimed, younger Royal Navy ratings were into harder drugs. It was a suggestion the Ministry of Defence would refute but that resurfaced a couple of years later when a number of sailors were court-martialled and jailed for offences including the possession, supply and importation of, among other substances, cocaine.

Senior defence advisers, worried about the effects on Britain's reputation for efficiency and reliability, urged the Navy's Special Investigation Service to look into the whispers. They reported cocaine was available in Scotland but almost certainly beyond the pockets of the average seaman. That hope brought little comfort to the top brass, especially as between 1978 and 1983 eight mariners were dismissed because of drug offences. Having spaced-out ratings running about submarines carrying the means to end the world was a serious business.

A top-level inquiry into cocaine smuggling would have brought MI5 into the equation because this is the arm of the intelligence services responsible for protecting Britain against threats to national security. It was heavy-duty stuff and the Happy Dust Gang would come within a whisker of gaining the attentions of senior civil servants at the highest levels in Whitehall, indeed even in the Cabinet.

But it would not come to that. The hard work and routine slog around contacts and informants by the members of the Strathclyde Police drug squad was about to pay off. Like that of Brian Doran, the name Andy Tait now began cropping up. And Alan Bartlett was about to enter the police log. Had he been superstitious, then he and brother Ronnie might have locked their door and refused visits on 13 February 1982, but they did not. Before the day was out, they would wish they had.

The telephone rang and at the other end of the line was Brian Doran.

'Hi, Alan, it's Brian. I'm on my way around to see you.'

'You have something for me?'

'Yes, but I have something to do in a hurry, so I need you to do me a wee favour.'

'What's that?'

'Nothing major, tell you when I see you.'

Had the police been watching Alan Bartlett's flat on

Highburgh Road at around six in the evening, they would have seen Doran pull up in his car a few minutes after the telephone conversation and disappear inside. But they did not need to be there. Someone would give them all the information they needed. Inside the flat, Alan and Ronnie Bartlett were waiting.

'Brian, hello.'

'Hi Alan, Ronnie.'

'You got anything for us?'

'One ounce. Here it is.'

'And you mentioned a favour on the telephone.'

'Yes, I have to nip to the hairdresser's. While I'm out, can you cut half of this stuff and put it into smaller packages. I'll get them when I come back.'

'No problem. How long will you be?'

'Shouldn't be more than an hour, maybe just half that. We can sort the money out when I'm back.'

Doran left Highburgh Road and a half-hour later the telephone rang in Alan's flat.

'Alan, it's Brian. Do me a favour. That stuff I left; some of it is for a couple of customers. I've asked them to call at your place to collect it. That OK?'

'Sure, who are they?'

'One will say he's picking up for a publican and the other guy you might recognise.'

'Who is he?'

'Tom Ferrie, the disc jockey.'

'Tom Ferrie! Fucking hell, I didn't know you supplied him.'

The fact was he should not have known. But the knowledge demonstrated how indiscreet Tait had been. George regularly complained to Thomas that when he showed up to make a delivery at The Pantry, Tait was unable to stop himself naming well-known customers or even telephoning them to announce the Parachutist had arrived. It was information that would prove crucial to the strategy George would ultimately work out with the forces of law and order.

'Nor does anybody else. Keep it under your hat.'

'Sure.'

Another hour later, the telephone rang again and Alan Bartlett picked it up.

'Alan, Brian Doran.'

'Yes, Brian.'

'I've a wee problem. Been delayed, so I'll be later getting there.'

'That's OK, Brian. See you when we see you.'

Within minutes of that call, a telephone rang at the Turnbull Street offices of the drug squad. In the next brief moments, a voice destroyed the days, weeks, months and years of the Happy Dust Gang.

About eight o'clock that evening, the doorbell rang at his flat, followed immediately by thuds on the door. Alan Bartlett, who would turn out to be the weak link in a chain the length of which the police could not be sure, answered to be greeted by two officers holding up their warrant cards and with the glad tidings, 'Alan Bartlett? We are police officers. This is a warrant authorising us to search your house because we have reason to believe you have cocaine hydrochloride on the premises.'

Opening the door and admitting the police, Alan Bartlett stopped in the hallway. He did not hesitate to think about what he was to say next. 'I know why you are here. I'll give you the gear.' He handed over a little bag filled with white powder, which turned out to be 23 grammes of cocaine. The search produced £800 cash.

The dam had burst. Trouble was about to flood forth.

'Where did this come from?' asked Detective Sergeant Ronald Edgar.

'From Brian Doran,' answered Alan.

12

TRICKY DICKIE

Brian Doran and Andrew Tait expressed surprise when news came on the grapevine that their friend Alan Bartlett and his teenage brother were being held in a police cell. George Duncan and Thomas Sim were not at all shocked. Duncan had been warning the others for months that they were talking too freely. Through friends, he knew that when word went round he was coming to town nightspots would be packed with lust-dust-hungry young people begging for invitations to house parties at which there was a chance he would be among the guests. 'We're getting gear, the Parachutist's here,' would be the word speeding through the rumour mill.

Shortly before the arrest, he telephoned Doran from Utrecht to complain, 'People are even openly saying that the Parachutist is on his way to The Pantry. When I get there, Tait picks up the phone and starts doing the rounds, boasting that I've just walked in, as if he is masterminding some big deal. It's crazy. The police are bound to find out what's going on.' His concerns were ignored and the consequences would not be long in emerging.

It was not only Duncan who urged a policy of remaining

mute. Advocates the world over tell their clients that in the event of being taken into custody and cautioned to the effect that they are 'not obliged to say anything but that anything they do say may be taken down and given in evidence', then the best policy is to say nothing. Silence is golden, at least until they have a lawyer alongside. No one could say for certain that in the case of Alan Bartlett that advice was not valued, but the fact was that after speaking with him, detectives collared first Doran and then Tait. They appeared briefly in court charged with possessing and supplying cocaine and were remanded on bail. A month later, in March 1982, Detective Sergeant Edgar was in his office when a constable informed him he had a visitor.

'Who is it?' the detective wanted to know.

'Someone calling himself Brian Doran.'

The travel agent was anxious to speak in private. 'I'm wondering if we can help one another,' he said.

'In what way?' asked the police officer.

'Well, in fact I know I can help you considerably. But if I do, I'll be looking for something in return.'

'If you have something to tell me, why not say what it is and we'll take it from there.'

'I need some assurance beforehand that by giving you information you will do something for me. What I have to say will be a huge help to you.'

'And what is it you want from me?'

'I want you to drop the charges.'

'Look, Brian, there's no way I can do that. It's impossible.'

'It's been done before.'

'Maybe it has, but a policeman just cannot say to someone, "You've helped me, now go home and forget about everything." The system doesn't work that way. I can promise that if you have information and give it to me, if it turns out to be useful that I'll do what I can for you.'

'Right, in that case I need to think this over.'

'OK, you have my number and know where I am. Get back to me anytime.'

Eight days later, Doran rang the detective sergeant and asked for a meeting in the offices of his travel agency. It was a worried man the officers spoke with that day and the conversation mirrored the one in the police station earlier. Doran asked for a further meeting, but when Detective Constable Joe Corrigan and his colleague arrived for that, they were surprised to discover the businessman was not alone. With him was Andrew Tait.

'I've been thinking over our conversation of last month,' Doran said, 'and have a proposal to put to you.'

'And what is it?'

'Well, the people you really want are the guys who have been bringing coke in. We're just pawns. If it hadn't been there in the first place, we wouldn't have become involved.'

'Brian, that's for a jury to decide. What is it you want?'

'If you drop the charges against us, we'll set up the courier for you. We'll give you the time, date and place where he will be with 100 grammes of Charlie. You'll be able to pick him up red-handed.'

'I've already explained that under no circumstances can the charges be dropped. What I can say is this: I will ask one of my bosses if I can speak to the fiscal on your behalf, should you give information and it turns out to get us the courier. That is as far as I can go. I promise to speak to one of our gaffers, but what happens after that isn't up to me.'

'All right. When will you know if you get the go-ahead?'

'Ring me in an hour.'

Sixty minutes later, Doran called and was told Edgar had been given the nod. The travel agent asked if they would meet him that evening at the Sherbrooke Castle Hotel.

'We can hardly talk about something like this in the bar, Brian,' Edgar told him.

'Don't worry, I'll organise a room.'

A time was arranged for that same night. In the bedroom, Doran condemned the two men who had been his friends. 'The courier is Simmy, Thomas Sim, and he'll be with George

144

Duncan. We can set them up for you. But we are trusting you to ask the fiscal if this gets us off the hook.'

The police were astonished at the way in which Doran had caved in. He was looked upon as smart, hard talking and generally a tough cookie. Tait, too, had a reputation for being shrewd. The decision to arrest these men had not been taken lightly.

Both were prominent in the business world, and Doran, in particular, was a popular figure in Glasgow society – powerful, wealthy and with many connections. He cut a dazzling figure at the wheel of his Rolls-Royce with a personalised registration number BGD 1 and was known throughout the city as a 'big, kind-hearted guy' who went out of his way to make sure people around him had a great time. Of course, there were the occasional few who laughed at him behind his back – an ex-Celtic player who used to turn out for the businessman's football team once transplanted from a building site a giant sign bearing the construction firm's name – 'Dickie' (one of Brian's nicknames was 'Dickie Doran') – and drove it to Pollokshields, planting it in the Dorans' front garden. A handful of locals saw the joke, that here for the man who had everything was the biggest nameplate in the city. His arrest would cause a sensation.

The police in Glasgow knew that before accusing Doran and Tait of dealing in highly illicit cocaine, as serious a drugs offence as Scotland had seen, they had to be sure of not just having *sufficient* evidence but evidence that would stick. But so rife had been the talk about their involvement, that it was more than mere speculation. In addition, after interviewing Bartlett, the confidence of the detectives had grown. Brian Doran, the football-mad millionaire, was about to kick off on the game of his life.

Police will never admit to making deals, offering to go easy on one suspect in return for his or her cooperation in nailing another. In Scotland, the usual response to a plea for mercy is to agree to pass on details of any collaboration to the procurator fiscal, the pursuer of wrongdoers on behalf of the public. Sitting in the bedroom at the Sherbrooke, the reality of their respective situations came home with a jolt. Tait and Doran somehow needed to lessen the blow. And they thought that potentially the best way of achieving that was to grovel to the police. To collaborate. Grass. Inform. The police tactic had been to convince them they were in an impossible position. And it had succeeded. They believed themselves to be in deep, deep trouble, facing ruin, humiliation, disgrace and many years in prison. Their dilemma was that neither knew the extent of the police's case against them. Should they gamble that the police had little on them, hold out, paper over the fact that vast amounts of cocaine had been smuggled to them and hope a watered-down version of the truth would be accepted? Or was the wisest policy to gently suggest that if the detectives promised to go easy, they would spill the beans, give a full, complete, unexpurgated version of the story from start to finish, being careful, of course, to paint themselves as stupid, naive, willing servants of the real villains, gullible individuals of whom a weakness had been taken advantage by the men who actually supplied happy dust?

On their part, the police needed only to sit back and wait, to drop a hint here, a bluff there. They had their men, but they wanted the whole gang. What the police lacked was a link to Duncan and Sim. They were positive they were the smugglers, but could they prove it without catching them with cocaine? The answer to that was probably in the negative. Courts were unlikely to convict the pair solely on the word of men who, it would be argued by the defence, had everything to gain and nothing to lose by slandering others. If Tait and Doran sat back and said nothing, took their punishment and did their time, then the two Scots from Utrecht would walk away, shaken perhaps but free nevertheless. There would never be any doubt that the two businessmen talked and in a few seconds of betrayal added to the destruction of the Happy Dust Gang. As Alan Bartlett had implicated them, so they blamed Duncan and Sim.

146

In hindsight, they would come to realise it was a wrong move.

'You sure you can give us a time and place?'

'Definitely.'

'When will this be?'

'It only takes a phone call. A week at the most.'

'Where does the cocaine come from?'

'Holland.'

'How is it brought over?'

'Don't know that.'

'Why deal with Duncan and Sim? You could have gone to some of the small-timers in the housing schemes and asked them to get the stuff for you.'

'Because the two of them suggested they could get us as much as we needed.'

'So it was their idea?'

'Yes. They pointed out that we were paying through the nose for what little there was going around because the guys who had it looked on us as being well off and able to afford whatever they asked. These people had been selling any old shit, passing it off as clean when it wasn't. But when you're desperate, you'll try anything.'

'So what was different about Sim and Duncan?'

'They didn't want money up front. They told us if we weren't happy with what they brought they would take it back, and they were offering it more cheaply.'

'How much?'

'£45 a gramme compared with about £80 to a ton.'

'So they set the thing up?'

'Yes.'

'And you're in this mess because of them?'

'That's it. It's down to them. It was their idea.'

'Where is it hidden?'

'With his big pal Robert Bruce in Paisley Road West.'

That remark showed how naive Tait and Doran could be, and how little they understood George Duncan. He knew the penalties for being caught in possession of cocaine and there was no way he would have put the liberty of Robert Bruce at risk by leaving the drug at the butcher's home. At the end of the meeting, Edgar told a colleague, 'Doran is the big fish here and Tait is only his lieutenant. They're in a helluva panic. At the very first sign of any trouble, they were only too happy to give me Sim and Duncan on a plate.'

The result of the confab was the raid on the flat as Robert and his friend unloaded the Alfa Romeo. But, apart from a tiny sample of Andrews Liver Salts, the police took away nothing. The elusive cocaine hideout remained that way. But the Judas kiss was about to be planted like knives in the backs of the men from Holland.

13

HAPPY HOOKER

The police had done their work well. Having hung out Alan Bartlett at the end of their line, they now had two others wriggling there, squirming in the knowledge that their only hope of getting off the hook was by deceiving two men they had looked upon as friends into taking their places. Treachery and jungle law were foreign to Doran and Tait. It was true that to be successful in business required a degree of ruthlessness, but they now found themselves in a totally foreign situation. This was an animal fight for survival.

Ahead of them loomed grim prison walls, years surrounded by hardened low-life criminals who jealously despised pampered interlopers who had invaded and profited from a world of crime that was the domain of others. They were terrified by the prospect of attacks, abuse, filthy beds and foul food and the police had made sure both were aware of the fate into which they would be cast. As they headed back into the centre of Glasgow after leaving the private room at the Sherbrooke, both knew their only get-out would be at the expense of Duncan and Sim – the former, in particular.

Treachery has been changing the course of lives since Delilah's infamous hatchet job on Samson's hair. In more modern times, the word has become almost synonymous with criminal enterprises. Had Whacko and the baker recalled the story of Al Capone, they might have thought twice about their betrayal. Capone was fiercely loyal to his troops and loathed the thought of any of them being disloyal. When he discovered that his three top enforcers were plotting his downfall, he threw a banquet and invited them along. Albert Anselmi, Joseph 'Hop Toad' Guinta and John Scalise turned up in their best dinner suits to the bash on 7 May 1929. After the soup course, they had their brains smashed in by Capone, who then had them shot to make sure they had been finished off. It was a lesson others remembered.

Mayer Lansky, the Polish-born racketeer who dominated the American crime scene between the two world wars, boasted his underworld syndicate was bigger than the giant US Steel Corporation. He made sure he retained his grip by setting up his drug-trafficker friend Louis Lepke Buchalter with the FBI, an example of foul play that took Buchalter to the electric chair and gave Lansky virtual immunity from harassment.

FBI agent Joe Pistone infiltrated a Mafia mob but became so embroiled in his role as a hood that his marriage disintegrated. When the local don suspected him of being a policeman, Pistone sacrificed his friend and mentor, fellow Mafia man Lefty Ruggiero, to save his own skin. The true story was made into a film, *Donnie Brasco*, starring Al Pacino.

While the Happy Dust Gang flourished in Glasgow, in New York the Gambino Mafia family headed by John 'The Bull' Gotti, known as 'The Teflon Don' because no charges ever stuck, was presiding over an empire that appeared untouchable. It is unlikely he had ever heard of Tait or Doran, but nine years after they were singing to the Glasgow drug squad, Gotti would wish he had. His trusted lieutenant Salvatore 'Sammy the Bull' Gravano, a mass killer with at least 19 victims to his name, betrayed the don and 36 other mafiosi, condemning them to sit out the rest of their lives behind bars. The adage that there was no honour among thieves applied equally well to those in the drugs trade.

The two informers did not know it as they plotted the downfall of their victims, but a major spanner was about to be thrown in the works. Fed up with his warnings about loose talk being ignored, George Duncan had decided that in future there would be a change of routine. Instead of travelling across himself to hand over his little packets, he would leave that to Sim. It was a show of confidence in the other man he would live to regret.

Before the next delivery, he discovered his worst fears had been realised. During a routine telephone conversation with a friend in Glasgow, he was told about the arrest of Alan Bartlett. He wanted to know if there had been anyone else involved.

'What about Brian and Big Andy?' he asked.

His informant could not help. However, George was sure he knew the answer. As he replaced the receiver, his expression was grim.

His fears were eased soon after, when he received a call from Tait requesting a further drop. Before making the call, the baker had discussed the next move with Doran. They needed to keep the police sweet and that meant dishing up the others. To achieve that, they would need to be persuaded to come to Glasgow with dust and the police would need to be tipped off when and where. After that, it was up to the teams of detectives. But that would not be as easy as it sounded. They had no idea of the route used by Sim or even if it was really his friend who acted as courier with Sim as a decoy to distract anyone who might be taking an unhealthy interest.

Late in February 1982, they set about finding out the answers by asking for the further delivery. Tait placed the order with Duncan and a date was fixed for the following week.

'We'll be seeing you?' George was asked.

'Yes, of course,' he lied. 'Why not?'

'Just wondering. Presumably you've heard about Bartlett?'

'Yes, he and his younger brother Ronald have both been lifted.'

'What about Brian and yourself?'

'What about us?'

'Have the police been to see you?'

'No. Why do you ask?'

'Remember I've been warning you all to keep your heads down. The reason has been that I always assumed if Bartlett was hauled in by the police, he'd sing his head off and put you and Brian in the frame.'

'Well, he must have clammed up. We've heard nothing.'

'OK, but from now on play it very cool.'

When Thomas Sim arrived at The Pantry the following week and made the handover, Tait was clearly ill at ease.

'Where's the Parachutist?' he demanded. 'He said he'd be here.'

Sim told him he couldn't make it. 'There's not a problem, is there?'

The big man opposite him was sweating, and with good cause. He had promised his police masters the duo they wanted were as good as in handcuffs. Detectives had been watching for Sim, and if they moved in now, the cat would be out of the bag. He had promised to signal them once both men were in the shop but had no option but to do nothing other than hand over the money and let his visitor leave.

'George hasn't shown,' he told the officers.

'Why not?'

'Simmy just said he couldn't make it and I didn't want to make things too obvious by asking a lot of questions.'

'Could he be over here but just hasn't turned up?'

'I honestly don't know. There would be no reason for him not to show his face.'

'You sure you haven't said anything that might scare him off?'

'Definitely not. Everything was absolutely normal.'

'Andy, you know the rules of this game. We're doing this for your and Brian's benefit. Without the others, then we have nothing to put to the fiscal.'

'OK, OK. I'll ask for another drop and just say I prefer dealing directly with George. Maybe that will work.'

'For your sakes, it better.'

The police knew George Duncan was not in town. Flights into Glasgow airport had been watched, the Dutch police at Schiphol had checked on departures in case he might have used another route and all his usual haunts had been given the once over.

A week later, the telephone shrilled at George's home. It was Tait.

'Hi, George, you OK?'

'Sure. Any news on the Bartletts?'

'Nothing. Don't worry, they're sound. How about you? Everything OK?'

'Yes, thanks. What's up?'

'We need some more.'

'You should have taken a bigger delivery.'

'Yes, I know that, but so many people want a slice nowadays it's difficult to keep pace.'

'That's good.'

'But, George, I don't like dealing with Simmy. No offence, but I don't really know the guy and everybody is very nervous since Alan Bartlett was nicked. I'd prefer it, and so would Brian, if you'd come over. People were asking about Simmy.'

'Why should that be a problem?'

'It's not really a problem, but you and I trust one another and I much prefer dealing with someone I know. Would you come, please?'

'OK, give me a couple of days and I'll bell you to let you know when.'

It would be easy, in retrospect, to wonder why George went ahead. He would admit to friends in Holland and to

Joop that he was nervous and slightly mystified as to why, the Bartletts having been caught, the others remained at large. It was a racing certainty Alan would have passed on the names of his contacts. Despite his worries, in mid-March he contacted Tait and announced he would be over sometime after the 20th of the month.

'And you'll be here?' asked the baker.

'Yes, but just don't tell anyone.'

He made the usual arrangement with Sim and Scouse Willie to use one of the ferry routes, and he would fly into Glasgow airport himself on 21 March. His friend Robert Bruce had been celebrating a birthday the previous day by having a short holiday in Utrecht and was returning on the same flight. At Schiphol, the two men struck up a conversation with an attractive, young brunette in her mid-20s, who told them she had been shopping in Amsterdam, filling in time while her husband worked long spells out of the country in the oil industry. She was clearly bored but had found something to perk up her interest. She was curious about her fellow travellers, both fit and tanned. On a whim, she announced that instead of heading straight off home to the west coast of Scotland on touchdown, she would book into a city hotel. They suggested one in Bellahouston, assuring her they knew it well. What they didn't mention was the fact it was only a few hundred yards from Robert's flat on Paisley Road West.

When she left them briefly in the departure lounge at Schiphol to telephone and make a reservation, Robert told his companion, 'Look, George, she's definitely up for it. Do me a favour, book into the same place when you get to Glasgow. Because I stay so close it might look odd if I checked in and the staff would tipple I was tapping up a bird. If I need a room, I'll just say I'm you. But don't worry, I'll convince her we should use hers – I'll tell her a business colleague might ring up and disturb us.'

George, game as ever, agreed, looking on this as a belated birthday present for his friend. He and the woman had been seated together on the flight over, but from the way she constantly turned to speak with Robert in the seat behind he realised the extent of her enthusiasm. And there was an unspoken message in her frequent references to her hotel. She was clearly interested in Robert.

But then others were interested in George. Unknown to him, the police had discreetly watched his arrival at Glasgow airport, having been tipped off by Tait and Doran he was expected from Holland. Undercover detectives saw him chat to Robert then walk with a mystery female to a car-hire desk and wave her off, him making for a telephone where he was overheard asking for a room at the same hotel where their later check with the car rental company showed she would be staying. George headed off with Robert to collect his car, clutching his overnight bag, but there would be no need to follow. The police knew where he was staying from his telephone call. Reaching the city, he dropped Robert off at his home. 'Good luck,' he told his friend with a wink and drove off.

As a result of not following, the police missed him meeting up with Thomas Sim, who had arrived by train. George drove in the direction of Byres Road, stopping a quarter of a mile from The Pantry and parking in a side street. Andy Tait was hard at work when he heard a familiar voice.

'Hello, Andy.'

'George!'

'The same.'

'Where did you come from? I wasn't expecting you so soon.'

'I said I'd be over.'

'Yes, but you didn't tell me the day. I was sure you'd let me know first.'

'What's up, Andy? Why the concern?'

'Nothing, no worries.'

'Well, there is a worry.'

'A worry? What about?'

'A worry for Brian and yourself. I have to charge more because of the extra expense.'

155

'What extra expense?'

'Andy, because you seemed in such a hurry to get the stuff I've not had time to make the usual arrangements. I've had to come over later in the day than I would have liked and had to book into a hotel tonight.'

'Yes, but you've got the stuff, haven't you?'

'Of course, why not?'

'I don't know, I've been on edge since Alan was picked up.'

'Well, cool it and stop worrying. Take it easy, the job is done.'

'What do you mean, the job is done?'

'Just what I say. It's delivered.'

'Delivered, but I haven't got it.'

'Yes, you have. It's already delivered.'

'George, honestly it hasn't. I haven't got it.'

'You've got it all right.'

'Where?'

'Around the corner. It's in your car.'

Andy Tait turned the colour of his flour. This was not going to plan. He had told police George would turn up and they would then discuss the handover. Sometimes this was at The Pantry, on other occasions they chose a club or nightspot when Brian Doran would be there, deliberately varying the routine. He wondered if the police were watching the shop right now and was in a funk at the prospect of them seeing George plant cocaine in his car and believing it was a double-cross.

As George had neared his destination, around the corner from the Byres Road bakery he spotted what he had been looking for: Tait's BMW. Removing a tiny screwdriver from his inside pocket, he had carefully opened the front passenger door, making sure not to damage the lock or paintwork. Having checked to make sure he was not being watched, he secured a plastic carrier bag in which was 100 grammes of cocaine under the passenger seat, closed and re-locked the door, and went off to look for his customer.

'When you drive home tonight, park your car close to your front door and when you go inside keep an eye on it.'

'Why?'

'Just to make sure there's nobody in the street watching.'

'Such as?'

'The fucking police, Andy. I told you to be careful. We don't know what Alan might have said to them.'

'I don't like this at all.'

'Stop panicking.'

'It's OK for you to say that. It's not your car. I have to pick up my wife and kids, and if anything happened, if the police stopped us and found it, they'd be arrested along with me.'

'Andy, nobody is going to be arrested.'

'I'm not having it in my car. Go out and take it back.'

George was worried by the man's tantrum and thought he was about to break down. He agreed to remove the bag but that left the problem of another meeting at which it could be exchanged for the cash. He suggested The Archies in Midland Street, but the proposal was turned down.

'I have an errand to run tonight,' Tait said. 'Can't we make it somewhere else? Somewhere quieter?'

'Such as?'

'I don't know, have you any other suggestions?'

'How about the Aldwych Café on Paisley Road West?'

'OK, George, just make sure you're there.'

Later, George would reflect on why he agreed to remove the bag from the BMW because by doing so he put himself in jeopardy and effectively undid a job that had already been done. He had delivered as promised. But he had built up a friendship with Tait and was uneasy at evidently having put him under pressure. There was also the little matter of keeping the customer happy. But, more importantly, George had become overconfident. This extended to changing the routine to allow Sim to act as delivery man. He did not know it then but taking the bag back from the car allowed the full extent of Tait's treachery to bear fruit. He had turned down

The Archies not because of a prior engagement but because in his talks with the police the detectives had instructed him to ensure the meeting would be in a location where George would be easily recognisable. Experience had shown the folly of arranging a rendezvous in a crowded bar where a suspect whose face was not instantly known to a surveillance team could easily slip away. The Archies could be one of the busiest clubs in the city and among its patrons it was odds-on somebody would be able to identify one or more of the police officers. After that, word of the police presence would spread like wildfire.

After George left the shop, Tait waited before looking outside. He was terrified at the thought of walking to his car only to see his visitor fiddling with the lock, trying to get inside. If he suddenly produced the key and opened the door, it would look odd to say the least. He fidgeted nervously for 20 minutes then cautiously strolled around the corner, trying to look unconcerned. The BMW was parked where he had left it earlier that morning. There was no sign of George. No trace of any tampering with the lock, and when he opened it and looked inside no package under any of the seats. To make certain, he checked the boot. That too revealed only familiar items. Knowing he was clean, he returned to The Pantry and called the police.

'It's all set.'

'Where?'

'The Aldwych Café.'

'Know it.'

'Where will you be?'

'We'll call on you tomorrow before you go. There are things to discuss.'

'Such as?'

'Wait until we see you.'

'You are going to mention this to the fiscal, aren't you?'

'Trust us, Andy, trust us.'

After leaving Tait and removing the package, George had slipped through the backstreets to rejoin Sim and given it to him to look after. He told his companion about the meeting the following day at the Aldwych Café, then dropped him near the home of a friend. 'I'll call you in the morning,' he said, before driving off to share a brief reunion and a drink with a friend of his own. But he clearly had other matters on his mind. Top of the list was a meeting with a lady.

He had been anxious to get rid of the highly dangerous package he had removed from Tait's car. The last thing he wanted now was to be pulled by a bobby on the beat looking for an excuse to shake someone down, suggesting that his face was familiar or accusing him that he looked like someone for whom an arrest warrant had been issued over an unpaid fine.

He knew of the extraordinary lengths to which some customers would go to avoid discovery of their guilty secret. One punter would book a room in the Central Hotel – famous for having the cowboy movie star Roy Rogers ride his horse Trigger down the spectacular staircase – and after the exchange, ring one of many massage parlours to hire a prostitute. When she arrived, she would be told to strip naked, don a bulky knee-length ladies' coat and be paid generously to walk to his car. He would accompany her, walking arm in arm and carrying her clothes in a carrier bag, the girl unaware that in an inside pocket was up to £4,500 worth of cocaine, enough to send her to prison for a lengthy stretch.

Once at the car, he would motor to a quiet industrial estate at Braehead where she would remove the coat, hand it back to him and replace her clothing before being driven back to her workplace. 'He says he gets turned on by the thought that I've got nothing on under the coat,' she told her partner. 'He's a weirdo, but then most of them are.' Her walking companion was in reality one of Glasgow's leading insurance brokers.

George headed for the hotel in Bellahouston, but by the time he arrived there was no sign of Robert or the woman. He guessed they had gone to bed and it was not until later the next day that Robert would tell of a remarkable night's events. Reaching the hotel, he found her waiting in the lounge, a drink on her table, and so he joined her. She had kissed him lightly on the cheek and said, 'I was beginning to give up hope.'

'I'm sorry, but I had some business to take care of,' he apologised. 'I promised I'd be here, though, and I always keep my word.'

'Well, you can trust me, too,' she said.

'Meaning?'

'Wasn't it your birthday yesterday? I decided to give you a present and trust it will be worth unwrapping. I've already ordered some drinks for my room, so how about joining me?'

In the bedroom, she stripped to display red underwear and then from her handbag produced a bottle of baby oil. She lay on her front inviting him to unhook her brassiere and begin kneading in the oil.

'Spank me,' she demanded.

He lightly flicked over her buttocks.

'No, spank me, spank me hard!'

Pulling down her panties, he did as he was ordered. The oil seemed to have the effect of exaggerating the sound. 'The people in the next room will hear,' he protested.

'Turn on the television then,' she said. 'But hit me hard.'

As he took to the task with gusto, she began groaning and finally shouting out until he became terrified of a furious rap on the wall or door. He heaved her onto her back. Her lovemaking showed how much she had been missing the attentions of her husband. Robert wondered if his work kept them apart for years at a time, not weeks.

At the height of their pleasure, he discovered, to the horror of them both, that the excitement had brought on an early period and the bedding was covered in blood. Robert used towels from the bathroom and spare sheets to clean them up, dumping the heavily bloodstained items in the bath before slipping from the hotel and returning to his nearby flat. There had never been any suggestion he would stay the night with her. She had her own hire car waiting in the car park and so too departed quietly and early, embarrassed over what had happened, simply leaving the room key on the reception desk while the sole member of staff was taking a telephone call in a back room.

George, meanwhile, was unaware police had monitored his arrival. There had been no need to babysit him through the night, since they knew where he was going the following day, but as the officers making up the early shift clocked on the next morning to resume surveillance they would find themselves in for a shock.

14

POWDERED PANTS

Unaware his friend Robert had already left the hotel, George also departed early the following morning, knowing a busy day lay ahead. He was keen to deliver his packets of happy dust. Tait was not his only customer; two others had asked for cocaine to be delivered and arrangements would need to be made to meet up with all three separately in Glasgow. Each had been told he could have 100 grammes. By the end of the day, George intended to be on his way back home to Holland with £13,500 in his bags. He would make his calls from coin boxes because dialling from his hotel room would leave a trace of the number he had rung.

First, though, he spoke with Sim and they arranged to meet in the city centre. Sim was looking after the 300 grammes and George suggested that to save time he should speak to the intended recipients and arrange to deliver to them before meeting him. Like George, Sim was eager to be going back to Utrecht and he agreed. George then rang the baker and the two arranged to rendezvous later at the Aldwych Café. He decided to contact his two remaining clients after seeing Tait, but first he had a shopping list to complete.

Andy Tait had spent a nervous early morning rushing to the telephone whenever it jangled. There had been several calls from the police asking if George had been in touch or whether he knew where he might be, and he detected a note of urgency as the minutes went by.

'You sure you haven't heard from him, Andy? You're not holding out on us, are you?'

'Look, I know what's at stake here. I'll call you the second he rings.'

'Make sure you do.'

'Why the panic?'

'Just call us.'

In fact, the police were worried. They had pulled up early at George's hotel waiting for him to emerge so one team could follow him while the other checked over his room, looking for any traces of cocaine. When there was no sign of life, they wandered into reception only to learn he had already checked out. As the officers debated which of them would break the bad news to their superiors, the receptionist had a bizarre story to tell them. The man they were asking about had been seen in the lounge the previous evening having a drink with a good-looking brunette, before leaving together, presumably to go to their respective bedrooms. A couple of hours later, a member of the night staff had discovered the female guest's bedroom key lying on the check-in counter. That morning, a cleaner had knocked on the woman's door and hearing nothing had eased her way inside to discover the bed in disarray and the bedding in a heap in the bath soaked in blood.

'We better take a look,' the police decided and headed upstairs.

As they waited for the cleaner with a key in the corridor outside the missing woman's room, the door of an adjoining room opened and a middle-aged male popped his head out.

'What's up?' he demanded to know.

'Nothing, sir. Nothing to worry about, I suggest you close your door,' was the reply.

'Look, I was woken up last night by a racket and now it's happened again. What the hell is going on?'

'What sort of racket?'

'Well, it sounded like some woman getting knocked about. Somebody was definitely getting hit and then the television was turned up, but I could hear a woman groaning.'

'What did you do?'

'I was about to thump on the wall and then it all went quiet. I heard the door close about half an hour later and nothing more after that.'

'Hang on in your room, will you, and we'll come back to see you in a few minutes.'

The door of the woman's room was by now open and the police rushed inside. Sure enough, lying in the bath were bloodstained sheets and bedding.

One of the detectives wrinkled his nose. 'What the fuck is that smell?'

'It's familiar, but I can't place it.'

'You know something, I know this sounds daft, but it smells like baby oil.'

'What the fuck's been going on?'

'Dunno. There's nothing to suggest a struggle. We better take a look in Duncan's room.'

George had left his bedroom in a pristine state. He had had no inkling of the frolics taking place elsewhere in the building. The police checked the bed and bathroom for signs of bloodstains but found nothing. Nor had George left anything behind, no white powder marks on the floor or furniture. Telling the hotel management to lock both rooms and not allow anyone inside, the officers decided to telephone their superiors. As they reached reception, they were handed a message pad with a telephone number on it. They called from their unmarked car to be told George had contacted Tait and the meeting at the Aldwych was on for later.

'Before we leave here, it might be an idea to get some people over.'

'Why?'

'He seems to have been with some bird and he was spotted talking to a smart-looking brunette at the airport when he flew in yesterday. There's blood all over her bedding, the room reeks of baby oil and a punter in the next room reckons he heard her being beaten up.'

'You sure? That doesn't sound like our man; he's a charmer.'

'Well, that's what the punter says.'

'Any struggle?'

'Not really. Apart from the blood, there doesn't seem to be any damage. Nothing knocked about.'

'OK, hang on a few minutes and we'll get a woman over. I've a feeling I know what might have happened.'

'What's that?'

'Not now. I'm having a sandwich.'

A few minutes later, a policewoman emerged from the bloody bathroom. 'You're neither of you married, are you?' she asked her colleagues.

'No, why?'

'Never mind. Give the hotel their rooms back.'

The guest next door was thanked for his contribution.

'What happened?' he asked.

'Minor accident. Nothing to worry about.'

'But somebody was getting a hiding.'

'Fun and games probably, that's all.'

Having solved one problem, the police were still clueless as to George's whereabouts and were forced to rely on him showing up for the transaction with Tait. They needed to set up a watch on the café but had to be careful: George might take a precautionary drive or walk past at any time and if he spotted or even sensed a police presence then the entire operation could be compromised. The officers knew that while he could be pulled in and searched, if he had nothing suspicious with him then they would struggle to find grounds for holding him.

In fact, at that moment, George was three miles away,

strolling along Argyle Street in the very heart of Glasgow's shopping area. Holland had many attractions but compared with Scotland it was expensive, especially when it came to clothing. During his visits back to his native country, he usually bought clothes and had decided to make use of this last-minute trip with happy dust to stock up. He knew what he wanted and where to get it and wandered through the double doors of Marks & Spencer, acknowledging a greeting from one of the floor staff who knew him from days gone by. He made for the gents section and ten minutes later emerged back onto Argyle Street clutching two familiar green plastic carriers bearing the famous gold lettering. Each held identical contents, George having decided, as a gesture of friendship, to buy for Thomas what he had purchased for himself. He had paid cash. His shopping done, he made for one of the many cafés, took a seat, ordered coffee and waited for his friend to join him.

Like the two smugglers, the police too had lots to organise. Temporarily losing sight of George was not a disaster. They knew he would be meeting up with Tait and had the time and place in their notebooks. They had no reason or intelligence to suggest he was supplying anyone other than fellow members of the Happy Dust Gang, although the detectives accepted this was a possibility. But for now, it was the rendezvous with Tait that was all-important. Senior members of the drug squad had discreetly called into the Aldwych Café to study the layout and had taken in every detail as they sipped tea and smoked cigarettes, giving the appearance of normal customers. Satisfied they had a workable plan, they made in the direction of Byres Road, choosing to drive through the Clyde Tunnel leaving others to keep observation on the café. They found Tait apprehensive, visibly becoming more agitated as the minutes passed and the time neared when he would climb into his BMW and drive to Paisley Road West.

'What if George doesn't show up?' he asked.

'Why shouldn't he?' the police replied.

'Maybe he's got wind something's up.'

'You saying you think he has?'

'No, but George is a very cautious man. Maybe he's suspicious at Brian and I insisting he come over in person.'

'Well, he came, didn't he? If he thought something was going on behind his back, there's no way he would have travelled over.'

'What if he says he hasn't got the gear?'

'You said he told you yesterday that he had it. What reason could there be for him not having it today?'

'I don't know. I just don't like any of this.'

'Andy, at the end of the day, it's either he and Sim or you and Brian. We've gone over this with you both. You agreed to hand them over to us on a plate, and let me tell you that if either of you get cold feet now and do anything to get these people off the hook, then it will go badly, very badly, for you. They get away with this and the pair of you will go down for their share as well as yours and Bartlett's.'

'It's OK. I know what's what. It's just the waiting I don't like. I wish it was over.'

'Right, that's understandable, but you've done fine so far. Now we need to run over with you something we've worked out.'

'Such as?'

'Such as what you need to do at the Aldwych Café. You know this place?'

'Not well, but we've met there before.'

'OK. Now, here's what we want you to do. If you're not sure, ask and we'll go over it again, but there can't be any fuck ups.'

For the next ten minutes, the police ran through what they wanted Andy Tait to do once he had met up with his friends. When the short briefing was complete, the police added, 'Of course, you understand we'll arrest you as well.'

'Arrest me? Why? I'm the one helping you.'

'Think about it, Andy. If we lift them and you walk, then they'll know straight away who set them up. This is for your own good.'

'How long are you going to keep me in?'

'Not long. You're already on police bail and we'll simply extend that.'

'You sure? I have your word?'

'Absolutely. Would we let you down?'

Tait made no reply. He was discovering the price of treachery and realising it could be a double-edged weapon.

Thomas joined George but had bad news for him. 'Couldn't get hold of either,' he said.

'Not to worry,' George told him. 'They're not expecting to hear from us until later on. I just thought it was worth chancing that they might be around. Let's get Big Andy sorted and then go on back to them. Where's the stuff?'

'I've brought it with me.'

'Well, stick his in your pocket and leave the rest somewhere safe.'

When George pulled up in the hire car outside the Aldwych, he and his companion spotted the BMW and realised the baker must be inside waiting. He was. He had been there for some time on the instruction of the police, who had told him precisely at which table they wanted him to sit so as to be visible to the others watching from outside. George went inside immediately, but before he left the car, he told Sim to stay put until he spotted their client and then to join them, bringing the 100 grammes.

'But don't show anything until we've made sure he has the money,' added George. On the back seat of the motor lay the two identical Marks & Spencer shopping bags.

As soon as he opened the door, he spotted Tait, sitting alone, a cup in front of him. There were a handful of other customers, including a young woman looking slightly out of place in a dingy headscarf, but, importantly as far as George was concerned, there was no one he recognised.

'Hi, Andy,' he said, sitting down. 'Everything OK?'

'Where's Simmy?'

'Outside, he'll be in here in a tick,' and as he said that Sim walked in and sat near them.

'You brought the gear?' the baker wanted to know.

'You got the money?' asked George.

'Of course, but have you brought the stuff?'

George made no reply, instead giving his companion the thumbs up.

'You got the kit with you?' he was again asked.

'It's here.'

'You got it on you?'

'Andy, it's here.'

'On you?'

'You're asking lots of questions, Andy. There a problem?'

'Sorry, just wanted to make sure.'

'Well, it's here.'

'Definitely?'

'Definitely. What's the worry? Why would we come if we didn't have any gear? I told you yesterday I had it. You could have had it then and again last night.'

'OK, we're just a bit desperate, to be honest. I need some cigarettes.' Tait stood up. 'Andy, where are you going?' George asked him. 'It's table service in here, you know that.'

But the baker was already striding to the counter.

That's odd, thought George. Why didn't he just stick up his arm like everybody else does and shout out what he wanted? His eyes went to his Happy Dust colleague and he noticed Tait appear to make a motion with his fingers, a faint beckoning to someone he could not see but who was obviously outside. For a split second, he wondered what was happening and guessed Tait had spotted a passing friend. Suddenly, he knew something was wrong, but before he could react the door was being pushed open and a squad of plain-clothes policemen were rushing in. There were loud cries of 'Police'. Tables were pushed over, chairs scattered, salt and pepper pots went flying and bewildered customers were clamouring.

'What the fuck?'

Andy Tait was dragged from the counter, where he was

still awaiting the arrival of his packet of cigarettes, to join Duncan and Sim, who were forced over a table and their hands cuffed behind their backs.

As the manacles snapped into place, George spat at the baker and hissed to him. 'Grass! You fucking grass, you set this up. You called us here for the police.'

Duncan and Sim were searched and the incriminating packet of 100 grammes of cocaine was produced triumphantly. But initially all that seemed of interest to the police were the keys to the hire car, which were removed from Thomas Sim. Then all three were dragged outside and pushed into police cars for the short journey to Govan police station on Orkney Street.

Seated in an interview room with the handcuffs removed, George was told to empty his pockets. He did and a few coins, his passport, some travel documents and banknotes were placed on the table. A detective double-checked and nodded to a superior that the suspect was hiding nothing. As he sat down, policemen crowded into the room. They were shaking hands, slapping one another on the back, celebrating, congratulating one another and telling him he was looking at a lengthy prison stretch. And from the officers' point of view, they had every reason to feel over the moon. Bartlett had led them to Doran and Tait who, in turn, had proffered the information that they were simply pawns in the big game and that the principals were the men from Holland who had supplied them. The Happy Dust Gang was in the net.

'Six years, George,' one of his inquisitors told him. 'If you're lucky.'

They noticed that their prisoner seemed unperturbed by his grim prospects. 'Why are you celebrating?' he asked them, 'Why am I here? What have I done? You've found nothing on me. Don't ask if I want to make a statement because there's nothing for me to tell you. So, just for the record, I don't want to make a statement, but you can get me a lawyer.'

And it was true. There was not a shred of evidence against George, other than the word of Andrew Tait, that they were both about to supply him with cocaine. He knew the packet destined for the baker and Doran had been uncovered, but Sim had held it and he himself was in the clear.

Fuck it, he thought. They've got Simmy with the 100 grammes, but I haven't been caught with anything. If it comes to the crunch, it's Tait's word against mine that I was in on it and I know Simmy will never incriminate me.

However, just as hope shone so brightly, the door opened and in walked a senior detective holding two Marks & Spencer bags. He upended them on the table and out fell neatly wrapped cellophane packets of a selection of coloured underpants. And two further objects. Two packages filled with white powder. An officer held them up to the light, then carefully undid the wrapping, licked his finger, dipped it in and tasted the grains of dust.

'Cocaine,' he announced, adding, 'must be about 200 grammes, I'd say.'

'Whoops,' said another.

Fuck, thought George, unaware that as he had been walking into the Aldwych, Thomas Sim was throwing the 200 undelivered grammes into one of the identical Marks & Spencer bags. George insisted it was not his bag. He was absolutely baffled as to how cocaine came to be in it. All he knew at that point was that he had not put it there. He wondered if it had been planted and police were trying to set him up, but then it hit him that Sim had decided that the 'somewhere safe' for the 200 grammes was in one of the green plastic bags holding new underpants.

His immediate reaction was that the police were trying to set him up. At that point, he didn't know it was Sim who had hidden the stash among his underwear.

'Where the fuck did they come from?' he asked. 'They're not mine.'

Had he been Benny Hill or Billy Connolly, he could not

171

have produced a more hilarious reaction. The police broke into peals of laughter, some sniggering.

'What's so funny?' he demanded.

'How do you explain this stuff? What is it?'

'Search me, how should I know. I never put it there.'

'It doesn't matter who put it in. The vehicle is in your name and the bags were in the vehicle. George, you're fucked.'

'That stuff is not mine.'

'These are your bags, aren't they?'

'One is, the other belongs to Thomas Sim.'

'And whose was the bag these packets were in?'

'Dunno. His, I think.'

'OK, whose name is the vehicle in? Who hired it?'

'I did.'

'The bags came out of the motor and the packet came out of the bags. That means it's your responsibility. It's down to you.'

'I never put that Charlie in that bag.'

'Look, there are two identical Marks & Spencer bags. One belongs to you and the other to Mr Sim. You're not arguing with that. It makes no difference which bag or whose it was. What matters is that it came out of a car hired to you.'

'I'm not stupid. I wouldn't do that. Do you think I would leave Charlie in a car I've signed for and which is in my name? You may think you've been clever, but you're still struggling.'

In the circumstances, it might have been the truth. But it was not the wisest of observations. As he was being questioned, George was offered a cigarette by one of the detectives sitting on the other side of the table from him. But when he went to take it, glad of the chance for a smoke, it was snatched away in an obvious attempt to goad him and the air of jocularity was replaced by one of hostility. George wondered about the mentality of officers who, having achieved their goal, were now making it such a personal matter. The atmosphere in the room was becoming heated and it was just as well that at this point Detective Inspector John Wilson walked into the room and ordered silence. He instructed his men to take George to the cells, where he was reunited with Thomas Sim.

Sim's role had been a minor one in the racket, following in George's footsteps in Holland as the scam was established, then carrying the cocaine from ferry terminals to Glasgow and handing it over to him. He was a courier, nothing more. 'Look, Simmy,' George said, 'I've done everything on my own until now; this is the first time you've really been involved and you've fucked it up. The fact is you have been caught with stuff in your inside pocket that was meant for Tait and the rest of it you go and leave in a car which is in my name. You shouldn't have had it with you in the first place. Why didn't you leave it somewhere else when you couldn't deliver it instead of bringing it with you? You're going to go to jail because of what they found on you. Why not put your hands up and say the stuff you threw in the bag was yours as well and I'll try getting you squared up with money for when you come out. Why not make something out of this mess.'

'No, George. I'm not happy about this and I'm not taking all the blame. Forget it.' When Sim refused the offer, Duncan decided to let the matter rest. In his heart, he was angry because it had been Sim's job to deliver the 200 grammes and the cocaine should never have been brought with him in the car. At the same time, he blamed himself for trusting Tait.

He realised Sim would not be able to cope with the pressure from the police if he put himself forward as the main man. 'OK,' George told him. 'I'll tell them I did everything. But I want you to listen very carefully. From now on, I don't want you to have anything at all to do with any of this. Just plead ignorance. Say I told you what to do from the outset and you only did as you were told. You know nothing about where the stuff came from. You only agreed to carry parcels you were given when you came off the ferry on holidays back to Glasgow. You didn't know what was in them. You guessed it might have been hash. Tell them it was all down to me.'

George was not merely being loyal to his lifetime friend; he now had other fish to fry.

15

THE BIG HOUSE

He and Sim were held overnight at Orkney Street and on 25 March appeared at Glasgow Sheriff Court charged with possessing and dealing in drugs and were remanded in custody.

George had been dismayed and confused by the change he had seen in those he had known and respected during the period between him and Sim leaving Glasgow for Spain and returning for the occasional holiday. Psychologists would possibly write complex papers on how the decline in moral standards was an offshoot of the cocaine trade, a double whammy in which using the drug changed personalities and being involved in the huge amounts of money it generated bred greed and disloyalty. The average man in 1980 earned around £50 a week, yet George had returned to find men he respected when he was younger paying three times that for powder to snort up their noses in a single evening. In addition, there was no quality or class about the way they did it, scuttling behind toilet doors. It reminded him of his early schooldays, when kids would sneak into lavatories for a furtive smoke to gain status in front of their classmates and avoid being caught by the head teacher. That very action guaranteed it was no secret at all. Now cocaine users were following the trend. That appalled him.

But now he was discovering an even worse aspect to this new society he had become involved with. These people had none of the scruples of the working classes, who shunned attempts by the police to make friends; instead, they were grasses, willing to sell their friends down the river to save themselves. Among the 1,000 men he and Sim were shortly to join at Barlinnie prison on the outskirts of Glasgow were many such traitors, who kept their heads down fearing discovery, knowing their punishment would either be to have their face hideously slashed or the contents of a slop bucket emptied on their head.

As the van taking Duncan and Sim to jail headed east along the M8, George knew he must have no misgivings about giving like for like. The two were in handcuffs looking through barred windows because of men they had trusted. Now he was on his own, but there would be time to pay back with interest.

Barlinnie, close to the motorway, is by far the biggest jail in Scotland. At one time, eight prisons had been necessary to house the lawbreakers of Glasgow and beyond, but by 1840 just two remained: on Duke Street and Glasgow Green. Overcrowding led to nightmare conditions for inmates and security headaches for staff, with the result that in 1879 work began building at Barlinnie on a 32-acre site bought from a local farmer for £9,750. Its opening meant the closure of the other jails and in the west of Scotland hangings were transferred there. Three days before Christmas 1960, Barlinnie entered the history books when it played host to the execution of Anthony Miller, aged 19, who became the last teenager to be hanged in Britain. It was said that the execution area, where men spent their last days, waiting to meet their maker, and then took a short walk to the death chamber, was haunted by the ghosts of some of those who had perished.

Bruce Grobbelaar, the legendary Liverpool goalkeeper
who spent a sleepless night at the Sherbrooke Castle Hotel.

In the colourful city of Amsterdam, George Duncan and Thomas Sim met the Dutchman who supplied them with cocaine taken at Glasgow sex parties.

Scouse Willie drove cars containing cocaine from the European mainland to the United Kingdom via North Sea and Channel ferries.

Friends knew travel agency boss Brian Doran as Whacko.
He fled abroad to escape the police but eventually
returned to Scotland to a prison cell.

The popular Glasgow baker Andrew 'Big Andy' Tait was jailed
after he became involved in the Happy Dust Gang.

Ronnie Edgar: the wily Glasgow detective answered the anonymous telephone call that set his team on the trail of the Happy Dust Gang.

Joe Corrigan was a master of disguise adept at infiltrating criminal gangs.

The Aldwych Café: it was here that police pounced on George Duncan and Thomas Sim after they arrived for a meeting with Andrew Tait. (David Leslie)

The Sherbrooke Castle Hotel was the setting for a top secret
meeting between Doran and detectives investigating the
Happy Dust Gang. (David Leslie)

Lord Donald Ross, the judge who jailed Andy Tait for four years
and issued a warrant for the arrest of Brian Doran.

Kenneth Togher, who teamed up with Brian Doran to plot
the smuggling of a multimillion-pound cocaine shipment
intercepted by Customs investigators.

Many noted criminals had walked into Barlinnie – Bar-L, the Big House – and had been carried out. Among them was Patrick Carraher from the Glasgow Gorbals. He had escaped death once in 1938 after killing a soldier and watching with relief as a jury reduced the murder charge to culpable homicide – but not a second time. When he left another soldier, this time a Seaforth Highlander, bleeding to death, he was hanged at Barlinnie in April 1946.

Peter Manuel faced the long last drop in July 1958 after leaving a trail of bodies across Scotland and the north-east of England. Police knew of seven victims but suspected him of many more.

Peter Manuel was caught because he talked too much about his wrongdoing. Thomas Sim, for one, wondered on the drive to Barlinnie just how much Bartlett, Doran and Tait had been gossiping within earshot of the police. He had mulled over the suggestion by his friend that he should take sole blame but admitted to himself he was not half so shrewd or streetwise as George and frankly feared the consequences of shouldering culpability on his own.

He would later confide to a friend, 'George could handle prison on his own. He knew people already inside and would be looked after. But it was different for me. I'd be a stranger and I just did not know what to expect. And I was worried about what might happen once they found out back in Holland. We were both on the verge of getting married and if I was parted from my fiancée for a long time, there was a chance she might not hang about. And if I was imprisoned, would the Dutch authorities try to prevent me from returning? What was even worse was wondering whether guys like the Monkey or Joop might decide their own situations were under threat from me and do something about it. I had read of men who went into Amsterdam, for instance, and simply vanished. I knew I was for the high jump because they found the 100 grammes on me, but if George hadn't gone to Marks & Spencer, then there wouldn't have been those bags lying on the back seat

177

of the car and I'd probably have been much more careful about hiding the other stuff. All the way to Barlinnie, I was kicking myself because it was those bags that tied George in. He knew that too, but never once turned around and blamed me.'

It was true that George had in his mind desires for recriminations. But his target was not Sim.

The two had been in the remand wing just a few days when the police came calling. 'How are you, George?'

'I'm fine. What do you want?'

'Want to tell us why you were meeting Big Andy Tait?'

'I've known him for a long time. Maybe he wanted me to set up some deal in Holland.'

'I'm troubled by that remark. Could you be saying that he and Doran paid you to act as a courier?'

'What do you think? I'm a roofer in Holland. Where would I get the money to pay for such big quantities of cocaine?'

'Come off it.'

'Look, you think you are so smart, but you are stupid bastards. You haven't a clue, have you? You think you have set me up with the help of Bartlett, Doran and Andy, but it's you who has been set up.'

'What do you mean, George?'

By the time the police returned to Barlinnie, George had been thinking hard. He knew the detectives could link him to the cocaine among the underpants because the car was in his name. He told his visitors, 'The people you have been dealing with are the so-called pillars of society. And you had the chance to get them, but you've let them turn the tables on you just so you could look good by picking up two couriers. Big deal. You've had the big fish in your net and you've let them escape so you could catch a couple of minnows instead.'

'What are you saying, George?'

'I'm saying that everybody knows you guys are mad to get promotion. All of you, because you get more money that way. Climb the ladder and you're in the big league and you get promoted because you make big collars. And you haven't got that here. What good will it do, you locking up a couple of couriers? Next week, the people who are paying for the stuff will just find two more and if somebody grasses on them, two more and so it goes on.'

'So?'

'Well, the others have told you they were just customers, haven't they?'

'Is that what you've heard?'

'It's what I know they would say. These people have everything to lose. They are important businessmen who have a long way to fall. They've been making out they were simply customers who couldn't resist buying, and Simmy and I were the big players who organised the lot.'

'We're not saying you are near the truth, George, but it would be in your interests to cooperate. How it appears at the moment is that you and Sim ran the entire thing with the help of some big people in Holland.'

'Listen, that's not the way it works. I was just a courier. Simmy knew absolutely nothing and just did what I told him to do. He's not in the picture. The people you seem to be suddenly good friends with ran everything. They paid the Monkey after I put them on to him and he got Scouse Willie to bring it over.'

'Hold on, George, who is the Monkey and who is Scouse Willie?'

'If this works out, I'll tell you later on, but for now all you need to know is that the people you have been speaking to gave me the money when I came over to Glasgow and I had to hand it over to the Monkey, who arranged for the stuff to get transported. All I did was deliver it when I got here. I'm a working guy. I don't get big wages and you have to have money to afford this stuff. There's no way I could get my hands on enough to finance an operation of this scale. It was Doran who financed it.'

'So, Brian Doran was the Mr Big?'

'I'm saying nothing more. I didn't even have to tell you

this, but I wanted to put the record straight. You've charged me with intent to supply cocaine and with possession, and I have to concentrate on my defence.'

'Maybe we can help you there, George.'

'And maybe I can help you, but I'm not saying anything more until I'm out of here.'

'You apply for bail and we won't oppose it.'

'Don't try kidding me that you're doing me a favour there. Simmy and I know we're getting bail. We'll have to hand back our passports, but at least we'll be out of here.' Duncan knew the police would oppose his application for bail because they wanted to keep him under pressure and could not be sure that if released he would stay in Scotland. But he was determined to see it through. 'Look, when I get bail, come and see me then,' he told them.

'Why not talk now, George?'

'Because I could be very helpful and you'd go away with the lot and decide you want me kept under lock and key.'

It would be in the police's interests for both suspects to remain in the remand wing of Barlinnie, making it easy to keep an eye on them and be sure at all times where they were, but the detectives, experienced men used to the devious ways of men and women under pressure, knew that if the pressure was to be eased then the promised cooperation might just as soon evaporate. Heat, the knowledge that police were so close they were breathing on you, is what any criminal dislikes; indeed, some are petrified by it. So, the drug squad determined to keep the heat on George and Thomas.

They returned for another informal chat at Barlinnie with Duncan. Inspector Wilson and Detective Sergeant Edgar seemed friendly and anxious to demonstrate their willingness to help. George had by now realised there was little point in denying he knew anything about the existence of the cocaine and possibly much to gain by dropping a helpful hint.

'Where did the cocaine come from, George?' they asked.

180

'Holland.'

'And where was it going?'

'To Mr Tait and Mr Doran.'

'How often had you delivered stuff to them?'

'Look, I'm not saying anything else now. Not until we are both out. And don't try pressing me because I've had a long think about what to do and I want more time to think. But not in prison.'

He and Sim had been assured by their lawyers they were about to be set free on bail, but before their cell doors were unlocked George had another visit from the police. The meeting lasted no more than ten minutes and was concerned only with establishing where and when they would rendezvous with him. The visit had another motive, however: it acted as a reminder that the police were, and always would be, close by. Despite police opposition on the grounds that they would abscond, Duncan and Sim were released on bail, a condition being that they reported daily to a police station in Cardonald, Glasgow.

16

SHADY CHARACTERS

Duncan and Sim were released into an atmosphere of mistrust. Tensions had been rising in the South Atlantic, with Argentina about to invade the Falkland Islands, insisting the time had come for it to take back the islands it knew as the Malvinas and which it considered the United Kingdom had stolen a century and a half earlier. Everywhere, families of British soldiers made ready to kiss loved ones goodbye; in the case of 255 troops, it would be for the last time. And, as ever, Scottish regiments would be at the forefront. In fact, the Scots Guards would play a major role in the retaking of the islands 8,000 miles away, but before the conflict was ended, all over Scotland the dirge of funeral pipes would be heard. The conflict distracted newspaper headlines from the problem of cocaine in Scotland, but George was well aware his own plight had not been forgotten.

Sim would later admit, 'George and I couldn't go back to Holland because it was a condition of our bail that our passports were surrendered. I tended to keep my head down, while George would go into the city every weekend to the old haunts. But he was conscious that many who had been his friends were now keeping their distance. These were people who used to flock around the Parachutist because they knew if he was in town then there would be lots of happy dust to share around. He brought them the means to have a good time and lots of sex. Now the Happy Dust Gang had been broken up, it was back to the bad old days of Charlie arriving in dribs and drabs. Anyone who had it was terrified of being caught because people knew the police were aware who might be using the stuff and that it was being brought over. And, once we had been arrested, it was, for a while, as if George especially was a leper to be avoided. It was understandable, people were scared that if they were seen in contact with him they might become implicated. Glasgow was still packed with hot tottie, young women showing off their tits and thighs, and sometimes middle-aged women dressing as if they were mad to pull. The trouble was that having been used to coke and the nice, easy, sensual feeling it gave, people were now getting stuck into hash as though it was going out of fashion because there was nothing else to act as a stimulant except booze.

'George was visiting Robert Bruce's pad on Paisley Road West one night. They had been to the Warehouse earlier and put the word around about a party at Robert's. Robert had a reputation at the time for pulling birds, who always loved his parties because they were always lots of fun. That night he had been visiting the home of a girlfriend, and her sister, who was still at school, came into the room. She was absolutely gorgeous, beautiful, a stunner and was wearing her school uniform. Robert asked if she would like to come to the Warehouse with him and the schoolgirl agreed.

'He took her along and had no difficulty getting in because he knew one of the guys on the door. But inside, everyone was staring at her because although she had changed out of her school uniform, she had left her school stockings on and it was obvious she was young, too young. Somebody whispered to Robert the girl was attracting attention, so he had a quiet word with her and suggested she go to the toilet and take off the stockings. She did and handed them to

183

him, but then decided she wanted to ring her uncle and ask him if he'd like to join them. The girl asked Robert to take her to the cloakroom where there was a telephone but as they arrived, he realised he was still holding the warm stockings. He thought it was time to go home and took her to his flat, where loads of people joined them.

'The party was going full pelt when a girl approached George and asked if he had any cocaine. He didn't, but the girl wouldn't take no for an answer. George remembered the story of the raid on the flat when the police had decided the contents of an Andrews Liver Salts tin was really Charlie, so he said to the girl, "Hang on a second," and went into the kitchen. He found the liver salts, mixed some baking flour into them and told her not to tell anyone else. She was a big blonde, who snorted the mixture, announced it was great gear and turned into a raving sex maniac, wanting to shag everyone in the room.

'Of course, the first thing she did was to blab to everyone else George had kit. Others started complaining they had been left out, that he was holding back, and so he had to cobble up some for them. Everybody seemed happy, especially a guy from Mosspark who was dancing around with the blonde's brassiere on his head like a pair of earmuffs and her bare breasted. Everything was going brilliantly until in the middle of the night there was a knock on the door and a nasty-looking guy was standing there, asking for Robert and demanding to know what he had done with his daughter, who had to be at school at nine that morning. Fortunately, she'd gone a few minutes before with one of her sister's pals.'

George could honestly say he had nothing on him because he didn't dare have even a trace of talcum powder on his clothing. That would have been excuse enough for him to be pulled up by the police. With two drugs charges already over his head, even the suspicion he was dealing would have meant an instant loss of bail and a slaughtering by a judge at the High Court. Try as he might, it was impossible to get home the message that he was clean. Even though Robert never had drugs in his flat, because he was a close friend of George's, it was automatically assumed he had stuff hidden away somewhere on the premises. Of course, every grey cloud had a silver lining. Both might have been genuinely drug-free, but George's reputation was enough to guarantee a full house at any party to which he was invited.

Glasgow has often been described as a big village, where keeping a secret is an impossibility. At first, George was treated warily, suspected of being responsible for the downfall of the Happy Dust Gang and the pleasures it had brought. But as the days and weeks passed, old friends began cautiously renewing contact, approaching and asking about his case. George was known to be a man who kept his counsel and he would merely answer that it was Tait and Doran who had grassed him but he was confident all would turn out well in the end. He told Sim, 'I say to them that because Doran and Tait are successful in business, they think they have been very smart but have actually got themselves into even more trouble through trying to act clever.'

George knew he was right and was about to make sure of the fact because the police had not been reticent in their contact with him once the walls of Barlinnie were left behind. He realised there would be no let-up from the police: having given them a taster off the menu, it was plain his guests were anxious to join him at the dinner table. He had the key to the whole puzzle. The police had one version of who was running the show but privately wanted to believe their wealthy informants had set out first and foremost to protect themselves because that was more beneficial to their businesses and careers. At the same time, they could not afford for him to escape a prison sentence. If that happened, it would hardly be a deterrent to those waiting in the wings to move in on the scene created by the Happy Dust Gang. Police intelligence reports suggested there were others eager to fill the vacuum. And while word of the arrest of the Scots had reached Amsterdam and the ears of the principal suppliers of cocaine in the Dutch city, these men would not be deterred from continuing their trade. They could not have cared less if those who bought their product ended up dead or in prison as a consequence, but what did make their ears prick up was the prospect of the trail leading back to them and facing imprisonment themselves or, worse, retribution from their masters in Colombia, who had proved in the past that prison cells, even solitary confinement, were no protection from tentacles with deadly stings. The men who ran the cocaine trade were ruthless when it came to ensuring the continuation of their own interests and fortunes. So, in Amsterdam, men like the Monkey and Joop needed to find out just how much, if anything, of their own activities had filtered back from interrogation rooms in Glasgow police stations to the headquarters of the politie. Until they could be satisfied of their own safety and that of others in the chain, they would be taking a step back from propositions by strangers with Scottish accents.

George was at the home of Robert Bruce one day when the telephone rang. The police were on the other end of the line and suggested a meeting. It took place the next day in the car park of a Safeway store on Paisley Road West. Another get-together occurred in the unlikely setting of the platform of Cessnock underground station to a backdrop of trains rumbling past when Duncan hinted he knew the names of people in the public eye who were cocaine customers. A third took place in Robert Bruce's flat.

'How's it going, George?' he was asked.

'How did you find out where I was staying?'

'Well, you hadn't exactly jumped over hoops to get in touch, so we thought we'd give you a reminder of our little agreement.'

'I told you I'd be in touch.'

'Never mind, we are now. You want to tell us anything?'

'How about you telling me something first.'

'Such as?'

'What have Bartlett, Doran and Tait told you?'

'George, how do you know they've told us anything relevant? And supposing they have, you know we can't tell you what it is.'

'You hinted while I was in Barlinnie that they'd put me there and it's no use saying Tait didn't set me up. The only reason I'm here is because they grassed Sim and me. Tell me what damage they've done to us and then I might want to put you in the whole picture.'

'Is that what you think? That they've set you up?'

'Tell me I'm wrong.'

'Come on, George, what transpires between us and the people we talk to is confidential. But maybe you're on the right track.'

'And maybe you've told them the same thing, that Simmy and I put them in the frame. I just don't know if I can trust you people.'

'Whether or not you want to trust us doesn't matter. What does is that unless you can come up with something that is going to be worthwhile to us, you are looking at a High Court judge and not going back to Holland for a very long time, if ever. Think about it. While your pals are partying, the most fun you'll have is watching a black-and-white television set with 30 other guys during prison recreation.'

After the third meeting, as the detectives stomped down the stairs, Robert asked his friend how it went. 'I don't know what to think,' was George's reply. 'They're a set of fucking shady characters.'

17

THE DEAL

The police could afford a smile as they drove away from Robert Bruce's flat. They had now, effectively, set the members of the Happy Dust Gang at one another's throats, a favoured ploy that often produced dividends when men and women who had once been close friends set to wondering if one apple in the barrel had turned bad. The raid at Alan Bartlett's in February so soon after Doran had made an excuse for not returning to pick up the cocaine he had dropped off with them had created a domino effect. It had left the brothers suspecting he had set them up so they grassed Doran. Doran and Tait had grassed Duncan, and so he turned the tables on them. For Duncan to avoid a long jail sentence, he needed to convince the police he was only a courier carrying a small amount of cocaine.

At his third meeting with the police, George had made his feelings crystal clear. 'I'm only prepared to help you because Brian Doran and Andrew Tait grassed me. But there are conditions attached to your getting my help.'

'You are not in a position to lay down what we will or will not do, George.'

'Listen, I'm the only person who knows the full story. I'm

not going to ask for anything unreasonable, but I can help you out.'

'Go on.'

'Well, I can help you, but you have to help me.'

'In what way?'

'I want the case heard by a sheriff, you cut the amount of cocaine and anything I tell you about the international drugs scene won't be used as evidence against me.'

'First things first, George. How can you help us? Remember, you're probably looking right now at coming in for something like three to five years.'

'I'm aware of that and that's one reason for what I'm doing. The other is that I want to get back at Mr Tait and Mr Doran. I'll give you enough witnesses to guarantee you have a watertight case against the two of them.'

'And who are these witnesses?'

'Never mind the names at this stage. You get those if we have a deal but, take it from me, I will give you ten people who will be first-rate witnesses, people who are clean, who have no criminal records. These are people you will never find in a million years, but I can provide them for you.'

'They were dealing with you, getting stuff from you?'

'Look, no names, nothing else now. Trust me, when the time comes, you will be given everything you need.'

'And in return?'

'You're telling me Sim and I are looking at something like five years. I want a guarantee of reduced sentences for us both and that will only be possible if you put us before the Sheriff Court and not the High Court. You can do that by reducing the value of the kit you found and instead of charging us with possession and intent to supply, drop the supply. That way it could be dealt with by a sheriff, whose powers of sentencing are much more limited.'

'The pair of you were nicked with 300 grammes' worth. Maybe on the very bottom line something like £60 a gramme, but more likely £100. Let's be friends and call it £18,000. How much are you saying you were caught with?'

'Less than 200 grammes. What if we forget about the "1" and call it £8,000?'

'£8,000? You're not serious. Be realistic, George.'

'That's precisely what I am being. You stick to your version and what do you get? The Bartletts for possessing and Simmy and me for carrying. You'll have nothing to pin on the main men.'

'We'll have the Bartletts saying Doran dropped the stuff for them.'

'Their word against his. Not enough and you know it. So, you went there after Doran had been and found kit. It could have been left by anybody. You have nothing to tie in him and Andy Tait. On the other hand, if you do a deal with us, you'll get us as witnesses, plus ten others I'll line up for you.'

It was a tempting offer, one that meant the disintegration of the Happy Dust Gang. 'Give us time to think about it, George. We'll have to have a chat with the fiscal.'

'Well, don't take too long. Remember our case is due up before the end of the year.'

George reported this conversation to his lawyer, Tom Bannigan, highly regarded by those who found themselves in a tight spot with the law. In his mid-40s and a criminal-law specialist, he was rapidly becoming the man to seek out in cases involving drug allegations, a mushrooming field of legal complexities that many lawyers were reluctant to enter.

The existence of the Happy Dust Gang was known about in the circles in which solicitors socialised, not least because a handful of members of that august and respected profession had been known in moments of weakness to sample the product in which the gang dealt. It was also rumoured the police were taking a deep interest in well-respected Glasgow citizens, including a baker and travel agent, and that criminal proceedings were already under way. There were many in the law who, for a variety of reasons, were keen to discover precisely what was going on and had more than a passing interest in Tom Bannigan and how he handled his case. In fact, he would be given the credit for the fact that what subsequently happened to his client, George Duncan, was looked upon with envy by others facing seemingly grim futures through becoming involved with drugs. That would stand him in good stead in a fiercely competitive business. Indeed, as the future rolled on, his name would frequently appear in newspaper reports of drug cases. In 1998, he was at the centre of a furore surrounding the daughter of then High Court judge Lord McCluskey. Police discovered 40 Ecstasy tablets in a crashed Ford Escort car owned by His Lordship's daughter Catherine. She was not involved, but her boyfriend, who had been at the wheel, faced the serious charge of dealing in Ecstasy though he was cleared and walked free. Bannigan, at the time a sheriff, took the controversial decision to throw out the case on the grounds that a police search of the vehicle, during which the tablets were found, had been illegal, a ruling later vindicated when a Crown Office proposal to appeal against it was dropped.

In 1982, Bannigan was facing another tricky legal minefield. His client had put his neck on the line by offering to help the police and, at the same time, effectively showing them his hand. If it went wrong, George and Sim would certainly be looking at a miserable future.

'Can you give them the witnesses?' he asked.

'Absolutely, and they'll swing it for the police.'

'You're sure about this.'

'I know what I'm doing, Mr Bannigan.'

'Well, as you've already been charged, the police will have to go to the procurator fiscal Len Higson and ask him to agree to a deal. I will speak to him and try sorting something out for you. I'll tell him you're prepared to fully cooperate.'

'We need to get the case out of the High Court and in front of a sheriff.'

'Don't worry, I know. Leave it to me. You've already shown good faith.'

191

He called back to announce the fiscal had agreed, adding, 'He wants you to make a statement. How do you feel about that?'

'If it helps Simmy and me, then I'll do it.'

Duncan made the statement at Strathclyde Police headquarters on Pitt Street, incriminating Tait and Doran. When it was done, he phoned the lawyer and then Sim to tell him what had happened.

'Can we trust them?' Thomas asked.

'No.'

He was still musing over his decision to put some of his cards on the table when Tom Bannigan called a few days afterwards. 'George, I've got bad news.'

'What?'

'The police, they've gone back on the deal.'

'Reneged?'

'Afraid so.'

'Bastards. Why?'

'They seem to think they can get a result on Doran and Tait with your statement.'

'Listen, Mr Bannigan, will you please get on to Len Higson. He must have been in on the decision to pull the plug on the deal. Tell him that if they renege on what they promised, when I go to court I will say my statement is a pack of lies and I was pressured by the police into making it. They said it would go really badly for Simmy and me if I didn't go along with them. If they don't keep their word, then I'll make sure everybody in Glasgow knows they can't be trusted.'

An hour later, the lawyer called back. 'We have a deal.'

'You've spoken to Mr Higson?'

'Yes. You are apparently in the Sheriff Court and the charge will only be one of possession. The prosecution will offer no evidence on the intent to supply and it might not even be mentioned. The maximum you can get is two years.'

'Is that what you think we'll get?'

'Don't take my word for it, I'm not the sheriff, but the

prosecution will make it known that you are helping the police with their investigations. I guess you'll be unlucky to even get 12 months, but please don't bank on what I say.'

'Thanks for the good news. I could not believe the police were backing out. I told a friend they were a dodgy bunch, but I hadn't realised just how dodgy.'

When he replaced the receiver, he knew one major step had been taken. But he had lots to do. Like finding ten witnesses. And arranging one more very important meeting.

18

THE OFFER

With the arrests of all five members of the Happy Dust Gang, the police were now in the driving seat. And the success of their operation to trap the smugglers was showing dividends. The then head of the Strathclyde Police drug squad, Detective Superintendent Charles Rogers, was delighted to be able to report good news to his chief constable, Patrick Hamill.

Until the break-up of the gang in early 1982, his team had regularly made seizures of cocaine. Now, hardly a grain crossed their paths. Was this down to users becoming more circumspect about their gossip? Or maybe discovering more secure hiding places? The more likely explanation, thought the police, was simply that the major trafficking route had been blocked and would-be smugglers were scared off by what had been thought of as a very tight operation being exposed.

'The drug has come to our notice only spasmodically,' said the superintendent, 'but we remain as vigilant as ever.' It was a comment that showed the huge impact of the Happy Dust Gang on the development of the drug scene in Scotland. And police would need to be on their toes. They regularly liaised with the Central Drug Intelligence Unit at

Scotland Yard, a specialised team that studied information gathered not only across the UK but also around the world, then looked for patterns that might give a clue as to the source of the drugs or the routes used by traffickers.

Details of the Happy Dust Gang now went into files at the unit, where experts acknowledged that, but for their betrayal, Duncan and Sim might have continued undiscovered for much longer. The vast majority of smugglers were identified because they had police records for involvement in the drug trade. Frequently, a check of a trafficker's past would show he or she had convictions for possession. What would have made Duncan and Sim so difficult to detect was that they were not known as criminals or for having connections to known drug dealers.

Men and women with a clean history were in huge demand as smugglers. In espionage circles, the most effective spies are 'sleepers', patriots whose loyalty to the cause is never questioned but who lie dormant for years, taking extreme pains not to attract attention, scrupulously avoiding even being issued with a parking ticket. When activated, they are beyond suspicion, unconnected to any controversial group or organisation, their very anonymity making them formidable. So it had been with Duncan and Sim, two Glaswegians living and working abroad and, like thousands of other Scots, briefly returning home from time to time. And the method they used had been so simple it had been almost foolproof. It was often the unorthodox, the ingenious, not the straightforward, that led to exposure. Skydiver Andrew Thornton, a former US police narcotics agent, strapped duffle bags to his body packed with enough Charlie to make him £10 million and leapt from a light aircraft over Tennessee to avoid Customs checks. Unfortunately for him, the parachute failed to open. And the same idea was adopted by two men in Florida: one threw two bags containing homing devices and cocaine from a twin-engined Cessna and a further four attached to parachutes, then leapt out after them. His chute opened, but he failed to spot the aircraft manned by Customs officers following him. On another flight, nearly 50 Eastern Airlines employees in America were arrested after Customs officials seized £250 million worth of cocaine stashed in the air-conditioning systems of two passenger jets. A 727 jet belonging to the same airline was discovered carrying cocaine in an electronics panel under the cockpit. In New York, an Old English Sheepdog was put on a flight from Bogotá to John F. Kennedy airport where an X-ray revealed packets of cocaine surgically implanted in her abdomen. She recovered after an operation.

Back in London, Horseferry Road magistrates heard the bizarre story of a 32-year-old Portuguese polio victim who smuggled snow worth £80,000 into Britain hidden in his leg callipers. Four men and a woman who hid cocaine worth £2.6 million by sandwiching it in between long-playing records when they flew from Colombia to Heathrow were jailed for a total of more than 80 years, while hidden in the canvas of a painting sent from the Middle East to a hotel in west London was a kilo of cocaine. Off the coast of East Sussex, £4 million worth of the drug was meant to be hidden on the seabed but was washed ashore onto the beach because the smuggler miscalculated the amount of weight necessary to hold the packets down. Junkies spent days patrolling the seafront, hoping for more to appear. Two female couriers were caught trying to smuggle cocaine worth £600,000 hidden in bottles of champagne on a flight arriving at Heathrow. They were jailed but defied threats to kill and maim them by turning Queen's Evidence against a millionaire drug baron who went down for 16 years. A university graduate, aged 24, on a trip to Ecuador to improve his Spanish, tried making a profit by swallowing at least 13 condoms filled with cocaine worth £10,000. After arriving back in Britain, one burst and he died in agony from cocaine poisoning. A 74-year-old pensioner returning from France was stopped by Customs officers as he drove his car from a ferry at Dover. He had previous smuggling convictions and hidden in lunch boxes and shampoo bottles was coke that would have been worth £2.5 million on the streets.

These were rackets that had gone wrong mainly as a result of accident, carelessness or the hunters playing a hunch. The biggest menace to any lawbreaker was the man or woman who told tales. They might be termed snitches, snouts, touts or whatever, but the effect of their treachery could be deadly. Ultimately, the downfall of the Bartletts, Doran and Tait would come as a result of an informant grassing to police. It was a fate fairly common to those involved in the dirty work of illicit drugs. Rival dealers often shopped one another to the authorities in order to lessen competition and while this was at the gentler end of the scale of revenge, occasionally opponents were savagely beaten or killed, or simply disappeared.

An informant who blew the whistle on a Mafia cocaine smuggling operation in Rome was sitting in a prison cell happy to be there for his own protection when a letter arrived and inside was a death note wrapped around the tongue of a close relative. He changed his mind about giving evidence. Closer to home, in London, wealthy Italian Sergio Vaccari, high-living son of a millionaire publisher, became embroiled in a row with Mafia associates running a smuggling enterprise known as the 'cocaine triangle' in which the drug was transported from Colombia into Britain via Italy. After the arrest of the Happy Dust Gang, Scots were believed to be among the customers who regularly called at his luxury flat in Holland Park to buy cocaine. It was where, in September 1982, a cleaner discovered his body riddled with stab wounds to the face, neck and chest. The killer has never been found, but Vaccari was probably murdered because he made it known he had discovered that Mafia members arranged the murder of multi-millionaire Roberto Calvi, known as 'God's Banker', found hanging from Blackfriars Bridge in June 1982. Apparently, he had threatened to pass this information to the police unless his debts were wiped off.

Revenge on this scale might not have been in the minds of Duncan and Sim, but they had every reason to feel bitter. While the easy option for one or both would have been to go to the police and pin the blame for everything on the others, Duncan still believed there was a way in which at least four of them could escape relatively unscathed, possibly even avoiding prison. It meant taking an astonishing gamble. He had already trusted the three Glasgow-based members and been badly let down for his troubles, while Sim had been unwilling to grasp a suggestion that would have allowed him to come out of prison with a substantial nest egg. History pages were packed with accounts of olive branches that had turned into poisonous vipers.

George was in love with a beautiful woman, though – he wanted to marry Rosa, put the troubles of the Happy Dust Gang behind him and get on with creating a new life. Sim, too, was contemplating marriage. Alan Bartlett was only weeks away from tying the knot with his fiancée Pamela Ritchie. And Andy Tait had a family who supported him, a wife who loved him and a business that needed his expertise and faultless work ethic. Brian Doran had a wife and six children who also needed their adoring father around, not least because one of his youngsters, Michael, was in tragically poor health. So every man had a motive for wanting to escape the worst the law could throw at him. Most of Duncan's sympathies were for Tait. He regarded the big baker as a gentleman sucked into an abyss by unexpected popularity but all too easily manipulated. He accepted the man had almost certainly lacked the guile to deceive the police over their plot to sucker him and Sim into the treachery at the Aldwych Café but to continue holding a grudge would only harbour resentment, which could distort his own future.

George had debated long and hard before asking Sim to be the fall guy. As he was considering putting the question to his friend, newspapers were recalling an incident of years earlier that had a peculiar relevance.

In 1969, when George was a 12-year-old schoolboy, he remembered adults discussing a murder in Ayr in which an elderly lady, Rachel Ross, aged 72, died as a result of being tortured and tied up by two men who robbed her and her husband Abraham as they sat in their home. A notorious safe-blower and petty villain called Patrick Meehan from Glasgow and a violent associate of his, James Griffiths, became the main suspects. At the time of the murder, the two had been passing through Ayr on their way back to Glasgow from Stranraer, where they had been setting up a break-in. Meehan vehemently protested his innocence, but he was effectively doomed when police went to arrest Griffiths, the only person who could confirm his story. The Englishman started a gun battle in which 13 people were wounded and he was killed. Meehan wanted the blame put on a noted thug named Ian Waddell, who, like Thomas Sim, would have none of it, even though there was no doubt he and a crony named William 'Tank' McGuinness were the real killers. In the end, Meehan was jailed for life for murder. He was eventually freed in 1976, but in 1982, at the time when Duncan was trying to negotiate deals with the police and his fellow conspirators, the row over the jailing and the amount of compensation he ought to receive still rumbled on. That May, the murdered body of Waddell was discovered in a shallow grave in the East End of Glasgow. In pubs and clubs in the city, many were asking, 'Is that what happens when you refuse to help out your friends?'

Thomas Sim, for one, was conscious of the similarity between his and Waddell's situation and began wondering whether he had been right to turn down George's offer of a substantial cash reward in exchange for shouldering the blame. Was it such a bad idea? After all, unless George could pull the legal equivalent of a rabbit out of a hat, he was going to jail anyway and why not emerge with enough in the bank to guarantee him and his new wife a decent start? Sim became increasingly aware of conversations about Waddell's grisly end. His problem was that he was purely

199

and simply terrified of prison, of being locked up with the sort of hard cases who murdered the Waddells of this world. And terrified too at being lumbered with a reputation as someone who would not go out on a limb for a friend. Sim was torn between a rock and a hard place.

The Happy Dust Gang had discovered just how dirty the business of drug smuggling could be. And it was about to get a good deal muckier. George was determined to find a way out of the pit into which the others had dug themselves using tools of lies and pretence. He reasoned that the platform from which he wanted to launch their escape had to be built on a foundation of honesty: that meant everyone being frank about their various roles and especially their dealings with the police. The Bartletts were ruled out of the equation – Ronald had never been a player and Alan only had a bit part in the gang's operations. In any case, he felt unable to rely on Alan, who, he later found out, had so readily coughed up to the police when they called at his flat. He knew the script as far as Sim and he were concerned, but what about Doran and Tait? What was their role with the police?

George phoned the travel agent and sought a meeting with them both. Doran was reluctant, fearing that if the police saw him and George together they might conclude happy dust was still circulating. The three met eventually, but Tait and Doran were adamant that they had never collaborated with the police and were not responsible for the set-up at the Aldwych. It was an attitude that both infuriated and disgusted Duncan. He felt it mirrored the middle-class view that those from the lower end of the social scale lacked subtlety and were easily manipulated. What Tait, Doran and Alan Bartlett failed to realise was that Duncan had not one, but two escape plans. He was convinced, though it was hard to accept it, that Doran, for all his learning and intelligence, believed he could stick his head in the sand and emerge to find the whole affair had blown over. The travel agent had one very major disadvantage when compared with the likes of Duncan and Sim: he was neither streetwise nor had he been coached in the rules of the tenement dwellers that to grass was to invite often terrible retribution. At further meetings, his attitude of 'we've done nothing wrong, nothing against you' persisted until the peacemaker wondered if he was wasting his time.

During one rendezvous, he had been talking with Doran when Tait approached. He rounded angrily on the baker, shouting accusingly, 'You set me up and it was you who gave the police enough information to arrest me.'

'No, I didn't,' Tait replied.

'Of course you did. You know it, Simmy knows it, and the police know it.'

Tait and Doran walked off but he was determined to get at the truth. When Doran telephoned and asked for another meeting, his suspicions were heightened. After Duncan had agreed, the travel agent continued the conversation with a warning. 'Don't come to my office,' he urged. 'I think the police are watching me.'

'Why should they do that?'

'I don't know, but I don't trust them.'

'Who can you trust these days?' Duncan asked. There was silence.

After a couple of seconds, Doran said, 'Let's make it at Andy's place. Give me a couple of hours.'

A voice in Duncan's head was telling him something was wrong. He decided to keep the rendezvous even though he knew it smelled of danger. Why did Doran need so much time to get to a meeting just a few minutes' drive away? Maybe he was busy, but warning bells were ringing and George decided not to take chances. He rang the office of the Glasgow procurator fiscal and asked for Len Higson. He introduced himself and told the lawman why he was calling.

'Mr Duncan, I can't stop you talking to anyone, providing you're not trying to induce them to change their story,' said the fiscal. 'But I'd be happier if you took along a small recorder and taped the conversation. What is it you want to ask Mr Doran?'

'Whether he told the truth. I know he's spoken to the police about Thomas Sim and myself, but I need to find out if he's exaggerated.'

'Fair enough. But I still think you should carry a tape.'

'I'm worried in case he checks if I have a recorder. What if we have this initial meeting to get his trust and then I arrange a second when I'll be taped up?'

'Keep me informed about what happens.'

George did not want any formal record kept of the forthcoming conversation because of what he was about to suggest.

He was driven to Byres Road by Robert Bruce. It was a fine day in late May, an early summer sun warming the streets and encouraging sturdily built female students to don short skirts and, the two noticed, even discard their brassieres.

'Don't know how long this will take, Robert.'

'Not to worry. Just be careful. I don't trust these two.'

'What will you do?'

'I might have a stroll around and buy an ice cream.'

'OK, see you later.'

He and Doran strolled in the sunshine and went into the University Café, a popular haunt for students and West End housewives. Looking about to make sure they had not been followed and that no one was listening to their conversation, he began. 'Brian, Andy and you must think you are out of the wood on this. You've put everything on to Simmy and me because you imagine that will get you into the police's good books. But maybe you don't realise just how thin the ice is that you are skating upon. Don't deny that you've helped the police to nail us. And don't go on telling yourselves that in return they are going to forget about the two of you because they aren't. They want you as much as they want us, if not more, and once they have us sewn up, they'll go for you two. We're small fry compared with you. The police want to make an example of rich people like you because it's the well off who can afford Charlie: if they weren't buying it in the first place, it wouldn't be brought in.'

'I'm listening. Go on.'

'Well, as far as I can see, the only people the police have found with cocaine are the Bartletts, and Simmy and me. They've found none on Andy or you.'

'Go on.'

'The Bartletts have dropped you both in it. But if you cooperate with me and say the police put you under pressure to make false statements, incriminating Simmy and me, I'll make sure that Simmy puts you in the clear.'

'How?'

'By making a statement to the effect that you and Andy had nothing to do with buying cocaine, and that it was the Bartletts who purchased it.'

'How will that help?'

'Look, the police only found a tiny amount at Alan Bartlett's flat. If Simmy says he was only bringing stuff to them, then that would sound plausible, that this was small scale, and it will throw doubt on what the police are trying to prove.'

'Which is?'

'That we conspired to import Charlie with intent to supply. We'll all be found not guilty.'

'How do you know they'll try pinning that on us?'

'Think about it. They want to make this look good.'

'George, this is all well and good, but you've missed one thing out.'

'I know what you're going to ask. Why will Simmy make a statement admitting he was bringing stuff in, landing himself in trouble and keeping the rest of us out of it?'

'That's it. Why would he do that?'

Before he set out with Robert Bruce, Duncan knew Doran would be so intrigued he could not stop himself asking that question. And because of the answer he was about to give, he'd rejected the plea by the procurator fiscal to carry a hidden tape recorder. No one had to hear what he was to say.

'Because you are going to offer him £15,000 to do it.'

'£15,000! You're joking.'

'Going to prison is no joke, Brian. And that's where we are all heading unless we do something. You put up the money and I'll get Simmy to go for it. Talk it over, the two of you.'

The two men rose and began to walk back to The Pantry. As they approached, Duncan said goodbye and just as he made for his friend's car he heard Doran's voice behind him. 'George, one moment, please. Can I have a word?'

'Go ahead.'

'That's a good idea about paying Simmy to take the blame, George. I think it might work, but I can't give you an answer until I've spoken with my lawyer.'

'Who's that?'

'Len Murray.'

'Ring him from a coin box here.'

'Sorry, can't do that. He's in Spain for me, trying to tie up a World Cup tickets deal. Right now he's in a meeting, but I'll ring him this evening.'

'OK, give me a call and let me know what he says. But we need to get moving.'

Climbing into the car, he asked Robert how he'd filled in his time.

'I told you. I bought an ice cream and went for a walk around.'

19

THE DECEIVER

It had been a condition of their bail that George Duncan and Thomas Sim remained in Scotland. George had been staying with his mother at Penilee in the north-west of the city. He was looking forward to returning there because Rosa was joining him for the weekend. After Robert dropped his friend off after the meeting, he drove back to his own flat, leaving George to await Rosa's arrival. Half an hour after she appeared, the gathering heard a commotion outside and, looking through the window, saw a gang of officers, most in plain clothes, drawing up in a convoy of cars and vans. George rushed into the living room, grabbed a sheet of paper and a pen and began writing frantically. He completed his task in seconds, in time to open the front door as fists banged upon it. The posse of police, waving a document before them, bowled him over as they stepped inside.

'George Duncan?' they asked.

'You know who I am.'

'This is a warrant for your arrest.'

'What for?'

'Earlier today you met Brian Doran and attempted to extort money from him.'

He was formally cautioned, then forced to bend almost double as his wrists were handcuffed behind his back.

'You're making a serious mistake,' he shouted, and told the police to look on his mother's telephone table and pick up the piece of paper on which he had been writing so furiously. On it was the name of the fiscal with whom he had earlier discussed meeting with Doran and his telephone number.

'Ring the number now!' he demanded.

'No need. We were watching you from the moment you and your pal Robert Bruce arrived on Byres Road until you left. Your every movement was filmed. We even have Robert licking his ice cream. He was definitely enjoying it.'

'If you don't ring the number, you'll make fools of yourselves.'

'Why?'

'Because when you do the fiscal will tell you he knew all about the meeting. He sanctioned the whole thing.'

It was clear the police were worried at this development. If George was telling the truth and they arrested a man who was effectively working for the procurator fiscal, harsh words would be sure to follow. There was a hurried conference and an officer went out to one of the waiting vehicles. A few minutes later, he returned, ordering the cuffs to be removed. 'We've spoken to Mr Higson and he confirms your story. Sorry, George, but we were given information suggesting you would try to bribe Brian Doran.'

'Would I phone the fiscal if I was intending to do anything wrong?' the prisoner of a few moments earlier angrily demanded to know. 'Well, now, I wonder if we can work out who tipped you off. By the way, any chance of a few copies of Robert with his ice cream?'

The next day, Brian Doran flew out of Glasgow to Marbella. He told friends he was taking his family on a well-deserved holiday, but it would be seven years before he returned. He had been out on £5,000 bail. When he failed to come back, the die was firmly cast in favour of the story that would be told by George Duncan to the police.

Doran had indeed told detectives about the meeting on Byres Road and that was why they were already there waiting when Robert and his passenger arrived. And after it was over, the travel agent had gone through his version of what had transpired, telling the officers how he had been asked to come up with £15,000 to bail out everyone except the Bartlett brothers and Sim. After it became plain the travel agent had flown out on a one-way ticket, the questions began: why, if he had nothing to fear, was he not returning? Had he been telling the truth?

George Duncan had a very different version for the police. 'I knew Doran and Tait had set us up at the Aldwych and told them if they had any decency left in them they should hold up their hands and admit to it. But they would not and that made me very angry. They realised I was going to leave. Doran was worried because he knew I could get him into serious trouble if I made a statement saying he was the Mr Big behind the whole operation, the man who had put up the finance and who had been the principal buyer. He said he could work out a way that would get both of us out of trouble. He said if I got Sim to say the cocaine belonged to him, he would pay him £15,000. I was horrified at being offered a bribe and said I wasn't interested.'

Of course, this was far from the truth, but who was to challenge his account? George knew he was in pole position. The days of the Happy Dust Gang might be over, but now it looked as though he had been telling the truth from the outset. There was now no point in George trying to protect Doran, even if that meant Andy Tait would be dragged down in the process. In any case, was Tait entitled to expect protection? He had been in on the Aldwych sting and on the tip-off about the Byres Road rendezvous. Like the Bartletts, and Duncan and Sim, he would have to take his chances in court.

When Doran left, there were many in Glasgow who refused to believe he would not return. Convinced he was only a customer of the dealers from Holland and could therefore expect only a slap on the wrist when he eventually appeared before the beak, they waited to see him once more surrounded by the best-looking women in town at Charlie Parker's, occupying his familiar stool, joking and sharing his largesse with anyone who cared to join in. They waited. And waited. And waited. But Whacko had gone to ground. He had other irons in the fire. Of two potential motives for his disappearing act, one would become evident within a couple of weeks; the other came close to coinciding with his flight.

His disappearance might have lightened the pockets of Glasgow's club owners, but it meant Duncan could now concentrate on fulfilling the promises he had made to the police and the procurator fiscal in exchange for their agreeing to the demands over his treatment. The principal of these was his offer to provide ten 'uncontaminated' witnesses. It was not a mammoth undertaking because he knew many of those to whom Tait and Doran had sold the Charlie he brought them. And he had been sufficiently shrewd to remember the names of his other customers' clients. The main problem was convincing those he approached that by agreeing to come forward they would be guaranteed immunity from prosecution. 'You can go along with me and when it's over still have not a stain on your character,' he advised, 'or wait for the police to knock on your door and haul you off in handcuffs. Do you want to put your families through that? Of course not. Here's your once and for all chance to wipe the slate clean.'

Some found it difficult to believe the police would keep their word. When asked to make statements, they expected, as they signed the foot of the final page, to be asked to stand up and be formally charged. That they were not came as a mixture of relief and astonishment despite previously being assured they had nothing to worry about.

George also had to prepare for his and Sim's court appearances. That meant explaining to their respective fiancées that they would almost certainly be locked away for months at least and even when they were freed would have their passports withheld until legal proceedings were over in the case against Andy Tait. And in the unlikely event of Doran returning to face the music that too would delay their return to Utrecht, although it was generally accepted that the prospect of that happening was now remote to say the least.

Three days after Doran left, the nightmare for the Bartlett brothers ended at Glasgow Sheriff Court. On 4 June 1982, Alan, aged 26 by now, described as a company director in his family's potato merchant business, and Ronald, 18, also said to work for the company but living with the brothers' parents in Airdrie, pleaded guilty to possessing cocaine hydrochloride with intent to supply it to another.

Prosecutor Jack Bell said, 'Police drug-squad officers received information that there was cocaine in Alan Bartlett's flat on Highburgh Road, Hyndland, and went there with a search warrant.' He did not say the raid came minutes after they had been visited by Whacko Doran or who had made the call that tipped off police but made it plain the Bartletts had offered no resistance and Alan had volunteered the bag of powder. Their lawyer, Ian Robertson, said neither had any intention to supply the cocaine to the public. Alan was fined £2,500 and Ronald £1,000. It was their one and only appearance in the dock; however, they would have to face yet further ordeals in the witness box.

The case seemed straightforward, but rather than solving mysteries it raised at least one unanswered question. According to Alan Bartlett, Doran told the brothers he had left one ounce of cocaine, equivalent to just over 28 grammes. The two customers had each collected what had been arranged and, as a result, police would later reveal their search produced just 23 grammes, officers estimating the value of this at £2,300 or £100 a gramme, a figure that raised eyebrows when the going rate charged by Doran and Tait was £60 a gramme. Inflating the value could be used to the benefit of both accuser and defender: for example, the higher the value, the bigger the racket would be made to sound. Conversely, from the point of view of those charged, as Duncan and Sim would come to be, a haul would seem much smaller when divided by £100 as opposed to £60.

20

WORLD CUP WOES

Like the television headmaster from whom his nickname emanated, Whacko was not one to let an opportunity slip past him. Both were wily but unlike the fictional character, Doran had boundless energy. He had become rich through first study, then putting his learning to good use, and if the sign of a good businessman is his sheer industry, then he was in the top drawer.

In the late 1970s and early '80s, Blue Sky Travel was unrivalled because customers had confidence that in him they were dealing with a man who knew what he was talking about. As a consequence, the bookings and commission had rolled in. Then, with the formation of the Happy Dust Gang, he had seen an opportunity to make money from his own habit. If he was willing to pay for the drug, then so would others whose canter to addiction would overcome any quibbles about paying top prices. He saw that there were vast fortunes to be made in drugs. Though he did not become addicted to cocaine itself, as time went by what did become an obsession was the idea of creating a vast fortune through its marketing.

It would be argued in the years ahead that Doran fled

to Spain to escape the police investigation into the Happy Dust Gang. That was not his original motive for going there, although it did become one, and once in Spain it became a reason to remain.

He had made plans to sell World Cup match tickets to tens of thousands of members of the Tartan Army including doing so at the various venues where the Scots would play. Only when he realised, after the meeting on Byres Road with George Duncan, that the game was up and the request for £15,000 might either be part of a police sting to set him up or the beginning of a crippling chain of blackmail demands, did he know that once in Spain to return to Glasgow would be to walk into a prison cell.

Doran had been over the moon when Scotland qualified for the finals of the World Cup and, like every other self-respecting member of the Tartan Army, was determined to be there to cheer on his side. That meant getting tickets for the matches, which he knew would be like gold dust. There were only a limited number available for the Scottish fans who would travel regardless of having a brief. Doran wanted to make their dreams of watching every game featuring Scotland come true – and become a millionaire at the same time. His Spanish was flawless and through contacts in the travel industry he discovered the competition organisers wanted tickets sold through the top clubs staging the various matches. Scotland, drawn in Group F with New Zealand, the USSR and one of the favourites, Brazil, would play their opening game against New Zealand at the Estadio La Rosaleda in Málaga on the 15th of the month. Their next game, against Brazil, was 100 miles inland at Estadio Benito Villamárin in Seville, and three days later they would return to Málaga to complete the Group games by playing the USSR on 22 June. If they managed to progress, then it would mean opening talks with officials of whichever clubs were selected for the further matches. But, by then, he was confident he could have made his fortune.

Around January 1982 he had begun talks by telephone

with a senior executive of the Málaga club, who seemed pleasantly taken with the suggestion that Doran would take tickets off their hands and sell these to Scots. From the point of view of the club, there were many advantages to this idea but mainly it would mean getting rid of a fair percentage of their allocation in one go and avoid time-consuming and often difficult conversations with fans whose knowledge of the language was poor. The conversation was brief but friendly, a deal was settled and a meeting arranged for May at which around £250,000 was handed over in exchange for thousands of tickets for the two games. At the same time, Doran set about making plans to launch a magazine targeting the Tartan Army.

Sales of match briefs from the Blue Sky offices opened slowly, but he hoped things would pick up as the games themselves drew near and fans began leaving for Spain. He had already booked his flight for the first week of June, together with a hotel in Málaga, and planned to stay on for most of the World Cup matches and then return home to Glasgow.

But by the time he landed in Spain at the beginning of June, he had double reason to be worried. He had discussed the Byres Road exchange with his highly regarded Glasgow lawyer, Len Murray. 'Len said he would make some enquiries and get back to me,' Doran would later tell friends. 'He did and warned me the talk was an attempt to frame me and have me done for attempting to pervert the course of justice. When I heard that, I knew it was impossible for me to go back to Glasgow. Every card was against me and it was obvious the police were determined to get me one way or another.' Now, with that grim prospect of having his freedom taken away hanging over him, Whacko knew he needed to work hard if he was not to also lose a fortune.

When the first enthusiasts from the Tartan Army started arriving, he had sold nowhere near the number of tickets he had hoped and it would be down to touting briefs outside the grounds. What had, weeks earlier, seemed a rosy future

213

was now looking bleak. He had gambled his savings on the World Cup, the venture had badly weakened his finances and he knew that back home knives were being sharpened over his double-dealing and back-stabbing, which had set the Happy Dust Gang at one another.

The game the fans really wanted to see was the match in Seville against Brazil. The opener against New Zealand gave him some limited success and the team a convincing 5–2 win through goals from Kenny Dalglish, John Robertson, Steve Archibald and a brace from John Wark. But as the busty female Brazilian supporters began thronging Seville, Doran, with two of his colleagues from Glasgow, Robert Torrance and Stephen Roche, were offering tickets outside the ground, having motored to Seville from their base in Marbella. Uniformed Spanish police officers made no attempt to stop the trio and because huge amounts of cash were being handed over, even took up position near the Scots in case someone had the idea of a snatch-and-grab theft. With the teams in the dressing-room preparing to take the field, trouble did come, but from an unlikely source. A Spanish market trader offering cheap souvenirs felt his trade was being hit through the ticket sales and formally complained that Doran, Torrance and Roche were breaking the law through not having a street sales licence.

The police had no option but to haul them to the local police station where Doran, bewildered, sat furious and devastated, staring at the useless briefs. What faint hope he had of rescuing his fortune had been devastated in a few moments. From the ground half a mile away came the sound of shouts of joy as underdogs Scotland took an unlikely lead in the 18th minute with a goal from Dundee United's David Narey. But from then on, neither the three nor the Scots fans would have much to shout about. Brazil drew level, then scored three more goals to run out 4–1 winners. Doran and his friends were held overnight and released only after police arranged for their passports to be collected from their Marbella hotel.

Len Murray was also holidaying in the area at the time and the three men turned to him for help. Doran had huge faith in his lawyer, and he was not alone. Murray had a long list of both notorious and celebrity clients, ranging from Tony Miller, the last teenager to be hanged in Britain, to Billy Connolly. He was also asked to advise Paul McCartney when he was caught growing cannabis plants at his farmhouse on the Mull of Kintyre. Shrewd and skilled he undoubtedly was, but even he could have had no idea of the celebrity status the man who had been touting tickets outside a football ground in Spain would go on to achieve.

Murray wanted to take in the World Cup but found himself receiving a frantic call asking if he could help out. He motored to Seville for a meeting in the Justiciary Department with the three ticket sellers and the local police. In the end, Doran was left with bundles of useless match briefs. As the Spanish police pointed out, there would have been no point in trying to get rid of the tickets for Scotland's third Group game back in Málaga against the USSR because he had no street-trading licence to sell there either. It would need only another complaint to see him and his friends being hauled off back into police custody. As it was, the game ended in a 2–2 draw and Scotland finished the Group with a win, draw, defeat and three points, an identical record to that of the USSR; however, the Russians would advance due to a better goal difference. Scotland had performed bravely and, as always, their fans were a credit to their country, but they would troop home disappointed, a sentiment that fell short of Doran's emotions.

The disastrous ticket and magazine venture depleted his funds by around £100,000, which didn't exactly leave him penniless but with the knowledge his life would never be the same. He had lost a fortune – a small one perhaps by his standards, but a lot nevertheless. He could not return to Scotland because of the suspicion that he would be instantly remanded in custody accused of trying to bribe at least one Crown witness. He had a wife and six children to consider,

215

especially the health of little Michael. And, in addition, as he debated his next move, news came from a friend in Glasgow that Blue Sky Travel had started legal proceedings against him, demanding £21,281, worth around £100,000 these days.

He had been expecting the action. In February, four months before he skipped bail for the sunshine of Spain, Blue Sky, for whom he was an agent, said it discovered that deposits paid in advance to him from other travel agents had been banked in a separate account in his name but on behalf of Blue Sky. And he had ignored demands for access to the account. Doran firmly denied doing anything wrong, claiming the account was his private property and insisting that if Blue Sky believed cheques had gone adrift they should tell him who had paid them and how much they were for. Blue Sky accountants would claim this left them in a catch-22 situation: they argued that they could not get details of the cheques because Doran would not let them access the account.

He would leave that matter for his lawyers to sort out; meanwhile, there was the business of organising a new life. He knew that having made one fortune, he could make another, and tried to look on the positive side. There were advantages to living in Spain, even if it was a far cry from his childhood days in a tenement opposite a police station in the suburb of Shettleston, a few miles from the centre of Glasgow. Old classmates at St Paul's primary school remembered Brian, at seven years old taking his First Holy Communion, as a timid little boy. As he grew older and moved on to St Mungo's senior secondary, his character developed into one which many looked on as overbearing; although this may have been down to him being smart, along with a penchant for languages, a gift that would be of immense use to him in later life and which helped him start off his working career as a travel courier in Spain. Now he was back and possibly for good, but much had happened in between.

Doran persuaded his wife Mary to move to Spain with the children, although the family retained the house on Terregles Avenue. They temporarily took over an apartment in Puerto Banus, but having found their feet and had the chance to take a good look at their surroundings, they opted to move to Marbella, renting a six-bedroom villa on the outskirts of the resort. It was ideal because there was plenty of room for the children and it was near to private schools. It seemed that in no time at all he had established the same social circle as he had enjoyed in Glasgow, calling at the best bars and the plushest hotels for meetings with men who had scars on their faces, who never walked about alone and who drove expensive motors. One of his favourites was the Coconut Grove country club.

Doran opened up an agency selling and leasing apartments and villas, but it was little more than a cover for building up connections in the drug trade. Doran could have set up home anywhere in Spain, but it was significant that he opted for Marbella in the heart of the Costa del Sol, better known then as the Costa del Crime because it was the spot which scores of criminals on the run from the United Kingdom had chosen for self-imposed exile. The prime advantage of settling there was that Spain, at that time, had no extradition agreement with Britain, partially as a result of long-standing ill feeling over the refusal of successive Westminster governments to negotiate the return of Gibraltar. In addition, Spain was the main stopping-off point for oceangoing yachts and container ships smuggling huge quantities of cocaine from South America. The Costa was within handy reach of the coast of North Africa, Morocco in particular, where most of the world's hashish was produced.

Among Doran's neighbours were Freddie Foreman, once a close associate of the Kray Twins; Ronnie Knight, one-time husband of Carry On star Barbara Windsor; and great train robber Charlie Wilson. Police from all over Britain regularly visited the area, trying to keep up to date with who was there and where. But these criminals inhabited a close-knit community and were wary of strangers.

The men exiled on the coast of Spain with their families had much in common with Doran. They were fugitives, most were rich – with few exceptions they enjoyed spending money on the good life – and all were careful to be constantly on the alert against occasional attempts by various police forces to plant an informer in their midst. The Scot, though, had one bonus: his fluency in the language and his encyclopaedic knowledge of the world's geography, built up through his time as a courier and then as a travel agent. It meant he could converse in the same tongue as the men who produced and controlled cocaine, and knew the chief exporters, Colombia and Bolivia, like the back of his hand. Those who controlled the cocaine routes decided this was a man they wanted to know better. He was becoming a jewel. A further problem for the UK police was that crooks in residence were frequently visited by other crooks who had good memories when it came to recalling the faces of detectives. The best intelligence came from local cops, who resented the presence of so many villains. They would much rather have kept an eye on the tens of thousands of young women who holidayed on the Costa, with their golden breasts and tanned thighs.

When Doran arrived and put it about that he intended staying, the first piece of advice he was given was: 'Keep your head down and don't under any circumstances cause trouble.' That was not only for his sake but for the welfare of others. Those who broke the rule quickly found themselves advised to clear off.

For Brian Doran, there was much to do: a business to get off the ground, contacts to establish, an income to be earned. For a time, the family seemed to settle down into a way of life that, for five of the children, would be the envy of their friends back in Glasgow. But it could not last. A tragedy was in the offing. It was one that no millions could preclude and that would force him into making the most heart-rending decision of his entire life.

21

THE BLESSING

Some reckoned Brian Doran to have had the luck of the devil on his side, leaving Glasgow without arousing any immediate suspicion. Others gave a knowing wink, wondering if a more powerful force had been at work. One thing was sure, his influence stretched into the most unlikely corners.

It was only in his dedication to the Catholic faith that his devotion to making money was equalled – a curious contradiction considering his weekly renunciation of wrongdoing. When it was announced that Pope John Paul II would be making a two-day pilgrimage to Scotland between 31 May and 1 June 1982, every single one of the country's 800,000 Catholics naturally wanted to see the great man in the flesh. Many would be disappointed. An open-air Mass at Bellahouston Park in Glasgow on the Saturday would allow 300,000 to come within sight of His Holiness, but Doran wanted more than a mere glimpse. A limited number of passes would be available to 'VIPs', who would be personally blessed by the pontiff. For the majority, it would be more than an immense privilege; it would be the crowning moment of their lives. It was an experience Doran did not want himself or his family to miss.

Entry was meant to be limited to deserving cases, and Brian could argue that his desperately ill son, Michael, was one. According to Matthew, Christ had said 'Suffer little children, and forbid them not, to come unto me: for of such is the kingdom of heaven.' Doran prayed for the son he so desperately loved to be taken before God's representative on earth, and if intensity of faith was the criterion by which the sharing out of VIP tickets would be gauged, then the Dorans would surely qualify. But then so would tens of thousands of others. There was talk of a draw, putting all the names of applicants into a hat and pulling out the lucky few. Doran could not and would not take chances. So, in order to secure his time with Glasgow's esteemed visitor, he made a few new friends, a meeting with one of whom was witnessed by a customer at Douglas Timmins' Parallel Bars bistro. 'There was a lot of talk going about, particularly in the East End of Glasgow, over the VIP section. Everybody wanted to be in it, but no one seemed to be able to find out how to go about getting tickets. Brian had clearly made his own enquiries. About two or three weeks before the visit, he came in with a stranger, rather scruffy and not the sort of person you would associate with Brian, who bought a couple of drinks and sat down to talk, making it plain he didn't want anybody else joining them. Brian was speaking very quietly but because his guest had a loud voice he had to constantly tap him on the forearm and make shushing sounds.

'The man was talking about the Pope's visit, how he could get tickets for anywhere in Bellahouston Park. We could hear snippets of Brian asking things like, "Are you sure?", "You won't let me down will you?" and "I really want this to be a big, big surprise for the family." And the other chap talking about "one bag", saying, "I can definitely get you eight but more than that will be difficult." When he left, Brian had a smile on his face as broad as the River Clyde and it was obvious he'd got whatever it was he was after.

'He was back the day before the Pope's visit and said he and the family would be getting a papal blessing. Someone asked him how he had managed that because you needed to be in a special section and Brian tapped the side of his nose with his finger. A couple of days after the big Mass, Brian popped in and said the whole family had been blessed. Somebody joked that it must have cost a fortune and he smiled and said, "My friend Charlie took care of it. It's amazing what a bag can get you." We never saw Brian again.'

Doran had been determined to wait until after the Holy Father had been to Glasgow before leaving. Later, when the conversation among his old crowd came around to his exile, there were many who were convinced that had it been a choice between getting away in safety or facing almost certain arrest over the bribery claim in order to be blessed, then he would have chosen the latter. Whatever the answer, it was certain that of all the many drug deals he arranged during his career as a smuggler, one, probably the smallest, had the most lasting effect. It would have been a good, pure memory to take with him to Spain.

* * *

As Brian Doran was getting to know his new neighbours and meeting criminals curious as to why such an obviously devoted family man had moved into their midst, George Duncan and Thomas Sim were bracing themselves for their own change of surroundings. The procurator fiscal had kept his word by having the amount of cocaine found among the packets of underpants fixed at 150 grammes, half the actual amount recovered, with the value given as £8,000, which worked out at just over £53 a gramme. If some thought this odd, considering the Bartlett brothers had been accused of dealing in cocaine from the same source only in their case it had been valued at £100 a gramme, then no one was complaining. Not the brothers, who were glad to have their case over, and certainly not Duncan and Sim, who, as a consequence, were avoiding a meeting with a bewigged High Court judge holding indefinite powers.

The two men knew they would be going to prison, and Sim especially was dreading his fate. His brief spell in Barlinnie on remand had left him with a loathing and fear of jail, and now whenever he went into a café or bar customers seemed to be discussing lawbreakers with a vehemence that in past times would have been heard around the scaffold or the guillotine. And the public perception that no mercy ought to be shown to those who dealt in drugs of whatever strength appeared to being heeded by judiciary everywhere.

'George is taking all this in his stride,' Sim told a friend, whom he bumped into in a pub on Paisley Road West. 'The more he tells me not to worry, the worse it seems to get. Maybe I should have taken up the offer of £15,000 to take the blame for us both. I'm going to jail anyway and as it stands now, I'll come out with nothing.

'People are looking at me when I walk in anywhere and I know they're accusing me of grassing on Big Andy and Doran. It's no use trying to tell anybody that that's not how it was, that they and the Bartletts dropped us in it. Brian's done the right thing by buggering off to Spain.'

The more he read newspapers, the worse things seemed to be. Sam McKechnie, aged 30, had been found with a huge haul of cannabis resin, claimed to be the largest seizure of the drug ever discovered in Scotland. The drug had none of the addictive properties of cocaine or heroin and was a relatively mild and cheap alternative, but a judge at the High Court in Glasgow handed McKechnie five years, a sentence that many felt to be savage, while Sim was near apoplectic with fear.

'He cops a five for hash! What the fuck will they do to us for Charlie?' he moaned to Duncan.

'Stop worrying, Simmy,' said his friend. 'Look, the guy went to the High Court. We're in front of a sheriff. The most he can give is two years and, take it from me, there's no way we'll get anything like that.'

It could have been a lot worse. Elsewhere they were executing drug dealers. In October 1982, a month before Duncan and Sim were scheduled to appear in court, painter and decorator Derrick Gregory, then aged 32, was arrested in Penang with £800,000 worth of heroin stuffed in his boots and a woman's girdle. Despite suffering mental illness, Gregory, from Richmond, Surrey, was convicted of drug trafficking and sentenced to death. Pleas for mercy from religious groups, his eight-year-old daughter and governments worldwide fell on the deaf ears of the Malaysian authorities. Gregory would wait seven years on death row while the last embers of the once brightly burning Happy Dust Gang were dying until early one morning in July 1989 he was taken from his cell at Kajang prison near Kuala Lumpur and hanged.

In an effort to forget his troubles, Sim tried rejoining the party scene, having dropped out after his arrest. He confided to Duncan, 'Every time I walk into a fucking house where there's a few of the crowd, they all think I've got Charlie with me. If I say, "I've got nothing," they think I'm trying it on to bump up the price and when I tell them I still don't have anything with me, they take the hump. They don't seem to want to know me.'

'Simmy, there's stuff around but hardly any coke. You've got to remember we were giving them all they wanted and now they have to send somebody to London to see if there's anybody there they can contact. Forgive the pun but they are paying through the nose and don't like it. I'm being asked why I don't ring home and get somebody else to bring stuff through.'

'And why don't we?'

'Think about it. How do you know we aren't still being watched? And who can we trust over here not to run straight to the cops? Nobody.'

'Couldn't we give Scouse Willie a call and ask him to come through?'

'Forget about Scouse Willie. Nobody knows who he or the Monkey are and that's the way we'll keep it.'

'But there is kit coming in; who's bringing it?'

'I don't know and I don't want to know. But it wouldn't surprise me if once Brian got himself sorted he set something up. He needs to make big money.'

Cocaine was still being smuggled into Scotland but in dribs and drabs. And the incompetence of the amateur smugglers had to be seen to be believed. Two young men in their early 20s had picked up a VW Golf at a Glasgow auction and headed to the Costa Brava in northern Spain, where, on a package holiday the previous year, they had met a North African who sold hashish but boasted he was in the market to supply anything they cared to name. The tourists, from Baillieston, had taken his telephone number and called, asking if he could arrange cocaine.

'Sure,' he'd said, 'but bring lots of pesetas.'

They found their man in Lloret de Mar and after a brief haggle settled on 20 grammes at the equivalent of £20 each, a fortune for them.

'Where will you hide it?' their supplier asked.

'We thought we'd put it in the back of the radio.'

'When you get to the French Customs point, that's the first place they'll look.'

'Shit. Where would you put it, if it were you?'

'Stop a few miles before the crossing and tape it to the underside. They'll never look there, means getting on their hands and knees and the lazy buggers don't want their trousers dirty.'

The Scots took his advice but, having difficulty in making the tape stick to rusting metal, bound it around the exhaust silencer box, assuring themselves that it was only for a few miles. Arriving at passport control, they found themselves in a long queue of traffic with Spanish police patrolling its length, urging drivers not to stop but to keep moving. By the time they were waved through, a gendarme having only peered inside the burning-hot vehicle, the temperature gauge was on red and as they picked up speed desperate to pull into the side of the road out of sight of the crossing point, where they could get underneath the VW without someone stopping to ask if they needed help, they heard a loud 'pop' and a cloud of white dust exploded from the underside, coating a van behind them and forcing the driver to turn on his windscreen wipers. To the fury of the other motorists, the driver screeched to a stop and the pair leapt out, scrabbling full length to peer underneath, where the melted fragments of a plastic bag and lengths of charred tape guiltily hung down.

On another occasion, a young married couple from Paisley decided their eight-day package holiday in Fuengirola should be made to pay for itself. On the terrace of a busy bar well away from those targeted by tourists, the girl's long, blonde tresses made her the subject of considerable interest from swarthy young men with black hair and wandering hands. The Spanish found their Scottish accents tricky to understand although the woman's polite but firm refusals to dance with them seemed clear enough. 'Non gracias' she would repeat, but the message did not appear to be getting home. 'Non gracias' too to offers of drinks.

Seeking sanctuary, she looked at her watch, meaning to suggest to her husband it was time to leave, but their uninvited guests took this to have another meaning.

'You buy watch?' they asked.

Her husband was quick to grasp the potential of sign language as his wife shook her head and was then offered 'Souvenirs?'

'Non gracias,' he said and made a motion first of holding a cigarette to his lips, then lowering his head, clearly sniffing from the table top. If the Spaniards had any knowledge whatever of drugs, then they would understand these universal actions of the hashish smoker and the cocaine snorter.

'You look for hash?' they asked.

'Hash, cocaine . . .' came the reply, and husband and wife looked at one another in triumph. At last, their meaning was understood. 'Hash cheap. Cocaine costs much money. It is dangerous. We get caught, prison. You get caught, both go to prison.'

'Cocaine, you can get cocaine?'

'Wait, please, I telephone somebody.'

Just a quarter of an hour later, a motorcycle drew up at the kerb alongside their table. The rider, his face marked by a scar along his left cheek that, for the Scots, was more reminiscent of the outcome of a misunderstanding in Saracen or Blackhill than in Fuengirola, with its splashing children and guitar music, joined them. Afterwards, the couple confided to close friends that for a while they wondered if they had walked into some kind of undercover police drugs operation and waited for the wail of sirens and flashing blue lights.

'You want cocaine?' the rider asked.

'Maybe, if the price is right.'

'I can get cocaine.'

'How much?'

'How much do you want?'

'No, sorry, how much will it cost?'

'How much do you want to pay?'

'£20 a gramme?'

'I think you're joking. Let us be serious. Nowhere will you get cocaine for that. How many grammes do you want?'

'Five.'

'Five grammes is too small. I deal in nothing less than ten grammes.'

'Five is all we want.'

'Where are you from, England?'

'No, Scotland.'

'Scotland. Right then Mr and Mrs from Scotland, as a special favour I will deal you 5 grammes, but the price will be £25 a gramme and you must pay in pesetas.'

'Pesetas?' said the Scot, scribbling on the inside of a cigarette packet. 'That's 18,300 pesetas.'

'I will take 18,000.'

'But why in pesetas?'

'It must be pesetas because if you pay me in English money, it attracts attention for me to have so much. People guess that someone like me carrying foreign notes is selling drugs and tells the police.'

'When can we buy?'

'As soon as you have the money.'

They walked with the dealer to a currency-exchange shop then strolled with him along the beach between courting and copulating couples to a clump of palm trees where he opened a plastic shopping bag and invited the husband to dip his finger into another package inside. Having tasted the wares, the buyer nodded to his wife. The dealer gave the goods to the woman, who carefully placed them into her handbag while her husband handed over the money. All three then casually wandered back towards the bright lights of the Fuengirola centre before parting with handshakes, the dealer giving them a scrap of paper on which was written a telephone number.

'Next time you come, ring first,' he said. '*Buen viaje. Bon voyage.*'

This left only the problem of where to hide their contraband for the journey home. They settled on a carton of talcum powder, removing the cap on the morning they flew back to Scotland, pouring out half its contents, popping in the little polythene packet of happy dust and, after topping up with talc, employed the favourite prisoners' trick of using toothpaste as an adhesive to ensure the cap stayed firmly in place. They were stopped, along with the family immediately ahead of them, as they passed through the Customs check at Glasgow airport and asked if they had anything to declare. Each answered in the negative and was then told to place their various bags on a low counter and open them.

The pair from Paisley looked on in terror as one officer began searching through the family's baggage immediately, while another uniformed official first chatted to them amiably about their holiday before beginning his own check. They watched, appalled and mute, as the officer searching the family's luggage discovered in the mother's toilet bag a carton of talcum powder, the cap of which was loose.

'Why has the top been removed?' he wanted to know.

'It came off and wouldn't stick back on,' came what seemed a reasonable and innocent reply.

Regardless, from beneath the counter, the man produced a clear plastic bag and into it emptied the contents of the carton. Calling his colleague over, who was by now delving deeply into the Paisley couple's belongings, he asked him to check what was inside.

'Talcum powder,' he pronounced, after probing and sniffing. Returning to his own task, he produced the incriminating carton. A slight turn of the metal cap opened a series of holes through which the powder flowed. He gingerly shook a dusting onto his palm, as the girl, by now experiencing the sinking sensation of a deep wrong discovered, waited for the toothpaste to fail them. It did not. The cap remained in place and no more than two minutes later, drenched in the sweat of fear and dreading their legs would buckle, they were waved on their way.

Things would not go so well for Duncan and Sim, although both would later agree the outcome of their visit to Glasgow Sheriff Court on 26 November 1982 could have been worse. Both admitted to possessing cocaine eight months earlier in March at Glasgow airport and various pubs and cafés in the city. The prosecution was handled by Leonard Higson, who said officers from the drug squad had been watching when Duncan stepped off a flight from Amsterdam. His every move over the following two days, including a reunion with Sim, had been watched and the two arrested eventually in the Aldwych Café, where a search uncovered cocaine worth £8,000. Both, said the fiscal, had cooperated with the police, Duncan offering the explanation that they had been paid £500 for bringing in the drug. Duncan's lawyer, Tom Bannigan, said both had fallen into temptation because they were saving hard to get married and the offer to carry something with them on a routine trip to visit family in Glasgow had been impossible to turn down. It would bring nearer to fruition their plans to marry and be with the women they loved.

The prosecution's and the defence's versions were broadly based on fact and if there were holes in the stories, then who was complaining? They had been caught, hadn't they? Sheriff Archibald McKay was certainly satisfied and said he would treat both with leniency for a variety of reasons, not least that until then they had clean records. Each was jailed for six months and ordered to pay a fine of £500 or face a further spell behind bars. Duncan and Sim knew that if they stayed trouble-free, they would be out at the end of March 1983, having served two-thirds of their sentences.

It could, Duncan reflected, have been considerably worse. But could it? Without them, the prosecution would struggle badly. And at least one more member of the Happy Dust Gang would face his own personal Armageddon – that member being Andy Tait. As the two waited for a van to take them on the short drive to Barlinnie, Big Andy was taking his own turn to step into the dock at the Sheriff Court. In his case, though, the situation was more serious. While the prosecution had decided to treat Sim and Duncan as mere couriers, Tait was being portrayed as a major player. They were charged with possessing cocaine, but the allegation against the baker on 26 November was a step higher in the league of transgressions. He was accused of possessing cocaine in city bars and cafés with the intention of supplying it to others. Tait made no plea during a brief hearing and his bail was continued. As he set off back to his home in Cathcart, he had every reason to be worried because as far as he was concerned things were going to get a whole lot worse.

Sim's experience of prison life had revolved around his short spell on remand. Things were more regimented now as a convicted prisoner, but unlike the transitory population on the remand wing, where futures were uncertain and dependent on the whim of a jury or judge, he now found himself among men who knew what lay ahead and the dates when they would be free of their shackles. For Sim, as he'd expected, prison was a nightmare. He found himself sharing a cell with a stranger, petrified in case others should categorise him as a dreaded informant because of his role in the predicament of Tait and Doran. Duncan did his best to calm his friend's trepidations, communicating with him via the pipework that criss-crossed the prison, running through cells. He himself knew some of his fellow inmates but in prison the golden rule is that it is every man for himself. At meal times and recreation periods, Sim became a loner, shunning company and wanting only to return to what he saw as the safety of his cell.

'Stand up for yourself, Simmy,' George told him.

'It's OK for you to say that. You've got loads of mates in here. I don't know anybody. All I want is to get out and go home to Utrecht.'

Like animals, many prisoners exploit weakness and fear in others. For Sim, matters came to a head in a furious row over the distribution of tea. The steaming liquid slopped around inside large urns as it made its way around the prison population. Inmates dipped in their mugs to get a drink, but because some mugs held a full pint, occasionally, by the time the urn reached the end of the line, it was empty and some would have to go without. Tea is like gold inside prison walls, and a universal stimulant and comforter; back then, it adopted the medicinal role now dominated by smuggled drugs. On this occasion, it happened that Sim poured himself the last cup. The next man along was a prisoner convicted of violence and said to have strong IRA connections. He demanded Sim's cup and when refused, punched him. The ensuing row attracted prison officers, who knew only that Sim had been assaulted but not the identity of his attacker. They took a course commonly used in such circumstances and slapped Sim in solitary confinement for his own protection and safety. It was known as 'going behind the door'.

Not only did this *seem* unfair, especially to Sim, but it *was* unfair. What else, though, warders would ask, could they do without being able to take the guilty party out of circulation? Duncan felt he had to intervene. Each morning, he pushed a note beneath the door of Sim's cell telling him not to worry, but the man was clearly depressed and frightened. He could not let Sim suffer unjustly. After the IRA sympathiser was pointed out to him, he cornered the culprit in the toilet area and demanded an explanation. This scoundrel had already received threats over the Sim affair from others.

'These bastards are giving me pelters,' he complained.

'Well, go and tell the governor you punched my mate, so he can get out of solcon. He won't grass you nor will anybody else, but unless you own up he's in there for the next four months.'

'Fuck him,' was the response. 'He asked for it.'

'No, he didn't. He didn't know the score. He and I have four months to do and neither of us wants any trouble. But I promise you that unless you get him from behind the door, there'll be a war in here and you'll be on your own.'

The man stared at George. He thought himself a celebrity because of his terrorist connections but looming over him was an inmate who was as powerful as he looked, being a regular in the prison gym. He noted Duncan's bulging muscles and grim look and the conversation ended. He headed to the desk of the nearest prison officer and began talking.

After the attacker owned up, he was put in solitary, but at least he gained respect for having won the release of the innocent party. Some might have expected Sim to be grateful for his release, but he was not and became ever more morose and introverted.

For Duncan, the weeks parted from Rosa were difficult, but he made friends quickly and as spring approached was looking forward to freedom, although he knew Sim and he would not get their passports until they had given evidence against Tait and, should he decide to return to face the music, Doran. That trial was fixed for April.

In early March, two detectives visited Duncan in Barlinnie. They looked worried and told him another problem had arisen. 'George, if we are going to help one another then we must put our cards on the table and show our hands.'

'Sure, what's wrong?'

'Well, you told us you were only a courier and didn't have the sort of money to finance a cocaine-smuggling operation, didn't you?'

'Yes, because that's the truth.'

'OK, how do you explain the fact that we've discovered you have an account in a building society worth £18,000? Where did that come from?'

George had been expecting this, realising the police would have been scouting for any assets, hidden or otherwise. And he was aware that if what he told them was not accepted, then the money, a considerable amount then, would almost surely be confiscated. 'Oh, that's an easy one. After I left Scotland, I started buying a flat in Glasgow, thinking I would come back some day and live in it. I rented it out but sold it a while back. I got more money from a mortgage deal in Glasgow to buy a place abroad for my fiancée, Rosa, and me. That's what accounts for the £18,000. Some of it belongs to her. I know what you might be thinking, but you'd be wrong. I knew you would find that if you looked, but it was never hidden. I'd deposited it in the building society in my own name and, let's be honest, if I had meant it not to be found, I would have taken the money abroad.'

'You sure about this?'

'Absolutely. Why the concern?'

'Because if the defence had found out about this and we produced you as a prosecution witness, they'd have a field day. It would put us in an impossible position. They'd want to know why you'd only been charged with possession.'

'Look, I'm telling you the money is legitimate.'

'And if you are asked about it in court, you'll stick to that story?'

'Definitely. It's the truth and remembering the truth is easy.'

Later that day, Sim asked what the police had wanted.

'Nothing, they just wanted to be sure I was still on board.'

'And are you?'

'Simmy, we try jumping ship now and we'll be wallowing in deep water for the rest of our lives.'

22

CRUCIFIED

Child killers, cops who murder, arsonists, bombers, robbers, rapists – all have through the decades passed before Scotland's most senior judges, many en route to prison or probation, some to swing on the gallows and others to have their sentences suspended. But by the late 1970s, a new breed of transgressor was on the increase: the drug peddler.

At first, cases tended to be minor, involving small amounts of cannabis. It was a worrying trend, but what was really of concern were reports from England and the rest of Europe of more deadly drugs, cocaine and heroin, creeping ever further north. Most hash came from Morocco, driven from the Rif mountains at night to the coastline, where it was taken by small boats with outboard motors to waiting yachts that whisked it to Spain. From there, it was moved on in dozens of different ways. Much of the cocaine sourced in Colombia arrived at busy ports in Spain and Italy but principally went to Rotterdam via the Caribbean. Afghanistan and the area known as the Golden Triangle made up of Burma, Thailand and Laos supplied the bulk of the world's heroin. Via overland trails with romantic names such as the Silk Route, the drugs reached markets in the USA and Europe.

Although other gangs would eventually follow in their footsteps, the appearance on the scene of the Happy Dust Gang had spelled the arrival in Scotland of the first bulk delivery of cocaine. Charlie had landed big-style. And the authorities were determined to show they meant business. So as Andy Tait climbed the steps to the Glasgow High Court in April 1983 to surrender to his bail, he was a worried and frightened man. War had been declared and his was the head above the parapet.

Occasionally, he looked about for his fellow accused, Brian Doran, wondering if Whacko might show. He knew it was a forlorn hope because his friend appeared settled in Spain, and why should he return? No one could force him, there were no extradition regulations demanding the Spanish police arrest the Scot and stick him on a plane back to Glasgow, and Doran was sufficiently smart to know the prospects would be grim if the outcome went against his accomplice. So what if Doran had agreed to put up £5,000 bail. Losing that was to drop a crumb at a banquet. The travel agent knew all that was happening in Glasgow through frequent telephone calls to family and Tait and from news brought first-hand through an unceasing string of visitors from home. Doran realised his friend the baker had been hung out to dry but was nevertheless convinced he was making the right decision.

While he waited for his case to be called, the accused man had every right to feel bitter. He had been drawn into an intrigue not of his making but one that had ended with him as the fall guy. The Bartlett brothers, he reflected, had effectively escaped with what was seen as, for them, no more than a slap on the wrist. The Parachutist and his apprentice, Sim, had, it was true, gone to prison, but their stay in Barlinnie would last only four months. Had it not been for them, none of this might have happened. And while he looked at the green-painted walls of the custody area, his associate Brian Doran was in Spain already involved with other, bigger smuggling ventures. It was no secret why the

235

Bartletts, Sim and Duncan had been treated so leniently in the circumstances. All had been persuaded to give evidence against him. So had others who had come cap in hand to him in the past begging for a line or two of Charlie. He had helped them out, in return for money, of course, but now they too would repay him as Brutus returned the affections of Caesar. And for a mere £15,000, the price of Sim's silence, none of this would have happened.

Was his loyalty to others – to Doran, in particular – worth what he now faced, he wondered? Close friends would say not. Even at the last minute, Duncan had held out an olive branch. In the weeks between their freedom from jail and the start of the trial, he had approached Tait four times, taking care that the meetings were not monitored by the drug squad because inferences might be drawn that would have serious consequences, that either Tait was trying to buy Duncan's silence or the latter was endeavouring to blackmail the baker.

In truth, according to Sim, neither was the case. 'George felt sorry for the big man, why I could never work out, because had it not been for him and his pal Doran trying to weasel their way out of their own troubles by selling us down the river, we would have been in easy street. As he saw it, Brian did a runner, leaving Andy to take the blame. He went to see Andy a few times, trying to find out what had gone on, asking him what had transpired between him and Doran and the drug squad. He even promised Andy that if he came clean when he went into the witness box, he'd tone down his evidence and give him a break.

'Andy was a pathetic figure around this time. We'd often bump into him in clubs or pubs at night. His wife was about to give birth, but there was no sign of the joys of fatherhood in his face. Only despair, misery and hopelessness. He was terrified about what was going to happen in court. Once in Pzazz he even broke down in tears. It was hard not to be sympathetic, but at the end of the day he and Doran brought it on themselves, and the rest of us.

'But Andy was too stubborn. Right up to the day of his trial, he kept to his story that there had been no contact with the police and he'd had nothing to do with our arrest. By maintaining that, Andy effectively put the noose around his own neck. He was crazy to try making us believe it had only been a coincidence that the cops lifted us at the meeting he'd set up at the Aldwych.

'What Andy didn't know was that George had kept his word with the police. They'd tried to renege on the deal he'd made, but he had still found the witnesses he had promised them. George had gone to each of them and said they could either agree to give evidence for the prosecution and then walk away, or refuse and find themselves in the same boat as him and me. All they had to do was cooperate to wipe the slate clean. Neither of us could believe how easy it all was, but then the police were desperate to make a success of this case and agreed to almost anything, at the end of the day, to get a result. And the people he roped in to be witnesses came from the class that took the attitude of "Fuck everyone else, so long as I'm OK."'

The opening day of the trial, 11 April, was dramatic. For Andy Tait, it was an anticlimax; he never even made it to the dock. He was told there was a delay, that his bail was continued and he should go home and return the next day. The custodians of the law might have known that of two accused just one would be turning up but, all the same, justice had to take its course. Brian Doran's name had to be called, and so it was. The judge, Lord Ross, was told Doran faced three charges: importing cocaine into Britain, supplying the drug to others and attempting to pervert the course of justice. The eminent judge knew, of course, the accused would not be appearing, but this was an open courtroom – the case of the Happy Dust Gang had attracted huge interest – and justice had to be seen to be done. There was always a faint possibility that, at the last moment, Doran would rush into the High Court to answer the charges. But he did not, and Advocate Depute Donald Mackay was ready with an explanation.

As soon as Lord Ross announced, 'Yes, Mr Mackay?' the prosecutor was on his feet.

'Mr Doran is at present in Spain,' he explained. 'Communications have been received through his solicitors to the effect that he has no intention of returning at this time.'

Brian Doran was effectively sticking two fingers up at the court, a gesture that would have earned any schoolboy six of the best. In this case, it cost Whacko his bail money. The judge ruled the £5,000 would be forfeit. It would go into a legal pot, slosh its way around and eventually act as a contribution towards the prosecution bill. Lord Ross also issued a warrant for Doran's arrest, a serious step because by doing so he placed an onus on police forces worldwide to help in his apprehension – provided their own countries had extradition agreements with the United Kingdom government. Of course, Spain did not, but if Doran should venture into a state that did, then he could be arrested on sight and kept in prison while the authorities in Scotland decided whether they still wanted him. In his case, they would never cease in their efforts to get their man, the resolve of the police in particular never weakening despite the passing of years.

The next morning, Andy Tait was back, and this time it was for real. In the dock, he looked about like a sailor trying to get his bearings. He was invited by the judge to take a seat, a gesture that had lulled many before him and since into believing this was a good sign, that the man in charge was already showing sympathy. In fact, it was merely a formality while the jury were sworn in, a ritual regarded with extreme ceremony and seriousness. Many learned counsel have had their knuckles publicly rapped by judges for shuffling unduly or whispering during this brief rite.

When it was over, the jury were told the accused man faced two charges. The first that between 1 December 1980 and 23 March 1982 he was allegedly concerned in the importation of cocaine from the ferry ports of Hull, Harwich and Dover. The second, the more serious, that between 1 December 1980 and 23 March 1982 at a number of places in Glasgow, including public houses, restaurants, his own shop on Byres Road and the offices of Blue Sky Travel on Queen Street, he had supplied the drug to other people. He pleaded not guilty to both charges.

What followed over the next two weeks was akin to a reunion of young men who had once been old friends; however, now they queued up to heap woe and disgrace on one of their number. Alan Bartlett said he and his wife, Pamela, used to dine out socially with the Taits. He had known Brian Doran for around five years and it was the travel agent who introduced him to cocaine. Doran had twice sold him a gramme, charging around £55 on each occasion.

Soon the story of how the Happy Dust Gang came into being unfolded. Alan had met 'a man from Holland', who sold him 20 grammes for £800, each gramme giving him about 15 snorts, usually through a rolled-up £5 note. This lasted around three months. Doran and Tait were both there and bought similar amounts. All three, said Mr Bartlett, sniffed the drug to make sure it was genuine and were satisfied. But in his case, he had bought cocaine solely for his own use. 'It became the in-thing,' Bartlett said, 'for wealthy people to snort cocaine in clubs and restaurants.'

One Saturday in February 1982, Bartlett said, Doran had turned up at his flat in Hyndland with an ounce of cocaine in a plastic bag, and asked him and his brother, Ronnie, to keep it for him, but split half into small packets. After they did this, the drug squad arrived and they were arrested. It was a story that had been told at their own hearing in June the previous year when they had been fined. Bartlett and his brother had little trouble remembering names and faces. But two other prosecution witnesses were given a ticking off by the judge for their reluctance to give names.

The evidence of one of the culprits, publican Jacob Kinsell, showed how the taking of happy dust spread and how it was effectively advertised. He said he used his gold Porsche about ten times on trips to The Pantry to collect cocaine for customers, paying up to £60 a gramme. There was laughter when he confessed to charging clients '£5 petrol money'. But while Kinsell admitted giving cocaine samples to young people for free, he refuted suggestions this was to encourage business.

'Who were these people?' he was asked.

'I'm afraid it's so long ago and I was never told their names,' he replied, urging a mild rebuke from Lord Ross.

Another young businessman, Ronald McCulloch, aged 30, a familiar face on the nightclub scene and involved in a company that ran various businesses, including the fashionable Rock Garden bar and restaurant in the city centre, would deny a prosecution suggestion that he was 'part of a high-living set who passed cocaine around like cigarettes or drink'. Although he admitted knowing Alan Bartlett, Tait and Doran, he knocked back suggestions he was part of their social group. 'I occasionally met Tait socially but just by bumping into him in pubs or restaurants. Not by arrangement,' he said. Asked if he had ever used cocaine, he replied, 'I tried it once about three years ago when I was in London, but I have never carried it around, had it in my possession.' He was unable to remember who gave him the cocaine in London.

If the evidence of Kinsell produced laughter, the appearance of another prosecution witness was looked on as nothing less than a sensation, even meriting front-page headlines in the following day's *Daily Record*. Tom Ferrie was, at the time, an icon for tens of thousands of young Scots, the disc jockey having made his name through a highly popular show on Radio Clyde before turning freelance broadcaster and moving to the BBC. Ferrie was typical of the smart, bright, well-paid class who ventured into cocaine and he told of how a conversation, while he was in company during the summer of 1981, had turned to the drug. The speaker, he said, appeared familiar with cocaine and Ferrie had asked if he could buy some. As a result, he had twice done so. The first deal was in the basement of Tait's bakery, where he was given a small piece of paper containing a tiny amount of the drug; the second at the Highburgh Road flat, where he chatted with the Bartletts and was given cocaine in a packet for which he paid £50.

'Why,' asked the prosecutor, 'were you buying cocaine in the first place?'

The DJ had an answer. The deals, he said, were part of an investigation he was undertaking into the Glasgow drugs scene and after briefly trying cocaine, he washed it down the toilet.

Another witness agreed that cocaine was limited to the wealthy, but they could afford to hand lines of it about like the working classes proffered cigarettes.

Neither the Bartletts nor Ferrie were kept long in the witness box. Nor were others. One prosecution witness in particular had an almost instant moment of glory. The man, who for legal reasons has to remain anonymous, had been holding his own court with the others, who were nervous, even terrified, as they waited to take the stand. He decided his own experiences should be recounted. 'You've nothing to worry about,' he told them, 'it's a doddle. Nothing like as bad as having to own up to your wife you've been seeing some other woman. I've been through all this before and it was so easy. I've given evidence in stacks of cases, even once at the Old Bailey, and didn't even break into a sweat.' It was at this point that his name was called and off he went.

Seconds later, the waiting witnesses heard a thud followed by a commotion. 'What happened?' one asked, when an official eventually appeared.

'That last witness, nervous as a kitten, climbed into the box in a sweat and collapsed in a faint. Somebody decided to pour the contents of one of the fire buckets over him. It was filled with sawdust. We've sent him home.'

George Duncan, who had been waiting with the other

witnesses and had been interrogated by them as to why he had given their names to the police as customers of Tait and Doran's, realised there could be no such get-out for him. He knew he was in for a lengthy session such was the importance of his role, especially when it came to being questioned by Kevin Drummond, the advocate leading the defence team. He did not know it then, but he would also face being asked for help from an unexpected source.

In the witness box, he could afford to relax as he knew he was in a position to tell virtually any story he wished because no one could either challenge or confirm what he said. He explained how the Happy Dust Gang began, when he had met Doran in Charlie Parker's, then after the conversation moved to the subject of cocaine how he was introduced to Tait. His version of the story was that he had been asked if cocaine was available in Holland, and when told how the country was looked on as the major European importer, he was asked if he would buy the drug.

From there, the die was cast, but the names of powerful men such as Joop would never be mentioned. Instead, the tale would be one of buying from the Monkey and how over a 15-month period around 1,000 grammes had been brought across but never by him. It was a huge underestimate, but no one could challenge the figure because only the men from Utrecht knew the truth. If no one had asked them about other customers, then why volunteer that information? When the happy dust arrived, said George, it would be delivered to Tait at The Pantry.

But, he said, he had blamed Tait for setting up him and Sim at the Aldwych. If the police had hoped to keep private the fact that a deal had been done with Duncan for his collaboration and the details of what had been agreed, they would be disappointed. The Parachutist recounted the three points conceded to him in return for naming the other members of the Happy Dust Gang – his appearance before a sheriff, dropping the value of the cocaine in the underpants and no action being taken against him over information about the international drugs scene.

'Had you asked for the three conditions before making any statement to the drug squad?'

'Yes.'

'Did the time come when you were aware that the Crown was prepared to accept your plea on the basis that you suggested?'

'Yes.'

The following day, he was again in the witness box, admitting to having organised the smuggling into Glasgow of cocaine worth at least £50,000 from Amsterdam. During the lunch break, he strolled to a bar in the nearby Saltmarket for a brief pub lunch of pie and beans followed by treacle pudding. It was not by chance that Tait, allowed from the dock during each break, walked in as well.

'George, can I have a word with you?'

'Take a seat.'

'No, at the bar.'

'What's wrong with here?'

'I don't want anybody listening in.'

At the bar, the two men faced one another, heads bent together, and George could not fail to notice or be moved by the tears in the eyes of the big baker.

'Help me, George. They are crucifying me in there.'

'Why won't you tell me what happened?'

'OK. We had arranged a meeting, Brian and me, at the Sherbrooke Castle with Inspector Wilson.'

'So, what went on?'

'The police were only interested in jailing Simmy and you.'

'Why wouldn't you tell me this before, Andy?'

'Because you helped put me where I am and I didn't know who to trust. But I'm asking you now to help.'

'It's too late, Andy,' Duncan told him and walked off.

On the brief walk back to the courtroom, he mulled over what had been said and decided that maybe it was time to forgive, if not to forget. And what could be the harm in helping – after all, Doran had fled, leaving his friend to carry the can. Nothing he said would make matters worse for Doran. He decided he would do what he could to help Tait, to make it appear that Doran was the main man in the Happy Dust Gang.

So it was that the jury were told the idea of Sim being paid £15,000 to shoulder the blame came from Doran at the same meeting, which had been watched by the police as much concerned with Robert Bruce's ice cream as with them, it appeared. 'Doran knew I could get him into serious trouble. He said he could work a way out for both of us. He said that if I got Sim to say the cocaine belonged to him, he would pay him £15,000. I rejected the suggestion.'

Of course, in reality the reverse had been the case and the suggestion ignored by the travel agent. It was all the more bizarre, therefore, that Doran had been charged with perverting the course of justice by offering a bribe. To emphasise the seriousness of what had been offered, George Duncan was asked by the prosecutor to read out that charge.

The building of the case against the hapless Tait continued like the Creation and on the fifth day Thomas Sim told how the Happy Dust Gang smuggled cocaine hidden behind the dashboard of cars driven by Scouse Willie, who was paid £200 plus expenses, his movements monitored by Sim, who then carried the drug by train to Glasgow, where Duncan took it to The Pantry.

Sim had not wanted to give evidence. While he knew he had nothing to tell, he was still terrified of saying too much and risking retribution from the men with whom they had dealt in Holland, or too little and being whisked back to Barlinnie. When he left the witness box, he wanted only to return to Utrecht. He had decided some considerable time ago while in solitary confinement at the Big House that it would have been better had he never heard of George, Doran, Tait, the Monkey, Joop, Scouse Willie or happy dust. If he took risks in future, they would be on Dutch roofs.

George Duncan felt he had done his best to help take the onus from Tait, even though he had known from the second it happened that Tait's pretence of buying cigarettes at the Aldwych Café was a signal to someone waiting outside. Confirmation came from Detective Sergeant Ronald Edgar, who repeated what he had told a colleague months earlier, that Doran was the boss and Tait a subordinate. 'We met them in a hotel bedroom in Glasgow, where they said they were ready to set up Duncan and Sim if we would arrange a deal for them. The arrangement was that Tait was to meet Duncan and Sim and signal to us if they were carrying cocaine. The cue was for him to go to the counter for cigarettes, at which point we would arrest them. After that, Duncan and Sim offered to make statements in exchange for a deal of their own.'

The fact that the police too were willing to heap blame on Doran was backed up by Inspector John Wilson. 'We found evidence of a cocaine-smuggling network between Amsterdam and Glasgow, and Doran was the main man in it. After he was arrested in April 1982, Doran approached us and asked me what I could do for him. I told him I did not understand what he meant. He said he would be prepared to provide certain information that would assist the police and asked, if it was good enough, if we could get him off the charges. I said I would approach the procurator fiscal to see if there was any way of reducing the charges. Doran indicated there was a run from Amsterdam and two men were involved. He was willing to do something about it, but he had to be told the procurator fiscal was not interested.'

Tait would spend just three hours in the witness box and would later confide, 'They were the worst and longest three hours of my life.' Friends expressed astonishment that immediately before him had come police witnesses who held up Doran as the culprit-in-chief. And then he made the mistake of shifting the emphasis to Duncan. Tait gave a moving account of his financial troubles, of how Doran had loaned him money in return for his putting up the family home as security, how the pressures had led to him being unable to sleep until cocaine had been suggested as a possible help. That was the only reason he used it. He wasn't part of a rich social circle that snorted cocaine. His friend, Alan Bartlett, had suggested Duncan could get him the drug and in one year he bought only 30 grammes, two-thirds of it from the man from Holland and the rest from Jacob Kinsell.

'How much did that cost?' he was asked.

'£1,500.'

'Hadn't he supplied cocaine to Tom Ferrie?' he was asked.

'Never,' came the reply. He said he had never been involved with Doran in importing cocaine and it was Duncan who had supplied him with the drug four or five times.

Tait would pay dearly for his loyalty to Doran, who, he admitted, had made a telephone call from Spain as the trial progressed to ask how it was going. Kevin Drummond told the jury, in a plea to clear him, that 'Tait was the dummy who was so naive that he was the only one, in a trial full of double-dealing, who failed to make a deal for himself with the police'.

The prosecution naturally saw it differently. Donald Mackay said, 'It is inconceivable that a man earning £15,000 a year, who admits spending a tenth of it on cocaine, did not know what was going on. It is curious that, although it was the defence who introduced the idea of a group of wealthy people in Glasgow using cocaine and passing it around like packs of cigarettes, Tait denied all knowledge in his evidence about being a member. This is particularly strange considering that all the witnesses who talked about using cocaine were friends of Tait and on his own admission he was using it regularly.'

Three hours after they were asked by the judge to consider their verdicts, the jury of eight men and seven women returned to their seats. Many experienced in the ways of the court examined their faces, convinced by the old theory that if jurors don't look an accused in the eye it means they are too ashamed to do so because they have decided he or she is guilty. In this case, some did and some did not. Tait, for his part, sat still, alone, while the man for whom he had gambled with his own future was collecting a Spanish suntan. By majority verdicts, they found him guilty on both charges.

The following day, a newspaper reported that the baker stood 'ashen-faced' as Lord Ross told him, 'I accept that Doran played the major role and yours was subordinate. It must be clearly understood that persons importing drugs and supplying them to others can expect little mercy in these courts. I am prepared to accept that you were, in a sense, under an obligation to Doran for financial assistance, which may have induced you to become involved in these activities. I take into account your family circumstances and background, but the part you played in the importation of the drug was an important one.'

Two minutes later, Big Andy Tait, close to collapse, was being helped to the court cells below the dock after being sentenced to two years for supplying cocaine and four years for importing it. Because the judge said the terms would be concurrent, it meant a maximum of four years.

Even today, more than two decades later, many believe he was treated unfairly and there are grounds for supporting that view, one enhanced by what would subsequently happen to Brian Doran. The Bartletts had collaborated with the police and had, in relative terms, got away with fines both could easily afford. Duncan and Sim had done a deal and escaped lightly. Doran had simply escaped, cocking a snook at justice in the process. Andy Tait, who went along with the police plan to set up and catch the couriers red-handed, whose sense of old-fashioned honour meant he did his best for a runaway friend, lost his liberty, family and business. Was it right, many asked, that a previously respected and successful businessman should be jailed on the word of self-confessed drugs couriers? Lord Ross replied as follows: 'The evidence of Duncan and Sim should be treated with special scrutiny, but the Crown was perfectly entitled to agree to their conditions. As you should appreciate, unless the Crown does a deal with informers, there is often no possibility of prosecuting anyone.'

Then why was Tait prosecuted when his case was clearly in tandem with that of Doran, who fled? Was it fair that he should carry the can for Doran as well as for himself? Normally an individual is legally responsible only for offences he or she commits. There are some exceptions to this rule, one covering an enterprise in which a group or a gang, no matter how large or small, are all more or less equally involved in the same crime. In such a case, each gang or group member is judged to be accountable for what the others have done. The Crown successfully argued that the actions of Tait and Doran were so closely intertwined it was impossible to separate the share of the responsibility each should take. It was the Crown case that the two ordered the cocaine supplies, paid for them and distributed them once they had been smuggled to Glasgow. So, Tait should be made to shoulder the blame for what Doran had done, even though Whacko was not around to face the music. Had it been Tait who had fled then Doran would have had to face the music and answer for the baker's actions. Tait did not help himself. George Duncan heaped the blame on Doran, and so did the police, but either by accident or design Andy Tait had not done that. And as a result, he had cooked his own goose.

23

THE GANG BUSTERS

By busting the Happy Dust Gang, the police smashed the first serious drug-smuggling racket to infiltrate Scotland. It was a triumph for old-fashioned detective work and showed how effective a combination of nurturing contacts, playing suspects off one another, and luck could be. It was through old-style coppering that the police had their first sniff something was amiss, that the moneyed class had a new toy from which to get their kicks.

'Just before and after the start of the 1980s, there was cocaine about but very little,' said one of the men who worked closely with the drug squad on the case of the Happy Dust Gang. 'It wasn't a drug people had experienced much, mainly because it was so difficult to get and so expensive. You'd come across the odd tenner bag of heroin, but cocaine was a drug you associated with people who were well off, and there was so much poverty about at the time those who had money stood out. It was well known that Brian Doran was into cocaine but actually being able to ascertain where he got it from was another matter. There was a suspicion the odd gramme might have been brought into Glasgow on flights from the Spanish resorts to which he was continually arranging holidays but never any proof.

'Doran had a huge coterie of hangers-on. Where he went, they went and many were like him – lots of money to spend but determined their enjoyment came first even if it meant upsetting others. He and his crowd might roll up somewhere and because of their loud behaviour start a rammy, upsetting other customers. Doran would just go to whoever owned the place, pull a couple of hundred pounds out of his pocket and say, "There you are, that should take care of it." Some would describe the behaviour of his crowd as boorish, like that of many present-day footballers or minor celebrities – too much money and too many people wanting to help you spend it. He loved being the centre of attention and could be very funny at times, but there were many who didn't like him because when he went into a club or a restaurant, he wanted to take the place over.

'Police were constantly getting information about drugs. The drugs culture had been around but because there wasn't a lot of the stuff, it was still a bit of a novelty and the vast majority of people hadn't the means of either knowing how to get drugs or, even if they did, being able to afford them. A lot of calls started coming in from informers, saying there was suddenly much more cocaine about. This was a concern. As far as was possible, we tried checking everything and while a lot of the information turned out to be wide of the mark, there were so many snouts talking about cocaine that we knew there had to be something in it. Frequently, the name Brian Doran would be mentioned during these calls. The difficulty was finding out who had it and where it was coming from.'

It was just before six on the night of Saturday, 13 February 1982. In the East End of Glasgow, there was an air of despondency because that afternoon Celtic had been knocked out of the Scottish Cup, losing by a solitary goal at Aberdeen while along at Govan there was jubilation thanks to Rangers blasting out Dumbarton by four goals to nil. In May, the two victors would meet in the final, the Dons taking the trophy 4–1 after extra-time. There was a light-hearted air in the offices of the drug squad with the day shift about to go home. Some of the officers, including Ronnie Edgar and Joe Corrigan, already had on their hats and coats when the telephone rang. It was picked up by Edgar, who heard the voice of a woman at the other end of the line.

'I don't want to give you my name, but I have information as to where the police can find a lot of cocaine. It is there now.'

He was about to ask the standard questions, but experience told him this was one of those situations where it was best to let the informant have her say first – sometimes even a single question at the wrong moment could scare off a valuable caller and instead of listening to pure verbal gold an officer might hear only the burr of a line after the receiver had been hung up mid-sentence. So he let her continue.

'Go to the home of Alan and Ronnie Bartlett on Highburgh Road in the West End of Glasgow. There is cocaine in it now. At this minute. Go to Alan Bartlett's flat.'

Then she was gone. Ronnie Edgar looked at Joe Corrigan.

'Joe, keep your coat on, but we're not going home. We need a warrant. Immediately.'

Following her instructions was not so straightforward. It meant scouring lists to find a Justice of the Peace who was available. Fortunately for the police, they were in luck. But it was almost eight o'clock before they had sworn on oath that they had information about the whereabouts of cocaine, specified where they wanted to search, got together a team of seven or eight officers and arrived at Highburgh Road. There the problems were only beginning. Their caller had not given the exact address of the Bartlett flat and the detectives had to hunt about before they found it in a luxury Victorian terrace. Alan's name was on a bell outside, but they could not afford to ring the bell and wait for him to answer. In any police raid on a drug dealer, the emphasis is on surprise and speed. Once a suspect knows the police are about to pounce, it takes only seconds to flush gear down a toilet or throw it out of a window and thereby destroy the evidence.

They forced the outside door but inside found there were four flats, none of them showing the name of the occupant. Time was of the essence and so while the detectives waited outside each door, Ronnie Edgar told one of his men to go outside and push Alan Bartlett's bell. They then listened for the flat in which it sounded. The idea was to bang on the door and order him to open up. If he didn't, they would burst the door down. However, as soon as they knocked and shouted, 'Police,' it was opened straight away. And immediately Alan admitted he had cocaine.

In the kitchen on a table was a tiny spoon they had been using as a measure and some pieces of paper for wraps. He even helpfully told them how much a level spoon would weigh. His then girlfriend Pamela was in a bedroom, unhappy at being told she was being arrested along with the brothers. She was carted off nonetheless. As police were making the arrests and carrying out a search of the flat, an officer keeping watch on Highburgh Road reported that Brian Doran had appeared to motor up but, seeing police activity, drove off without stopping.

The brothers and Pamela were taken to Turnbull Street and placed in cells, where the men were visited by their father, who advised them to come clean and tell everything they knew to the police. Pamela was given a procurator fiscal's release the following morning and was never charged with any offence. Their lawyer, Len Murray, was called in. Also being Doran's lawyer, the police wondered if, in telling all they knew, the brothers would implicate Doran. Mr Murray advised them to say nothing, but they insisted that, on the instructions of their father, they would make full confessions.

When they made their initial appearance in court, the fiscal decided to carry out a judicial examination, a procedure not normally done at a first appearance. Under it, an accused person can be brought before a sheriff at a very early stage in the proceedings to be questioned by the prosecutor. But Ronnie Edgar was anxious to question Alan Bartlett himself before this was done, and sent a note into the fiscal asking for permission to do so. Bartlett had indicated he wanted to tell all and the detective wanted to strike while the iron was hot. Later on, police would agree the accused man had answered everything he was asked truthfully.

Meanwhile, on the happy dust grapevine, Doran had been given word of the Bartletts' arrest and telephoned, asking to see Ronnie Edgar and Joe Corrigan. The meeting was arranged at the Blue Sky Travel offices after the rest of the staff had gone for the day. When Edgar and Corrigan arrived, they discovered Doran was alone. He offered a deal in which he would implicate those responsible if any likely charges against him were dropped. During the discussion, he dropped in the name of Andy Tait.

At a further meeting at Blue Sky, Tait joined Doran, the businessmen proposing to spill the beans on Duncan and Sim. In the light of what was being suggested, the officers visited their boss, Charles Rogers, to seek permission to continue speaking to Doran and Tait. He gave the green light and another meeting was arranged for that evening at the Sherbrooke Castle Hotel. Doran arrived with the two officers, walked in with them, went up to the reception desk, asked for his 'usual room' and was handed a key. It was clear he regularly used the hotel and the officers suspected it was usually to take girlfriends back there. During the discussion, Doran told the policemen he realised they knew who they were after and in answer to their question who, named George Duncan and Thomas Sim. He promised the officers they would get 'the actual time, date and place where they could get Duncan and Sim in possession of a substantial amount of cocaine'. When the detectives asked how much cocaine, they were told 'hundreds of grammes'. It was, for them, an exciting and astonishing offer. This would be the biggest capture of its type, a mega hit.

They knew cocaine was flowing into the country but had not realised the scale of the smuggling. It was at the Sherbrooke that arrangements were put in hand for the Aldwych Café arrests.

That day, as Tait arrived, a policewoman, her face partially but deliberately obscured by a headscarf, was already in place sipping coffee. It had been decided none of the officers who Duncan or Sim might recognise should be inside. The arrangement would be for Tait to find out if the two had brought the kit and, if so, to signal to the policewoman, who would in turn signal to the officers waiting outside, who would jump in. When it was over, detainers and detainees alike were taken to Govan police station.

'I know I've been set up by Doran and Tait,' Duncan told Edgar and Corrigan. 'One bad turn deserves another.'

The detectives remained silent. Words were unnecessary. It was all too obvious what had happened. A former drug-squad detective said, 'After George Duncan had been released on bail, Ronnie Edgar arrived at his office one day to be handed a message asking him to call a Glasgow telephone number. When he dialled, he recognised George's voice telling him he wanted to see him. They met and he offered Ronnie information about the exact importation details, and the number of times deliveries had been made and cocaine brought into the country on behalf of Doran. George had even kept counterfoils of receipts for tickets used during his journeys so he could be sure of exact dates, places and times. One of the features of cocaine is that when you are in a tight spot, your resolve goes and you pass the buck. It has the effect of loosening your tongue. Strictly speaking, because he had been charged, the police should not have been talking to him and to cover their backs the officers approached Fiscal Len Higson to tell him of the offer.

'The fiscal had been involved in the case of the Bartletts, so he knew the background. He was also aware of the effect a full statement from George Duncan could have on Tait and Doran. The policemen submitted a report and at the end of the day an arrangement was arrived at whereby George Duncan and Thomas Sim would plead guilty to effectively reduced charges and make statements after being sentenced. But it was of such significance, and potentially such a legal hot potato, that eventually the matter was decided by Lord Mackay of Clashfern QC, the Lord Advocate himself, who gave the go-ahead for the deal. The Lord Advocate is Scotland's principal law officer and has the ultimate responsibility for criminal prosecutions. For him to intervene in action being taken in a lower court was unique, but in this case it was justified because he was effectively giving permission for the case of Duncan and Sim to be downgraded from one of High Court level. As a result, immediately the two men from Holland pleaded guilty in front of the sheriff and were sentenced.

'Ronnie and Joe were free to interview them. They were brought from Barlinnie prison to Turnbull Street in Glasgow and George, in particular, spent an entire day making a copious statement. It was extremely detailed and absolutely nothing was left out. He even told them of the banks and building societies where he had exchanged the money paid to him by Doran and Tait into Dutch guilders. From the police aspect, the atmosphere was amiable. There was a feeling everyone just wanted the whole thing out in the open and finished with.

'Andy Tait had been arrested by this time. When the police came for him at his home, he was crestfallen. Andy was a big guy, who became caught up in the whole thing, sucked into a circle in which he was out of his depth, and was carried along on a wave of near hysteria.

'In the police's eyes, one of the few people to come out of the whole business with any credit was Tom Ferrie. Ronnie and Joe sat outside the BBC studios in Glasgow one night listening to his show on the car radio. When it was finished and Tom came out of the building, they followed him home then knocked on his door, showed him a warrant and searched it. They found him a thoroughly nice guy and still listen to him.'

While Doran was on the run, the police, of course, knew where he was. It was never a secret and, in any case, all they needed to do was to read the newspapers from time to time and see his name mentioned among the criminal community that had bedded down in Spain. In between house moves, he would book into hotels, such as the four-star Andalucia Plaza in Puerto Banus, and occasionally receive a telephone call from Ronnie Edgar. The policeman made sure Doran was aware of the fate of Andy Tait after the baker's trial.

'Hello, Brian, how's the weather?'

'Warmer here than where you are, I bet.'

'How are things?'

'Look, you didn't ring me to pass the time of day. It's about Andy, isn't it?'

'Thought I'd bring you up to speed.'

'What happened to him?'

'Guilty, possessing and supplying.'

'And?'

'Two years for one and four on the other.'

'Concurrent?'

'Yes, but I gather he'll appeal.'

'I know.'

'You and he been keeping in touch?'

'You know we have, you've been tapping his phone.'

'Wrong there, no need, as well you know. Anyway, I thought I'd pass on some advice.'

'Meaning?'

'It may get too hot for you there, if you're not careful.'

'What do you mean?'

'They're not going to allow guys like you to stay there forever.'

256

'Well, the time to worry about that is when it happens.'

'What are you up to these days?'

'I have one or two things going.'

'Not drugs, I hope. They're very hard on people they catch running gear there.'

'I'm not involved in drugs and never have been.'

'Well, why not come home?'

'After what happened to Andy? No way. I won't get a fair deal and I'm not going to sit around in Barlinnie waiting to find that out.'

24

GROUCHO MARX

Almost as soon as Andy Tait reached the reception area at Barlinnie prison, where he would suffer the humiliation of being stripped and having his every last possession taken from him, questions were already being asked among now forlorn and bereft happy dust users. What, they wondered, had gone wrong? Were others now in the firing line? And what would Brian Doran do?

The answer to the last question would emerge later and it wouldn't surprise anyone, especially those who knew Whacko. As for the other two, it was back to the old routine for the police. As the advent of the Happy Dust Gang had caused an explosion in the amount of cocaine entering Scotland, so its demise coincided with an equally dramatic collapse of the trade. Detectives would continue sounding out snouts for any sign of another group taking up the mantle but none had immediately sprung up. As for what had gone wrong, among the smart set it was acknowledged that the wheel of fortune had fallen off with the anonymous telephone call to the police, telling them the Bartletts had cocaine at the Highburgh flat. That had sparked the concatenation that led Big Andy to jail and

Doran to self-imposed exile. So who made it? And, more importantly, why?

Theories abounded. Had the police told the truth in saying the call came from a female? If this was correct, then it possibly ruled out the natural suspect, Doran himself. He had already been arrested and, in the web of double-dealing and deceit which followed, it would have been only natural for him to save his own skin by making it appear someone else had handed over the others. He could easily have organised one of his many women friends to make the fateful call. And, crucially, apart from him and the Bartlett brothers, who else knew about the drop? But if he had been so helpful, why the need for flight? Surely, as part of any deal with the police, he would have ensured for himself what the brothers and the men from Utrecht had arranged: an appearance before the sheriff and lenient treatment. In fact, those closest to Doran would put his absconding down to nothing other than vanity. One remembers, 'Nobody who really knew Brian blamed him, but there were many who did, saying he did the dirty on his pals then saved himself. In normal circumstances, he would have swallowed the pill and taken a fine, but he was such a big face in Glasgow he was convinced any scandal would have finished him. He probably believed that to bow down to the law would be to lose face. To many of his hangers-on, Brian was bigger than the law. Yet, if he had taken the fine, no one would have thought the worse of him. Instead, he chose to go in the other direction – he thought he was unbeatable and had suddenly discovered he was as vulnerable as the next man or woman.

'One or two suggested that at the time of the call, he and the police had not put their heads together, and he was probably thinking that if he was lifted why should the others not suffer also? But he was intelligent enough to know that if the Charlie was found, the Bartletts were the weak link, and the real extent of what the Happy Dust Gang had been up to would emerge and that could only worsen the trouble he was in already. Some wondered if it had come from a wife whose husband had become hooked on cocaine and was blowing the marriage and the family fortune. Or had it come from a woman whose husband had gone off with some girl he'd met at a party where gear had been flowing and she wanted revenge on those she saw as responsible?

'There were countless possibilities, but what many saw as the most likely explanation was that the call came from a girl who had been given a full nose of Charlie and while she was in seventh heaven had got her kit off for a string of men, something foreign to her nature. She'd only remembered what she'd done the next day, or even the one after, and had asked the Bartletts when the next drop was being made so she could get kit. Maybe she even sat and watched while Brian delivered and then put the call in to the police. Who knows? Of course, there were yet others who maintained there had never been a tip-off, that the police had simply been following Doran but used the call as an excuse for getting a search warrant to look over the flat.' These were the imponderable questions that would plague the party circuit for months to come.

As for the principals, Duncan and Sim went back to Utrecht, but not before the drug squad had reminded them that when – not if – Doran was brought to trial, they would be needed back to give evidence. The Bartletts threw themselves into learning the vegetable business. Andy Tait had a meeting with his legal team after which an appeal was formally made against his conviction and a successful application made for him to be given bail until the hearing.

Meanwhile, Brian Doran was setting about rebuilding his life. If he had hoped that would be with his family around him, he was in for a disappointment. Mary and he had tried their best to help the children settle. Their new surroundings would have made the youngsters the envy of their pals in Glasgow – a swimming pool in the garden, ever-present sunshine, beaches to play on and sea to swim in – but they missed their friends back home. And when Michael had to return for treatment, his mother and brothers and sisters went with him, leaving their father to fend for himself. It was a heartbreaking and distressing parting.

In Glasgow, it was agreed things were not the same without Whacko and the Parachutist around, the latter being missed for the pleasure he brought and the former for his generosity. And people really did see Doran as both kind and generous. One of his Blue Sky clients remembers, 'Brian went to work for an older chap who ran the agency and was such a good worker that the owner took a real shine to him and eventually left him to operate the business. He exuded an attitude that nothing was too much trouble – he was effectively Mr Holidays in Glasgow. If you wanted a decent holiday abroad, the first person you tried was Brian, and when he dealt with you personally you left the agency feeling as though you had been in the presence of royalty. You'd go along and enquire about a holiday that would cost around £100 and if you were a friend he'd let you have it for £70. The point was everybody felt they were his friend. He had properties in Magaluf, which he rented out and even arranged flights to them. No wonder he was rich.

'There was a rumour that one of his employees had been bragging of having been with Brian one night when he worked out his share of the proceeds from the travel company for the week and it came to £14,000, an absolute fortune then. In those days, there were no credit cards, everything was in cash, so it was difficult for the taxman to keep an eye on how much he was due. When Brian skipped to Spain, even the police were losers because they were among his biggest customers. They would think they were being given a special cut-price rate because of who they were – he would do a deal and tell them to keep it to themselves, but they didn't realise that was what he said to everyone.'

So prolific was the package-holiday business that flowed through the Blue Sky offices that in the early stages of the investigation into the source of the ever-increasing quantities of cocaine circulating in the west of Scotland, some police officers wondered if flights from Spanish resorts were being used by smugglers. It was a reasonable theory. Spain was a source of the drug and the man who ran the holiday trade at the Scottish end appeared to have become suddenly and sensationally wealthy, able to spread largesse at will. Whether it was mere guesswork or carefully conceived supposition, it was a suspicion that came close to hitting the bullseye.

Other demonstrations of his generosity would be missed too. One of scores of stories illustrating his thoughtless beneficence concerned a character well known among the upper echelons of Glasgow society as a provider of high-quality regalia. Some unkindly spoke of this individual as being a dealer in 'dodgy' goods – the word frequently being misunderstood to suggest his offerings might be fake, whereas this was far from the truth: they were very much the genuine article. The dodgy element came in their source. It was considered impolite to ask from where they had been derived and definitely bad form to use the expression 'nicked' in his company. One evening, Brian Doran was seen in concentrated conversation with the dealer. It would later transpire he had bought two Cartier watches, one costing £3,000, the other £1,500, with the total being paid over in ready cash. Brian gave the more expensive to a female friend and the other to his very pretty wife Mary, though his actions brought a rebuke from an older confidant. 'Fuck sake, Brian, I don't understand you doing that,' complained the man. Doran anticipated moral outrage. 'Don't you know how life works? Give a bird a present now and again, but always give the most expensive item to your wife because that way you know whatever happens it is going to stay in the family.'

However, it was in the party world that Doran and George Duncan were missed most of all. Wherever there had been cocaine, there had been a party, and wherever there had been a party, there had been Brian Doran. It was a remarkable situation. In his early 30s, having sired six children, created a fortune, built a reputation that was the envy of business rivals and associates everywhere, he ought to have been putting his feet up to enjoy the fruits of his loins and his labours.

It was rumoured that he had been introduced to cocaine by a friend who had himself discovered the drug and its effects in a bizarre way. One afternoon, this man had decided to splash out and give himself a rather special and private treat. He entered the New Solar sauna off Argyle Street, Glasgow, and hired the establishment's only two available prostitutes. They had locked the door and adjourned to a cubicle, where all three quickly removed their clothing, the customer having paid to watch the women perform a lesbian sex act he had seen in an American pornographic film and which he now described in detail to them. The girls were willing but wondered if their lack of enthusiasm might be too obvious until one briefly left and returned with a tiny packet from which she invited the others to sniff.

'What is it?' the man asked.

'Cocaine,' one of the girls replied.

Soon afterwards, the pair was able to give a virtuoso performance and their clearly satisfied spectator now wondered if he had been on a short trip to paradise. 'Where did you get it?' he asked

'On a weekend in Amsterdam.'

'Got any more?'

'Not enough. If you're caught bringing it in, you're in trouble. Ask somebody going there to bring some. You'll pay about £50 a gramme but tell them not to get caught.' He mentioned the experience to a business colleague who had connections in Belgium and several weeks later was telephoned by a Dutch lorry driver who had arrived in Greenock after a journey via Hull suggesting they meet up. After doing so and taking delivery of cocaine from the driver, when he next met up with Doran he offered a sample to the travel agent, who was instantly hooked. Once tried,

263

everyone wanted more happy dust and the meeting with Duncan and Sim established an apparently bottomless pit of happiness.

Others would tell of how, within minutes of snorting, they felt a wave of relaxation sweep over them and fantasies that floated past were so real they had to be lived. Sexual fantasies especially. Give cocaine to a woman inclined towards pleasure and she was all yours.

What was remarkable was that this should have happened to a man to whom, according to the laws of physics, women should not have been attracted. He did not appear to have much going for him: married with a big family to whom he was devoted, balding, showing signs of the beginnings of a middle-aged spread, bespectacled and with a moustache that sometimes earned him the sobriquet 'Groucho Marx'. At other times, he'd receive the compliment of being 'a big, nice, ugly bugger' and could, like the famous Marx brother, be remarkably sarcastic to the point of being offensive. Mostly he managed to get away with his barbs, but sometimes a friend would need to step in and tell him to stop it. He would then instantly turn on charm, as a tap pouring affability. 'You can't helping liking Brian,' many would say. 'But how does he do it?' The answer lay in a single word: power.

Throughout the ages, men and women have been attracted to those with power. Wealth brings power, and Brian Doran was rich. So he had power. He could buy whatever he wished and that included cocaine. Women were drawn by his power and succumbed to his cocaine. He made the unbelievable discovery that a man with cocaine did not need to be good looking, that regardless of what stared back at him from the mirror women saw only power and desire. Being intelligent helped. He was able to enter any conversation and positively contribute on any topic. That added to his magnetism. Very soon he had an entourage, a following of men and women who wanted to be seen with him; he had not asked them to become his disciples, they simply tagged along. A well-known model who would later turn her talents to television was said to be besotted by Doran. The daughter of a highly respected Glasgow business family who discovered cocaine when she became one of the many hangers-on who seemed to follow Doran and his circle eventually fell from grace and became known as 'Margarine Legs' because they were said to spread so easily. Blonde-haired Linda McShane, a former beauty queen who, according to the local press, could 'set temperatures soaring even on the coldest winter day', was, for a time, his girlfriend. He had spotted her photograph on a Tennent's lager can. For a brief time after he moved to Spain he and Linda remained friends, but they parted for good shortly after Tait's trial. When a newspaper implied in January 1984 that they were 'shacked up in a Spanish love nest', it received a letter from a firm of Glasgow lawyers reading, 'The article implies that our client is Mr Doran's girlfriend. Whilst that was the case, she has not seen him since 7 June 1983.'

Eventually, everyone was talking about Brian Doran and everyone wanted to know him and what he was up to. Had Glasgow been able to boast a newspaper with a gossip diary, then his name would have appeared daily. It was said that taking cocaine had given him a new confidence, one that allowed him to enjoy the myriad stories circulating about his exploits.

One of these was that he would occasionally drive about in his Rolls-Royce offering rides in the front passenger seat to voluptuous young women, the only condition being that en route they removed their tops and brassieres and flashed their naked breasts at passers-by – it was certainly possible, with plenty of young women sufficiently confident in the condition of their breasts and daring enough to sally forth on such an adventure. Then, too, he was in a position to ask young hopefuls, 'Do you want a cheap holiday?' or 'Do you want to work in one of my Blue Sky hotels abroad?' or 'Would you want to work as a travel representative?'

His friends believed he was experiencing his second adolescence. Having spent so much of his youth seeing the birth of his family, he now wanted it back. Women, especially attractive young women, they were certain, were what he had missed. While contemporaries had been sowing their oats, he had been at home playing with his babies. Now he needed to catch up and he had the means to do so. Females loved being in his company because he promised fun, money, flash cars, the finest restaurants, best clubs, gifts of jewellery and happy dust. He had discovered a new lease of life.

Andy Tait went along with it. Through their reputations as playboys, they acquired celebrity stature. That these men, nearer 40 than 30, chose to dress in suits designed for a young Adonis half their age mattered not to them. They were in utopia. If, say, Douglas Timmins organised a beauty contest at his club, among the judges might well be these matadors of the Glasgow scene. At one club, which had taken up Timmins' theme, the entrants were invited to take part in a special after-hours competition in front of a select audience. Contestants would each receive happy dust and a few pounds extra in their purses, the only stipulation being that the young beauties parade topless. Five took up the challenge, their breasts bouncing as they showed what they were made of in front of a couple of dozen cheering, clapping men and women.

A Miss Nude Glasgow contest, held in a West End flat with a £10-a-head levy on hand-picked spectators including free lines of cocaine, was rumoured to have attracted half a dozen entries, and when it was over one of the also-rans and her boyfriend performed an extract from the Kama Sutra. This was Scotland before the onset of Aids. Contraception was held to be mainly the responsibility of the female, who relied on the birth control pill to make sure a night of fun had no unfortunate long-term consequences.

The young men and women who liked to be thought of as part of Doran's circle would party up to three times a week, meeting first in one of the well-established clubs or pubs, where they would arrange the remainder of the menu. The men would take it in turn to host an occasional gathering at their homes and liked to ensure there was always a surfeit of girls present. They had a selection formula based on experience. For instance, while everyone was enjoying themselves at the Warehouse, up to 30 young women would be invited to one of these select gatherings. 'We've a party going, do you fancy coming along? Loads of booze and if you behave we might have some gear. If you misbehave, we'll definitely have some,' knowing the average take-up ratio was around two out of three, and of the twenty or so who turned up about ten would be in the mood for letting their hair down – and their clothes. For every two girls, there would be one male, but once the party was under way it was every man for himself. If someone had cocaine during a shortage, it was unlikely it would be shared with friends.

In between parties, there were informal gatherings, an excuse for sex and cocaine. Doran arrived at such a tête-à-tête at a flat in Cessnock one evening. Inside were two of his friends and three women, all five in their birthday suits, enjoying in blissful comfort the cocaine powder still in evidence on a glass-topped table. One of the girls, a Scot, was handsome rather than attractive, but the giveaway was in her nickname, 'Monster Mash'. The owner of the flat, clearly still in a state of excitement from her efforts, answered the rap on his door to see Whacko standing there, a girl on his arm. Bowing his head slightly, Doran immediately took in the situation. 'Goodness, I always suspected you were the same as me, king-sized,' he said, stepping inside.

The same straining for fun could not be said to have extended to the Bartlett brothers. Alan would be described as quiet, even dour; a man constantly terrified by the effect on his business career of being caught with drugs. It was a terror that would become reality and leave him and Ronald isolated. The younger Bartlett did at least make an effort to become one of the boys. He arrived at a flat around 4 a.m.

one morning and was pleasantly surprised by the sight which greeted him: a teenage girl, her short brown hair in ringlets, lying on a couch wearing only briefs and for some reason painting her nipples with vivid red lipstick.

'Go on, Ronnie, she's all yours,' he was told, but, being nervous and a gentleman, he first asked the girl if she would mind. Stoned on cocaine, hot and horny, she rose and led him into a bedroom. He came out a quarter of an hour later, a huge smile across his face.

'You don't know what you've missed,' he said.

'No, we don't – because we haven't missed anything,' they replied.

'What do you mean?'

'We all had her before you came, you were her fourth tonight.'

The young man's face fell, his moment of glory destroyed.

This, then, was the world of salacious sex, power and promiscuity that Doran abandoned for Spain. But while he had departed in ignominy, his reputation remained. One of his most trusted friends, who wore spectacles not unlike those of Whacko, was partying in Paisley one night. 'There was a lot of gear flying about,' he said, 'and I had my spectacles on to see a line when this bird comes up and says, "I know who you are." I asked her who she meant and she replied, "You're Brian Doran. I thought the police were looking for you." I thought to myself, stupid cow, Brian has been away for more than a year out in Spain, but tomorrow she's going to go around telling everybody, "Guess who I saw last night? Brian Doran, and I shagged him." It seemed a shame to spoil her fantasy, so I did.'

In Spain, Doran busied himself buying into a club, running his property business and making contact with the men who ran the drug-smuggling trade along the Costa del Sol. He knew how the Happy Dust Gang had made fortunes, certainly George and, to a lesser extent, Sim. Buying drugs in bulk was the way to riches and having been in business, successfully, he knew the bigger the outlay, the bigger the return – accepting, of course, that the same applied to the risks involved. Like any clever criminal, he was conscious that when a chance came, it had to be taken. There was no gain in pondering what might or could be.

A man who would become a close confidant in the years ahead, one of the richest drug dealers to have been born in Scotland, had become a multi-millionaire simply by grasping such an unexpected opportunity. The man's name must remain anonymous because he has never been charged with the offence that set him on his path to plenty, so we will call him Del. Del was an associate of many of those who enjoyed the company of the Happy Dust Gang but because his occupation was humble and lowly paid he could not afford the escape from the humdrum cocaine brought. He supplemented his meagre income by stealing cars and had a reputation for being skilled and reliable in this field. He was approached one day and asked to keep his eye open for two Land Rovers, vehicles that were much sought after at the time. They were wanted by a man based in southern Spain, who had made it clear he had buyers for them and would pay handsomely. But they would have to be delivered to him. Late one afternoon, a friend of Del's happened to be collecting his car from a garage where it had been serviced and was putting the key in one of the doors when it fell through a drain grating. He was unable to recover it and returned to the garage, which advised him of a nearby locksmith, one of whose specialities was providing keys for all types of motor vehicles. The locksmith, whose integrity had at times come under suspicion by the police, explained that the vehicle had a code specifying the type and number of key required and detailed where this code could be found. We will not, in this story, go further than that. But the car owner returned, searched for the code, found it and the next day was provided with a new key. He told this story to Del, who had kept an eye on two brand new Land Rover vehicles in a Glasgow garage compound. On the pretext of buying one of these, Del approached a salesman and asked to look it over. He was allowed to do so at his leisure, during which time he ensured he found the key code. The following day, a sidekick did likewise with another Land Rover. The locksmith was then approached and asked to cut the relevant keys, being promised a handsome bonus in the process.

That night, the locks securing the compound were cut and the Land Rovers driven away. Disguised with fake registration plates, the cars crossed into Europe the following morning by ferry from Dover and were taken to the buyer in Spain. He had been caught unawares by their arrival and had only a portion of the agreed fee but offered to complete the deal by making up the remainder with hashish. Del was reluctant at first, but eventually agreed and returned to Glasgow with the drug in a suitcase. He sold it at an enormous profit, decided his future lay in drug dealing and set off back to Europe. In Spain, he made a base from which he talked his way into the leading European hash-smuggling gangs, several times evading capture by various police forces. He is still at large but has maintained a reputation for courtesy and discretion, plus a remarkable ability to think on his feet. As for the Land Rover vehicles, for many years they proudly wore the insignia of the Moroccan police authorities, having crossed the Strait of Gibraltar to their new owners.

Like Del, Doran was ready to seize his chance, but until he was established and secure there were other more pressing matters to resolve. His priority remained his family. Mary and the children made it out to the Marbella villa whenever they could, but Michael's deteriorating health made these trips increasingly difficult both practically and emotionally. Mary confided to a neighbour at the time, 'The ideal situation would be for Brian to be home with us. But it's something I just have to live with. He knows how much everybody misses him, as he misses his friends in Glasgow.'

One of those friends was car dealer Eric Rowan, who had fled to Spain in 1982 when the fraud squad began investigating his Glasgow businesses. While on the run, he married Yvonne Keenan, whose father Peter had been a much-admired bantamweight boxing champion. The law would eventually catch up with Eric, who is now a successful writer. But that was in the future. As far as Doran and Tait were concerned, both had yet to get over the hurdle of 1984. It was a year they would each want to forget.

Tait had been free since lodging an appeal against the conviction that had brought him a four-year jail sentence. He had walked the streets of Glasgow, a solemn, morose figure, complaining bitterly at the way he had been treated. His venom might have been justifiably directed at the man who ought to have been in the dock with him, but his friendship for Doran remained strong.

'Brian is not coming back and who can blame him? Especially after he's seen what happened to me,' he would tell anyone willing to listen. 'In Spain, he has the chance to make a fresh start, and good luck to him. This whole thing just got way out of hand. It's like a bad dream that won't go away. Not so long ago, I had a good business and everything was on the up. I followed some bad advice and the money started running out. When you are in that situation, you will turn anywhere if it means saving what you've worked for. I'm dreading how the appeal will go. My lawyers say I've a fighting chance but frankly, from where I stand, it's hard to see any light at the end of the tunnel.'

On 24 April 1984, Tait appeared before the Court of Session in Edinburgh asking the wise judges to agree with him that he should never have been found guilty. The argument put forward on his behalf was that statements made to the drug squad by Doran should never have been allowed to be used by the prosecution in their case against him. In doing so, the contents had swung the jury in favour of finding him guilty. The learned judges listened carefully to what was said by the baker's defence team but were not convinced.

271

They ruled that the statements had nothing in them that could be described as incriminating and they had therefore not affected the jury's findings. His appeal was lost and all hope of escaping prison gone. He was taken to Barlinnie, knowing that at least two years of grim routine lay ahead. Every morning he would wake up reminding himself that his surroundings were the price of membership of the most exclusive club in Scotland, the Happy Dust Gang.

If his punishment was harsh, it was nothing to that meted out to Doran by a higher judge. Only a month later, his son Michael died in Glasgow aged just six. The brave youngster had been born severely deformed and neither money nor prayer nor the undoubted love of his family and the skill of his doctors could save him from the inevitable. Doran had been kept up to date with every development in his son's condition.

After the boy's death, his father faced the agony of deciding whether to return to Glasgow for the funeral. He would, of course, be arrested instantly and in the end stayed away, an intention communicated to the police before the sad final ceremony. All the same, flights into Glasgow and Edinburgh were monitored, and a discreet watch was maintained on his palatial home on Terregles Avenue and during the funeral. He was left to grieve in Spain.

25

LOBSTER WITH CHIPS

Among Doran's friends of the day, there are some who still believe it was the death of Michael that set him on the road he would follow. He had been making a comfortable living, enough to keep him in style after ensuring there were sufficient funds to guarantee Mary and the children in Glasgow would never want. But now he became a man obsessed with success.

A former schoolmate, who kept in touch with him until the boy's death, said, 'Brian tortured himself over not being there at the end. He was not the sort to concern himself with what others might think, it was the view of his family that mattered, but even though they understood his dilemma, it would continually come back to haunt him that he had not been seen there alongside the others. He needed to take his mind from what had happened and set about concentrating on doing what he had shown he had always been good at, making money.

'He had kept in touch with a few of his old pals in Scotland and always looked forward to seeing those who went out to Marbella on package holidays and who made a point of looking him up. Brian was always desperate to keep up with what was going on, but you could see and sense that, as time went by, he was drifting away from the world in which he had been brought up. Whether it was with the intention of shocking, or just wanting to be gossiped about, he began to talk more and more about people living in Spain who were inviting him into their company. The reason some were so appalled was that these acquaintances were generally out and out criminals.

'He appeared to believe he was a member of a very select group of men who had exiled themselves in Spain to evade the police and who were big enough to stick up two fingers at the UK legal system. Brian was only there because he'd got himself involved with a gang shuffling cocaine about. Many of his new associates were in a different league, wanted for murder and armed robbery. Many of us wondered if Brian was getting out of his depth.'

Others, too, wondered about this Scot who had appeared out of the blue. For a man who spoke the language fluently, who was so obviously intelligent and had sacrificed so much, was it not odd he had thrown up so much over a relatively minor matter. Underworld contacts in Glasgow were sounded out and a leading East End underworld figure disappeared for a week. The Glasgow police wondered what had become of him; in fact, he was ensconced in a hotel in Marbella at which taxis would call from time to time to take him to expensive villas in the suburbs, where he was asked to go over the same story time after time while different sets of ears listened.

The trial of Andy Tait, with its allegations of lying, secret deals in hotel bedrooms with police officers, and set-ups for the benefit of detectives, raised the question of whether Doran was, in reality, a police or Customs 'plant' who had been allowed to escape justice. Was he an informant who had agreed to infiltrate the Costa drugs and crime networks? Crooks are never happy in the presence of others suspected of grassing, and uncovering informers, in or out of jail, is customarily the precursor to rough and harsh justice.

274

Brian Doran would never know it, although he must have wondered, but he was subjected to as vigorous a vetting as the most delicately placed security service employee. He might have had big plans for himself, but they would never have left the ground had there been the slightest doubt as to which side of the fence his sympathies lay.

Brian's face became familiar in the more sophisticated clubs around the resort. His natural generosity meant he was never alone, and being able to converse in Spanish gave him a huge advantage. The men buying vast amounts of hash and, in particular, cocaine frequently worried about their inability to fully understand many of their conversations with suppliers. Having a Spanish speaker around who could be trusted would give them a huge advantage. But the burning issue of trust remained.

In 1980, an American named Silas 'Olly' Hardy had appeared on the scene explaining he was wanted by the police in New Mexico over allegations of cocaine possession. It was by no means an especially serious matter, but there were problems with a wife and a girlfriend, a husband and unpaid maintenance, the usual accoutrements of a married man and an equally married mistress. Olive-skinned Olly said his appearance came from a Spanish mother; he even spoke the language and had worked his way over to Europe as a steward on a cruise liner before tiring of pandering to rich middle-aged women. He began inviting himself into the company of exiles but failed to understand that asking questions does not bring answers but suspicion. He had a special interest in cocaine, and quizzed them about who was buying and from which cartel. He was offered a small piece of action driving a carload of hash to the north with orders to abandon the vehicle with the keys under the driver's seat in a hotel car park in Tarragona and return to Fuengirola by train. Olly was never seen again, but it was whispered that in his absence his apartment had been burgled and detailed notes of conversations discovered in a tin of rice. It was said he had been offered an assignment helping load hash onto a seagoing yacht off the Moroccan coast and, falling overboard in darkness, had vanished.

Doran, on the other hand, did not need to ask questions. He already knew most of the answers. But as he slowly became accepted and party to secrets, there were still some who were wary. He was a man to be watched, in more ways than one.

Andy Tait, meanwhile, was also coming under curious scrutiny. He had been transferred to Perth prison, where men with longer sentences to serve were held. There he was regarded with amusement by some and awe by others. The Happy Dust Gang had, after all, been the most sensational set of drug smugglers of the time and Big Andy found himself treated by many of his fellow cons with the sort of respect that had been given years earlier to the great train robbers. Here was a big-time drugs dealer, a man of huge influence, from the middle classes, who had travelled and had run a successful business, and who knew which knife to use at dinner. He was best mates with a millionaire on the run. While he was required to wear prison-issue clothing most of the time, when it came to sports Andy ensured he was properly kitted out in the very best of outfits, brought into the prison during visiting hours by friends. His appearance in a spotless, coloured shirt only enhanced his image as a toff. He was well liked by the other inmates, a fact that made the time pass more quickly than he had feared.

Other cons wanted to know about the Happy Dust Gang, but it was a subject he tried to avoid. Questions about Doran, however, he fielded quite happily. 'Brian never gives up hoping something will pop up out of the blue to save him from having to come back and face the music. In a sense, just like me and the rest of us he's in a sort of prison as well, only his is in Spain and he can leave it any day. He's forever asking himself if he has done the right thing and is desperate to find a way out. After all, he's still got a wife and five kids in Glasgow. I'm honestly glad I'm not in his shoes. At least here I know when it will be over and when I can leave with a clean slate.

'You've got to feel sorry for him. Look at all the money he's had and where it's got him now. It's as if he's playing Monopoly and forever landing on the "Go to Jail" square.'

Tait was finally freed in 1984, but there would be no return to The Pantry or to his big house in Cathcart. His behaviour had destroyed his family and he moved into a tiny flat in Scotstoun, a horrendous come-down for a man who had not so long ago been the toast of the city.

His old pal Doran, though, had not forgotten him. In early 1987, Andy would head off to Spain and they would be reunited. Before departing, he told friends of an exciting new venture Whacko was planning.

'We're going to open a fish-and-chip shop in Marbella,' he said.

'You're going off to Spain to sell fish and chips?'

'No, this is a fish-and-chip place with a difference.'

'Whether it's in Maryhill or Marbella, a fish and chippie is a fish and chippie.'

'No, this will be a fish-and-chip restaurant. It will have the very best of everything, the decor, furnishings, and we'll be having lobster and smoked salmon on the menu.'

'And the Spanish are going to give paella the elbow and get stuck into chips?'

'Maybe, but we reckon we can pull in enough expats and holidaymakers to make it pay.'

'You sure this is what you're going there for, Andy?'

'Definitely, what else?' And, of course, there was something else, but the expression 'fish and chips' would hardly be appropriate. And so Andy Tait set off for Marbella.

Ironically, around the time he left Scotstoun, at Westminster, Lord Lane, the Lord Chief Justice, was exhorting Members of Parliament to bring in laws that would deprive drug traffickers of their profits, also suggesting that pressure be brought on drug-producing countries to crack down on the trade. 'There seem to be few signs of urgency,' he said.

'How many more years will go by, how many more children and young persons will have to die degrading deaths before action is taken? One would have thought that there would be few things more important for Parliament to get on with, and few things less contentious. At last people are beginning to realise the size of the problem and the appalling prospects for the future as cocaine vies with heroin for the privilege of being the leading destroyer of youth.' It was a message that would fall on deaf ears in Spain at least, where the drugs trade was very much on the up.

While Andy Tait waited and waited for the chippy with its lobster and salmon to surface, he worked in a local bar. Doran, meantime, had been steadily improving his prestige by entertaining in Marbella in the style that had made him so popular in Glasgow. There were girls aplenty at the bashes all right and lines of cocaine everywhere, with the host urging all and sundry, 'Please, help yourself,' but instead of trendy young men, the places of honour were reserved for those who made their fortunes by smuggling, principally drugs.

As the months passed, suspicions towards him eased. Introductions were made to men with North African and South American names. His advice on travel routes began to be sought, respected and taken. If someone needed to get a consignment of, say, rubber from X to Y without having to pass too many inquisitive Customs checks, they'd ask him which would be the best route and the most effective method. It became the done thing to 'ask Brian'. But naturally, not only the criminal element was interested in the Scot. As a foreigner who needed to register with the authorities each nine months to guarantee his stay in Spain, the various security services were able to start building files on him. Polite requests for information about him were made to police in Glasgow and his name was added to a list of men and women whose movements merited special filing.

* * *

After George Duncan and Thomas Sim had given evidence at the High Court trial of Andy Tait, they headed back to Holland. During the journey, Sim was quiet and withdrawn. George tried cheering him up by reminding him of some of their escapades as the Happy Dust Gang. The occasion, for instance, when a Dutch pal of the Monkey's had telephoned to say he had completed a contract in South America and instead of returning home to Amsterdam had been diverted by his employers to York. In his equipment, he had a sizeable stash of cocaine. Could the Monkey arrange to collect it? The Monkey approached George for help and made a generous offer. George said that when Scouse Willie next took over a stash behind a dashboard, if the Monkey could arrange for someone to meet him at the UK ferry terminal once he had seen Sim safely on his way to Glasgow, then he could bring the consignment with him on the return trip. The Monkey was delighted. He had two Dutch friends who would be happy to travel to a York hotel, meet the Dutch worker, then take the package to Scouse Willie. Their English was not the best, but he was sure they were up to this simple task. Still not wishing to give too much away to the Monkey, George proposed the Dutch couriers telephone him once they were in York so he could organise timings with Scouse Willie at Hull.

All seemed to be going well until the Dutchmen telephoned George in a panic. 'We have arrived but cannot find this place. It does not exist.'

'You sure?'

'Yes, we have had a terrible time getting here. We were told it was simple, but we have a very long aeroplane journey and now we cannot understand the language.'

'Where are you now?'

'Outside the police station. The police have given us a very bad time. They say they think we are drug dealers.'

'In York? They've never heard of drugs in York.'

'York? Where is York?'

'York. It's where you are to make the meet.'

'How are you spelling that?'

'How the fuck do you think? It's simple enough: Y-O-R-K. York. Fucking York.'

'Oh dear.'

'What the fuck do you mean by "oh dear".'

'We are in Cork.'

'Cork?'

'Yes, Cork.'

'Cork in fucking Ireland?'

'Yes, Cork. There seems to have been a mistake.'

'Mistake, you fucking bams. The mistake was in the Monkey letting you loose on your own.'

'What should we do?'

'Go to the police.'

'And what do we say?'

'Say you are drug dealers and can they tell you where you can buy a large amount of cocaine.'

'Are you serious?'

'Absolutely. And ask them to put you up for the night. Now, fuck off.'

At the time, the two Scots had roared with laughter, although it was some while before the Monkey saw the joke – the two had, in fact, been beaten up and robbed in Cork. But Sim's sense of humour had disappeared. He made it plain his friendship with George was over. It was best the two went their separate ways. George decided his future lay not on risky roofs but in the warmth and fun of clubland. He worked in casinos for a couple of years before investing in one of his own in Friesland in the north of Holland.

He was watching Dutch television at home one evening in late June 1987 when he almost fell from his chair. There on the screen was the face of Brian Doran. Whacko was handcuffed to a grim-faced officer, emerging from a police station and heading towards a van, its windows barred. Duncan turned up the volume and could hardly believe what he heard. Doran was among 16 people, including 11 from Britain, arrested in Marbella after a lengthy undercover investigation into an enormous hash-smuggling racket. Hashish had been transported by boat from North Africa, then sent all over Europe hidden in lorries carrying containers sealed by Customs. George briefly thought back to his trip around Rotterdam docks years earlier. Inquiries, the television report continued, were at an early stage, but this was the biggest-ever network to have been uncovered and early estimates were that the gang, said to have worked under the leadership of Doran, had a £50 million-a-year turnover. During the operation, police said they had seized 989 kilos of hashish, around a ton.

The scene switched to a villa, described as Doran's home, and to police in overalls hacking away at a false interior wall. Behind it, continued the commentary, had been discovered a fortune in a variety of foreign currencies. The programme was of interest to broadcasters in Holland because one of those arrested was a Dutch woman.

The item returned to the police station and a line of suspects being led, blinking, into the sunshine. Lo and behold, among them was Andy Tait, the Glasgow baker. George wondered if he was dreaming.

Watching the same news report was Robert Bruce, who would recall noticing a look of total unconcern on his old friend Brian's face, as if he had nothing whatsoever to worry about. He would later observe, 'He was being huckled out by Spanish cops, but it might have been Groucho Marx on his way to film another scene in *Go West*. He looked as though he didn't have a care in the world. It was as if he was saying, "Who, me? Never." Big Andy, on the other hand, looked as sick as a parrot. It was the perfect picture of a man who had just had his world taken from under him. He'd only been out there about three months. What a sickener!'

Almost as soon as he had been arrested, Andy Tait was released. There was no evidence to suggest he had done anything wrong. If it was a crime to know others were involved in wrongdoing then that was the extent of his lawbreaking, but it marked the beginning of the end of Andy's Spanish adventure and he would return home. Most of the others were freed also. There was a feeling the Spanish had jumped in too hastily and now needed to justify an operation involving 100 policia. The arrests were made by Chief Inspector Ignacio Bulanyos, who would make his mark ten years later in another major drugs bust involving Scots. In the later case, his victims were Robert Gillon and Donald Mathieson, both from Glasgow, picked up in a swoop on their villa near Fuengirola. The detective, by now known as 'El Latigo' or 'the Scourge', said he and his men discovered 470 kilos of hash. Gillon and Mathieson would ultimately be each jailed for three years.

The Scourge had less luck with Whacko. Doran spent months in jail protesting his innocence. He was transferred from the prison in Málaga to Cadiz then on to Madrid in what some saw as an attempt to sicken him so much he would throw up his hands and confess simply to be left in peace. If that was the motive, or at least part of the thinking behind the moves, then those responsible for its conception showed a remarkable ignorance of the man's character. Even when the odds were firmly against him, Doran never gave his persecutors an even break, standing for his ancient right of innocent until proven guilty and ensuring the prosecution were forced to prove guilt and not he his innocence. 'There's no way I'll be done for this,' he told friends who visited him. 'They've got no proof. They've fallen for the old trick of arresting someone and then hoping something will turn up in their favour. Nothing has and nothing will. They'll have to let me go.'

And they did. At the turn of the year, a judge ruled the evidence against Doran was weak and said that police needed to make further inquiries. In the meantime, he was freed on bail much to the dismay of El Latigo.

26

THE BRIBE

As Doran headed back to Marbella, technically still under investigation but for all practical purposes a free man, the storm clouds were gathering for Brits ensconced on the Costa del Crime. A century earlier, the government of Benjamin Disraeli had signed an agreement with Spain aimed at preventing the country from being a safe hiding place for UK villains. Piqued over the British refusal to hand over Gibraltar, Spain had ended that arrangement in 1978. However, after overtures from London, the Spanish had decided to offer up a compromise: future runaways would be handed back, while those already in their country could stay on, for now. It became clear time was running out for the exiles. Talks were already under way about banishing all fugitives back to their native soils.

Just a couple of weeks before Doran's arrest and that of the others on the hash-smuggling allegations, police had arrived from England to witness the wedding of Ronnie Knight and his bride Sue Haylock at one of Brian's favourite watering holes, the El Oceano Club in Marbella. It was more likely that they were watching the guests, but the gossip at the reception was that the officers were familiarising themselves with faces of men they would be handcuffing shortly themselves when they were urged off flights arriving at UK airports from Spain.

Doran had every reason to worry about what the future held. He was adamant his arrest had been a set-up and if that was the case, then it meant the Spanish police were out to get him. That possibility was not only of concern to him. He had built up a useful network of contacts among major drugs traders; these were men who could not afford to have their activities coming under the scrutiny of the police. That someone close to them was in that unhappy position was a worry. There had been major alarms when Doran was arrested: some realised that had his vast knowledge of the smuggling network made its way into police files, irreparable harm would have been done to a series of carefully worked out operations. The gangs and cartels waited: arrests or raids would be put down to his having talked. Nothing out of the ordinary happened and that fact alone was enough to raise Doran's reputation to great heights. To have spent six months in Spanish jails without squealing or begging for a deal was a considerable feat and his loyalty would be remembered.

However, it was assumed that El Latigo and his men had their eye firmly on the Scot, monitoring his every move and taking special note of those with whom he associated. It was a situation that could potentially endanger friends and a number took a pace backwards from their relationships with him. Doran was not a man to complain; he understood. But as the months of 1988 began passing by, he could have used some friends. The strain of maintaining a lavish lifestyle in Spain while supporting his family back in Glasgow was draining his resources. In Puerto Banus, he had been running Rokkos restaurant, but, as with most other bar owners along the Costa del Sol, he had to survive through the lean winter months until the tourist trade picked up in late spring. And while Rokkos provided a living, it would never fetch the sort of returns he had been making during the heyday of Blue Sky Travel.

In Marbella, he was conscious of the police presence and warnings from other exiles that time for them there was running out. The advice to get out would prove sound, some skipping to other European or North African countries, others leaving it too late and having to begin a seemingly endless round of prisons and lawyers' offices as they fought to stave off extradition. As for the police, Doran had not heard the last of the Scourge.

Towards the end of the year, Brian decided it was time to move on. He had been in Spain for almost six and a half years. Friends suggested he ought to get out of Europe altogether, but he could never abandon his family or go further from them. He looked about for a new haven and picked Amsterdam, the cocaine capital of the Continent.

In Glasgow, Doran might have been long gone but he was by no means forgotten. The police had never given up their quest to recapture him. Ronnie Edgar, by now promoted to detective inspector, was especially determined that the last of the Happy Dust Gang would be brought to heel. He had kept in regular contact with Duncan throughout his travels in Holland. George was now back in Utrecht involved in the building trade and the clubbing business, and the two men would occasionally chat. When George's wife Rosa told him there was a telephone call from Glasgow, he knew it was the detective ringing to ask how he was making out and the conversations would always end with a reminder that when, not if, Doran was brought to trial, George would be needed to give evidence against him as he had been a witness against Tait. It was a situation the man in Utrecht was not happy with. He felt Doran had been punished enough, having missed watching five members of his family growing up and the funeral of a sixth. It was terrible just imagining the grief of that alone.

Doran took over an apartment on the fringe of Amsterdam's red-light district, an area in which it is easy to lose oneself. The city was also home to many Colombians, some who had been advised that a trusted friend was

285

moving there from Marbella. In particular were members of the Ochoa family, one of whose number, Jorge Luis, had spent time in Spain trying to persuade hashish traffickers to switch their networks to the far more lucrative cocaine. The Ochoas were impressed with Doran, who knew he had an open invitation to visit them in Colombia any time. They admired his fluency in Spanish and his ability to pick up other languages with little difficulty. And they liked that he could think big – in quantities of cocaine and millions of pounds. Like him, they realised Spain was becoming too congested. There were too many criminals and too many Colombians – at one time, the Spanish government complained it was paying for the upkeep of 700 Colombian nationals in its prison system. The Ochoas asked contacts in Holland to keep a friendly eye out for the Scot.

His departure from Marbella had not gone unnoticed by others. It would always be officially denied, but the telephone line to 122 Terregles Avenue in Glasgow had been tapped. That made it easy for police in the city to keep tabs on the movements of Mary Doran's husband. He had regularly rung home from Spain, then the calls began coming from numbers in Amsterdam, sparking alarm bells. Police there were given the numbers and asked to look out for Doran, the Glasgow officers pointing out he was the subject of an international arrest warrant. The request came not from the drug squad but from the Scottish Crime Squad for, by now, the former had become the latter, so serious had the growth in drug traffic become. What the Happy Dust Gang had started, others had continued, recognising the huge profits that were seemingly there for the taking. Of course, there were risks, but some viewed the prospect of three or four years in prison as well worth it when there were tens of thousands of pounds to look forward to spending once they were released.

In early February 1989, Dutch police contacted their Scottish counterparts to confirm they knew where Doran was living. They were then asked to put him under surveillance.

This was not a request made lightly. Police forces in general constantly complain of being short-handed – to monitor a suspect requires a team of at least ten to a dozen men, so to ask the police in Holland to take such a step was to seek a huge favour; it might mean police there having to shelve one of their own major inquiries. In this case, officers came to an understanding that the watch would only be necessary until the Glaswegians could get together the necessary paperwork to seek their man's extradition. They had the documentation prepared by the middle of the month and a further call was made to Amsterdam asking for Doran's arrest. It was a move that came as a relief to the police there, who were inundated with pleas for help from forces all over the world, trying to track down runaways who always seemed to head for Holland.

Police who made the arrest would later say Doran appeared neither surprised nor particularly disappointed that his long journey had finally come to an end. 'When are they coming from Glasgow?' was all he asked. The only response they could think to give was 'possibly tomorrow'.

It would turn out to be unduly optimistic and Doran was to spend several weeks in prison, waiting for the courts to decide whether the strict and often nit-picking rules of extradition had been followed to the nth degree. It was ironic that after fleeing about Europe for so long, he should have finally settled just a half-hour car drive from the homes of the two men whose meeting with him that night in Charlie Parker's had started off the Happy Dust Gang. The arrest did not rate a mention in the Dutch media and merited only a paragraph back in Scotland.

As the weeks began to drag in the Amsterdam jail where Whacko was held, his lawyer, by now Mr Robert McCormack, flew from Glasgow for talks with him. Having recovered from the initial surprise of being lifted, he had determined to fight the attempt that would undoubtedly be made to haul him back to a belated appearance in the dock, where he had been expected to stand alongside Andy Tait.

By the beginning of June, almost four months after his arrest, he had fought the fight, lost and was now pinning his hopes on an appeal. That turned out to be as successful as it had been for Big Andy but for a different reason. Newspaper reports at the time revealed his Dutch lawyers had forgotten to lodge the necessary appeal papers within the required two weeks of the decision by a judge to extradite him to Scotland. As a consequence, it was now simply a matter of not if but when he would be turfed out of Holland.

When the two men spoke during a telephone conversation in 1983 about coming home, Ronnie Edgar had reminded Brian Doran, 'You'll have to face up to it sometime.'

'We'll see,' was the runaway's response.

'I know we will, Brian,' the policeman replied.

Six years on, the prediction came true. On the 28th of the month, two officers from the crime squad boarded a flight to Amsterdam. Fittingly, one was Ronnie Edgar and in his briefcase were documents formally requesting the handover of the prisoner. He and his colleague, Detective Sergeant Tom Sneddon, were not expecting to be out of the country for long. In fact, they had been booked on the next flight back. At the same time as they were fastening their seat belts, a prison official in Amsterdam was calling at the cell where Brian Doran had sat in frustration for months to tell him he would be leaving shortly and to collect his belongings. There was no need to mention the destination: Doran knew the worst. At Schiphol, the two officers were met and taken to a high-security police area within the giant airport. To save time, Doran had been driven under escort from the prison and was brought in to meet his old foe. In a brightly painted office, he was formally exchanged for the paperwork.

'Hello, Ronnie,' he said. 'You won't believe this, but I'm glad to be going back. I've been on the run too long.'

As they took their seats at the back of the aircraft, the prisoner turned to his captors, singling out his old foe Ronnie Edgar. 'Ronnie, how about a drink?'

'No way.'

'Why not?'

'I'm on duty, remember?'

'Yes, but I'm not.'

'No drinks.'

'Bastard.'

In Glasgow, he was driven in a police car to the remand wing of Barlinnie prison, but, before leaving, he made it plain he knew his rights. 'Remember, I am here as an extradite. You can't put any more charges to me,' he said. He was right, of course. The Dutch had agreed to return him only to face the specific charges listed on the extradition request; to have attempted to add further offences now would have been to risk an international legal row.

Getting their man back was only one hurdle to be crossed by the police. Now the real work began, getting hold of witnesses who had given evidence in the Tait case in April 1983, more than six years previously. They would need to be tracked down, interviewed once more to make sure their stories had not changed, and then visited by precognition agents acting for the defence, who needed to know what their evidence was likely to be. It was pretty much a formality. A visit to Glasgow's excellent Mitchell Library and a browse through newspaper reports of that trial would be enough to tell Doran's team what they were up against. But Ronnie Edgar had one very important call to make. As soon as Doran was safely in Barlinnie, he returned to his office, picked up the telephone and dialled the familiar number in Utrecht.

'Hello, George,' said the voice.

'Mr Edgar?'

'Yes, it's me. Have you heard the good news?'

'No, what news is that?'

'Brian Doran has been arrested. He's in Barlinnie.'

289

'When did this happen?'

'Today. George, we'll need you for his trial.'

'When will that be?'

'There's no date yet, three or four months' time. I'll let you know.'

'OK.'

George Duncan did not regard this as good news. He confided to a friend, 'I have the feeling that the police have been patronising me for years. They want me for their star witness, but I decided a long time ago that if they ever caught Brian they wouldn't get me to speak against him. I told myself that when they got him to court, I wouldn't go and hopefully the case against him would collapse. The police keep telling me how this man had to be brought to justice but to me it's more a personal vendetta between them and him. They think they will further their own careers by putting him behind bars. I told myself while I was sitting in Barlinnie with Simmy serving our six months that they could go fuck themselves, but I played along with what they said they would want me to do when he was caught. Hasn't the guy suffered enough?'

Sporadic calls from the police to his home continued until he was told Doran's trial had been fixed for the High Court in Glasgow on Monday, 9 October 1989. 'We'll want you to come over no later than the day before,' they told him.

There were those in Glasgow who were disappointed and dismayed at the prospect of Brian Doran, the one-time highly regarded and respected modern languages teacher at St Margaret's High School in Airdrie, facing a long stretch behind bars. But even greater was the sympathy being felt for Mary – they met while she was teaching there – especially after all the humiliations heaped on her in the past by her husband's roving eye. And had not their children suffered? Weren't they being punished unfairly for the crimes of their father? It may have been just those who felt sufficiently in unison with the Doran family who were determined to take positive steps and end the misery.

Five days before the trial was due to open, George Duncan arrived home from work to be told by Rosa he had visitors.

'Who?' he asked.

'They'll tell you themselves.'

'What do they want?'

'They didn't say but asked to speak to you in private.'

'Where are they?'

'In the park at the end of the road, waiting.'

'Didn't they want to wait in the house?'

'No, they were very polite but said they'd prefer if I wasn't involved in what they had to say.'

'Male or female?'

'You'll see.'

George Duncan went out to meet his unexpected visitors. He was surprised by their identities but not wholly by what they had to say. The conversation lasted less than an hour. During it, he was offered £110,000 not to appear at Doran's trial. He reiterated to them what he had told a friend in the past – that he had determined years earlier not to be a witness against Brian – and he explained why he had reached this conclusion. The visitors pointed out that he might still change his mind at the last minute and fly to Glasgow, but he was adamant, he had made up his mind and would not alter his stance. They also noted, unnecessarily, that £110,000 was a lot of money: when the police arrived to take Duncan to Scotland, as they undoubtedly would, it would guarantee him the means of being elsewhere. His guests did not look unduly disappointed when they left, refusing his offer of a meal, saying they felt they had to get back to Scotland. Duncan had suspected that something of this nature would occur from the moment he had received the telephone call from Ronnie Edgar saying Brian Doran had been recaptured. He was not surprised at the offer of so much money not to appear at the forthcoming Doran trial. What he found funny was that he was being offered a fortune to take a course of action he had already committed himself to. Why lose out by speaking up?

The awaited call from the police arrived, as he had known it would. But his wife had been well primed and told them she and George had split up and he was working away from home. Under pressure, she agreed he should telephone reasonably regularly and promised to pass on a message to him to ring Glasgow at the first opportunity. When he did not, the officers flew over to Amsterdam. It was Saturday and the trial would begin promptly on the Monday morning. They desperately needed their vital witness and sought collaboration from police in Amsterdam, who called Rosa with an instruction that she was to make sure George rang the city headquarters. He did, and a young Dutch inspector told him, 'You must come to the police station. This is something that cannot be discussed on the telephone. It is most important that we have a word with you.'

To stall for time he agreed to a rendezvous the following evening at 7 p.m., saying he was working on a contract with a harsh penalty clause attached if it was not completed in time. He was told to finish his work and then come in, but advised, 'Make sure you do. This is important.' That meant a day the police couldn't afford to lose had now been wasted.

He never had any intention of attending the meeting, at which he knew he would be handed a citation ordering him to attend court in Glasgow. Once it was in his possession, he had to comply otherwise he would be in contempt of court. This meant that on further visits to see friends and family at home he would get no further than passport control at Glasgow airport before being huckled off to the nearest police station in handcuffs. So, instead he used a coin box to make a telephone call to the inspector. 'It's George Duncan.'

'George, why aren't you here? The arrangement was for a meeting at seven.'

'I'm still at work,' he lied.

'OK, we'll wait.'

'Out of the question, it will be too late.'

'Well, why not come in tomorrow?'

'What's this all about?'

'Come in and we'll explain.'

'Listen, inspector, you have two police officers from the city of Glasgow sitting opposite you in your office right now. Put one of them on the phone.'

'George, it's Ronnie Edgar. Where are you?'

'Ronnie, I'm not coming in. I cannot get time off work. You think I am a yo-yo at the end of your string, but I have done my time and you have a statement from me. I won't be there in the morning to back you up.'

He rang off, chuckling to himself and reckoning that as far as the police were concerned the penny had dropped. He was deliberately stalling and had no intention of going to Glasgow to be a witness for the prosecution. At the same time, he knew the matter would not end there. Ronnie Edgar was an old-style cop whose motto was 'We always get our man', and now there was a chance his quarry, Doran, was going to get off lightly because the main witness was not going to show. He had wanted the police to know he had fucked them, and now, having conveyed that message, realised they would be furious. He had been tempted to say to Ronnie, 'I know you're upset, take an Alka-Seltzer,' but wisely did not do so. The game of wills had yet to be played out.

Next morning, as Glasgow awoke, four Dutch police officers arrived at Rosa's door with their Scottish colleagues. Angry and afraid, she telephoned George.

'The police have been here and have put a letter through the door. The letter is from the police in Glasgow. It's a citation.'

'Rosa, throw it back into the street.'

She did so, but minutes later there was a loud knock at the door. When she opened it, she was handed a letter. She rang her husband again.

'What do I do now?'

'Throw it back into the street and if they call again tell them I no longer live there.'

293

She followed his instructions, but it was clear the police were not giving up. They had waited more than seven years since when Doran went on the run and were determined that when they flew back into Glasgow, the chief witness would be with them. They had worked long and hard and would not risk their case being weakened.

'George?'

'Yes, Rosa.'

'The police are still outside the house.'

'Don't worry, leave it to me.'

He telephoned a relative of his wife's in Utrecht and told him, 'Go up to the house and the next time they put the letter through or hand it to anyone, tear it up and throw it into the street so the Dutch police will clearly see I haven't received or read it.'

Two hours later, the telephone jangled. It was Rosa to say the police had finally left.

On the aircraft taking him back to Glasgow, Doran had cursed when Ronnie Edgar had refused to allow him a drink. But that anger was nothing when compared with the fury of Edgar at his failure to persuade Duncan to travel to Scotland for the trial. His evidence was crucial and, in the eyes of the police, overwhelming in the more serious allegation of trafficking in cocaine, a charge that had earned Tait four years. Now, without him, there was no real likelihood of the prosecution succeeding. There had been frustration, too, at the fact that the Dutch police believed their own hands were tied by legislation barring them from actively supporting their Scottish colleagues.

27

WEEPING WHACKO

Dust had gathered on the court papers during the long
wait for the trial of Brian Doran, but even now, as the pink
ribbon around them was being untied, it almost did not
go ahead. Doran thought himself lucky to have secured
Donald Findlay QC, widely thought then, and still now,
to be the top criminal lawyer in the country, to defend
him, but Mr Findlay was heavily committed to another
trial that had overrun considerably. At the eleventh hour,
he had to stand down from the happy dust case. Doran
must have felt the odds stacked against him for, if that was
not bad enough, when he tried getting his trial postponed
for a month to allow Mr Findlay to be there, the request
was thrown out. It seemed a strange decision, implying
haste in settling a matter that had been in abeyance for
such a long time. The Faculty of Advocates, realising the
unfair position in which this left Whacko, asked another
eminent silk, Alexander Philip, to help the accused man,
but this offer was turned down, Doran arguing, with some
justification, that a month was not long enough in which
to brief a replacement counsel. This left the legal system
in an embarrassing quandary. It was not Doran's fault he

found himself in the position of a goalkeeper under attack from a well-drilled team and with no centre-half to protect him. Yet it was he who came up with a solution: he would defend himself.

The antiquated judicial set-up meant only recognised advocates could speak in the High Courts, unless an accused was given permission by the judge to conduct his own defence. There were many who believed this was but a form of self-protection for members of a very well-paid section of the legal profession. It certainly ruled out many brilliant solicitors from actively and publicly doing a better job of representing clients. The problem now was that Doran – an intelligent man perhaps but one at a definite, and possibly decisive, disadvantage when it came to arguing legal points – was the equivalent of a draughts player facing a chess master. The eventual solution was to allow his lawyer, Robert McCormack, to sit in court and pass on advice when it was requested. It was a bizarre situation and one that did the legal system no credit whatsoever.

Doran pleaded not guilty to three charges. The initial two had seen the downfall of Andrew Tait, alleging firstly that he was involved in smuggling cocaine into Scotland between December 1980 and March 1982 through ferry terminals at Sheerness, Hull, Dover and Harwich and alternatively that he came into possession of the drug after it had been brought into the United Kingdom illegally; and secondly that he supplied cocaine or was involved in its supply to a number of people in Glasgow between the same dates. In the third charge, he was accused that 'being conscious of his guilt, he absconded and fled from justice and failed to appear for trial at the High Court in Glasgow on the 11th April 1983'.

If some in the public gallery experienced a sense of déjà vu, it was no surprise. For many of the witnesses were the same ones who had helped condemn Tait and there was a familiar ring about their versions of what had transpired.

Alan Bartlett admitted he had used cocaine at his

luxury flat in Hyndland. Had he ever received anything from Brian Doran, the Advocate Depute Alexander Wylie, wanted to know? 'Cocaine,' was his reply. When asked how many times, he responded with 'Two or three.' The advocate depute continued, asking if Doran had ever sold him cocaine. 'Once, in mid-1981 I was sold a gramme for £50 or £60,' Bartlett said.

Had Doran ever given him the drug for free?

'Once, in Charlie Parker's.'

Had he ever bought cocaine from George Duncan? He replied that at about the end of 1981, Doran said Duncan was coming from Holland with cocaine and George met up with Doran and Tait at The Pantry before all three moved on to the Highburgh Road flat where he bought 20 grammes from Duncan for £1,000.

Had he used the drug, Mr Wylie asked.

'Some of it, usually sniffed through a £5 note.'

The judge, Lord Murray, then asked if a £10 note or £1 note could be used?

'Yes, but not a £1 coin,' Bartlett replied.

He then spoke of the night he had been arrested. Doran left cocaine at the flat, said he was off for a haircut and would be back in a couple of hours. Later, he was asked during a telephone call from either Doran or Tait, he could not recall which, to give two grammes each to two customers, one of them the broadcaster Tom Ferrie. Doran never returned; instead it was the police who called.

His version was challenged by Doran, who was allowed to cross-examine Bartlett, and accused him of 'telling porky pies', himself suggesting the cocaine had been left by a 'Thomas Jackson'. The fruit-and-vegetable businessman further rejected a claim he had done a deal with police to get a light sentence in exchange for incriminating Doran.

Ferrie said he had made a radio programme about heroin use and decided to follow it with one on the theme of cocaine. 'I spoke to a number of people in the city and eventually made contact with Brian Doran,' he said. The accused man, with whom he had booked holidays, handed him a piece of folded magazine paper, he explained. When he opened it up, there was a white powder inside, which he flushed down a toilet. Doran had given him the powder for free, but he bought similar packages from Tait at his bakery and from Alan Bartlett, in both cases also throwing the powder into a toilet bowl.

'Was it not a strange way to carry out an investigation, by flushing the evidence down the toilet?' Doran wanted to know.

'I had enough for my purpose. I was going on the premise that it was cocaine.'

But, the judge asked, could it have been bicarbonate of soda?

'Yes,' replied Ferrie.

Tait said he spoke to Doran about knowing of a man in Holland who could get cocaine and the travel agency boss told him to call him and 'get it'. Three weeks later, George Duncan had arrived with 100 grammes. After being tested, it was hidden in his shop and paid for as a result of the three men – Bartlett, Tait and Doran – chipping in £1,500 each. When he had sold the drug, the three men shared some of the proceeds, using the rest to buy more happy dust. In the months that had followed, more cocaine had come over from Holland, but he did not know how much he had bought or paid for it. 'I was using it myself at the time, snorting it through rolled-up £5 notes.'

The big man looked a shadow of the smart, confident playboy whose company had once been so sought after by the Glasgow jet set. Now, the one-time supplier of the Ibrox pies looked crestfallen, especially when he had to describe himself as the 'former' owner of The Pantry. Asked by his ex-Happy Dust Gang colleague, 'Is it true that despite knowing you were guilty, you pleaded not guilty?', he replied, 'Yes, I maintained I was innocent to try to stay out of prison.'

The courtroom was hushed when Doran began giving evidence. His story was the one most of those present had waited many years to hear and his version of what had happened was very different from that of the others. He told the jury that when Duncan and Sim heard he was facing charges over the activities of the Happy Dust Gang, a meeting was arranged between himself and Duncan who offered to pin the blame on somebody else to get off. Their asking price was £15,000, but he refused and told the police about the proposal. He heard nothing more and went off to Spain on holiday with his family. While they were there, his lawyer telephoned with news that shocked him. The police, he was told, intended charging him with trying to pervert the course of justice.

'After speaking to my lawyer on the phone, I decided to stay on in Spain and not go back for the trial because I felt that for some reason the police were out to get me,' he said. 'They were trying to frame me. I admit freely that I used cocaine but purely on a social basis and never took money for it.'

By giving evidence, he was open to cross-examination by the advocate depute, during which he maintained that Tait and the police had lied. 'At no time did I ever supply drugs for money. I would never have dreamed of charging anyone for cocaine. It was like taking someone to a restaurant for a meal. It is not something you take money for. It is between friends.' At Alan Bartlett's home, he snorted cocaine with friends. 'I would put my cocaine on the table and anyone who wanted could have some. Others did the same. It was like a gang hut in a childish sense.'

'A den?' asked Lord Murray.

'Yes, my lord, but not of iniquity,' he replied.

That little exchange produced laughter but in the hours that followed, Doran was in tears, openly weeping as he begged the jury not to find him guilty. 'I have been away from my wife and family for more than six years. All I ask is the opportunity to return home to them. You may ask yourselves why, when I had done nothing wrong, I did not just return to Scotland to face my accusers. The answer is simply that I did not want to have to sit idly and uselessly in Barlinnie prison for 110 days before I was given the chance to prove my innocence. I went to Holland from Spain to learn if there was a way in which I could legally return to this country and live once again with my family, but in Holland I was arrested. I was brought to Scotland and what happened? I was forced to sit in Barlinnie for almost 110 days before being given the opportunity to tell my side of the story. Now, it is within your grasp to fulfil that dream of togetherness for us.'

His tears did win over some of the jury members because it was only by a majority verdict that they found him guilty of supplying cocaine. The charge of absconding was dropped and on the direction of the judge the jury unanimously cleared him of importing the drug. Doran waited nervously as the judge shuffled through his papers, examined his notes and looked solemn.

Two minutes later, he was heading down the steps from the dock to the cells below, a sentence of two years ringing in his ears. It could have been considerably worse. It had been backdated to his arrest in Holland in February 1989, which meant that as he would be required to serve only two-thirds of the sentence – provided he behaved himself in jail – he would be freed in June 1990.

In jail, Doran was bitter at the outcome of the case. 'I never took money for cocaine from anyone,' he maintained. 'Others might have been out to make a profit, but I gave it away. This is how those I thought were my friends have repaid me. This is the trouble with being successful. Once you have climbed the ladder, so many want to see you toppled.'

Few were listening. They had heard it all before: every hard-luck story going, every frame-up, every lying witness, every bent policeman, every jury incapable of understanding the simplest of facts. In fact, most were surprised at his being sent down only for two years, especially bearing in mind the cost of keeping tabs on his movements during the years he had been on the run. And there were those whose many experiences with the law had left them considering themselves somewhat expert on the subject. They pointed to the comment of Lord Ross when he had jailed Tait in 1983: 'I accept that Doran played a major role and yours was subordinate.' Surely that was an indication that if and when Doran was apprehended, he would be in for much more severe treatment, being classed as the worse of the pair. But Lord Murray said the jury had convicted Doran of the same charge for which Tait had been jailed for two years and he would impose the same sentence. No mention was made of his learned colleague's observation.

It was purely coincidental that at the same time as Whacko was pleading with the jury for mercy, in an adjoining courtroom in the same building another jury was hearing the consequences of a different cocaine deal. Five men were accused of murdering Bristol drug courier Paul Thorne on bleak Fenwick Moor, south of Glasgow. He had delivered £30,000 worth of heroin and cocaine in October 1988, was treated to a fish supper, then forced to trudge across the moor carrying a spade and dig his own grave before being blasted in the back of the head. A mattress was dumped over the body and the spot filled in. Thorne's body has never been found. Twenty-four-year-old Glasgow hardman John Paul McFadyen was sentenced to life for the murder and to a total of 47 years for other drug offences. Spaniard Ricardo Blanco, 26, a former Foreign Legion soldier, was ordered to spend 15 years behind bars. Underworld gossip had it that Thorne had been attempting to steal some of the consignment he was paid to take to Scotland, then sell it and keep the proceeds. His assassination was carried out as a warning to others not to mess around. No one would ever know the truth. The Happy Dust Gang had operated on what was, at first, a friendly basis, which had then turned sour. At least the enmity that followed had not resulted in his having to dig his own grave, even if Doran, for one, felt he had been buried by those he looked on as friends.

As Doran was settling down to prison life, the telephone was ringing in the home of George Duncan. Unthinking, he picked it up.

'George Duncan.'

'Hello, George,' said a familiar voice, one he recognised from a Glasgow police station and elsewhere. 'Are you back with your wife again?'

'Yes, but what do you want?'

'Heard about your old pal Brian Doran?'

'No, why?'

'Found guilty.'

'What did he get? I know the police reckoned he could be looking at a 12.'

'Two years. He only got two fucking years.'

'Two years? That's bad enough.'

'He got two years because the main witness stayed away. How much did he pay you, George?'

'Listen. It was the police who wanted to get Doran, not me. I have put all that behind me. The Happy Dust Gang is in the past, long gone. The Brian Doran story ended with me years ago. I told the police that if they wanted me to come to Glasgow, they had to get in touch with me and give me sufficient time to make the proper arrangements. But they didn't do that. Instead, they turned up on my doorstep and expected me to drop everything immediately. If it went wrong, then that's the responsibility of the police, not me. I'm just not responsible any more. I've had no contact with Brian Doran. The police fucked up their own case because they wouldn't listen.'

He hung up, turned to Rosa and told her, 'You know, I've never felt so good in my life.'

28

LIPSTICK COLLAR

In the years that followed the break-up of the Happy Dust Gang, hundreds of others sought to take advantage of the idea of big-style drug smuggling inspired by the undoubted wealth the racket had created. Some, it was true, succeeded, but most failed. That they did so was because they frequently lacked an appreciation of what had made the gang tick.

The Happy Dust Gang was different from most smuggling groups in that it was made up not of criminals whose mugshots were already held on police records but of men from respectable backgrounds – intelligent, ordinary, outwardly decent businessmen who used their commercial acumen to set up an enterprise that could have made them all millionaires. They had devised a simple but near foolproof system of bypassing Customs and police checks, which had until then been looked on as being so effective. Sadly for them, it was their very success that proved their downfall. So much cocaine had begun flooding Glasgow that it became a talking point, one that inevitably led to the ears of policemen. And while throughout the gang's operation not a blow had been struck in anger, now, as hardened crooks began to enter the field, greed became a factor, disagreements led to violence and that, in turn, also gave clues to the police as to who the players were. Those teams that succeeded did so by and large because their controllers realised violence could not be afforded.

A Glasgow-based gang was using small coaches to transport hashish back to Scotland via Disneyland, Paris. This group would graduate to buying full-scale luxury coaches and raise the floor level to create sufficient space to hide 700 kilos of hashish at a time. As cover, it offered free holidays in luxury hotels on the Costa del Sol and Costa Blanca to first teams of young footballers and then impoverished families. The scam worked for seven years before it was uncovered. In that time, the gang netted almost £50 million and not a punch was thrown. It was a lesson also being heeded back in Spain.

Ten years on from the first days of the Happy Dust Gang, society had been transformed. People were richer now, and had developed a voracious appetite for an escape from the pressures of increasingly demanding employers. Likewise, they needed something to relieve the feeling of boredom that came when they discovered the unattainable was now within reach and that there was little to strive for. That relief came through illicit drugs. Possessing hash had become as near to commonplace as carrying a packet of cigarettes and provided gentle relaxation, but the thrill seekers demanded something stronger and more sensational. And instead of the enchantment of Charlie being limited to the well off, as it had been in the early '80s, the lot of the working classes had so improved it was now within their compass. They had heard how cocaine gave birth to a buzz that would disconnect them from the real world and waft them into Shangri-La, where an unseen genie would give reality to their every desire and fantasy. What they refused to believe was the misery cocaine use brought, the paranoia, the distrust of and secrecy towards even those nearest and dearest, the terror of having to share a final few lines with others, the eternally unfulfilled 'I'll give up tomorrow' pledge.

So it was as Brian Doran walked into the car park of Saughton jail in the western suburbs of Edinburgh early one morning in July 1990 a free man once more. Doran headed back to Glasgow but not to Terregles Avenue. His income at nil, the family had been forced to give up the mansion with its myriad bedrooms and bathrooms and move into a smaller property in Pollokshields. With the help of friends, he opened a business selling stock salvaged from fires and floods until, by a quirk of extraordinary fate, it was wiped out by a mystery blaze. When it seemed his luck could get no worse, it did. In 1991, he was arrested by police in Cambridge investigating allegations of passport application irregularities.

By the following year, he had teamed up with a pal from the past. Kenneth Togher, the younger by 19 years, was originally from Bellshill in Lanarkshire, a town ten miles to the south of Glasgow. But the partnership made an inauspicious start when the pair appeared at Stirling Sheriff Court and admitted fraudulently using a credit card to obtain jewellery, a china pot and lipstick from three local shops. They were fined £100 and ordered to pay £200 compensation to the Trustee Savings Bank. Whacko's lawyer said, 'This is a man down on his luck. He is resolved not to appear in the courts in the future, both as a matter of honour to himself and to his family.'

It was an extraordinary downturn in his fortunes and one that shocked a drug dealer who knew Doran from the past and had briefly spent time with him in Saughton prison: 'One night at the start of the '80s, I walked into Charlie Parker's with a girlfriend and there was Brian, lording it with a company of high rollers and a good-looking blonde at his side. He and she constantly turned and kissed one another lightly. There was nothing secretive about it, but it was strange seeing a married man with a big family acting so openly with another woman. As soon as he saw us, he waved us over and insisted we join them. Everything was on Brian and if he saw your glass was almost empty, he would have it topped up. His generosity was embarrassing to us, but the others seemed to take it for granted. This was at the time when he was running Blue Sky Travel. We all left at the same time – he was going on to a party and invited us, but I was working the next day. "Give me a bell next time you're going on holiday and I'll fix you up with a deal," he said.

'I was in Saughton when we read he had been extradited and a few days after his trial met him. It was hard to believe this was the same man who had been showing his money about in Charlie Parker's and I wondered where all his friends were now, the ones who had sponged from him. A lot of people from good backgrounds who go to prison feel sorry for themselves but not him. His concern was for his family. He felt he'd let them down by not being able to provide for them as well as he had once done. A lot of others wanted to know what he'd been up to in Spain, but Brian was giving nothing away. If you listened between the lines, though, you could tell he had made friends out there who he could turn to.

'After I was released, I bumped into somebody else who'd been in Saughton with us and he said Brian was giving the impression he was going to make a real go of doing something legitimate, but we both felt he had something bigger in mind. He was a very secretive individual, not going out of his way to give offence but making it clear he preferred his own company.'

It was a strange twist of fate that of the Happy Dust Gang the member who had been the richest and most powerful was now skint. Andy Tait, searching in Glasgow for a new opening, might not have been much better off, but he was at least a rung above Whacko. The Bartlett brothers had thrown themselves into a business that was expanding rapidly and proving increasingly successful and profitable. Across the North Sea in Holland, George Duncan was doing well for himself and although estranged from Thomas Sim knew that the other man, who had blown most of his earnings from happy dust, was still earning a good living through a demolition company.

However, while wheels might have come off Doran's wagon, it was still rolling, if only just. Through all his troubles, he had maintained his reputation in the eyes of the Colombians. They remembered his largesse in Marbella and Puerto Banus, and before he made the fateful decision to shift to Amsterdam had given an open invitation for him to contact them at any time. 'We'll be watching for you,' they had promised.

Someone else had promised to watch out for Whacko: El Latigo. The detective had been furious when his quarry was released by a Spanish judge and had defied repeated attempts, even by his superiors, to close the file on the 1987 hash bust. Some of his colleagues felt he had a downer on the British, lumping too many in with the exiles dotted around the Costa del Sol, who, he believed, attracted other lowlives, thereby adding to the problems for the police. But the Scourge would point to dramas, such as the shooting dead in 1987 at his home in Marbella of great train robber Charlie Wilson. It was without question a murder resulting from a drug deal that had gone wrong. One of the suspects, Walter Douglas from Glasgow, had been questioned repeatedly but in each case released without charge. Wattie, known as 'the Tartan Pimpernel' because of the inability of police forces to nab him, had been linked to a series of major drug busts and was wanted by police in Holland. There was one more significant factor that made him of special interest to the Spanish detective: Walter was a close pal of Brian Doran's.

29

EL JOCK

Colombia has two principal claims to fame and neither credits the state whose development has been steeped in violence. First, it locked up the England football captain Bobby Moore and accused him of being a thief. In June 1970, the owner of a jewellery shop in a hotel in Bogotá alleged the player had pocketed an emerald bracelet. The judge who freed the player after three days' detention told him, 'I hope everything goes well for you and that you score many goals.' It did not, and he did not. England, in South America for the World Cup in Mexico, lost the trophy they had won four years earlier and Moore had to wait three months for an embarrassing climbdown by the Colombian authorities.

Second, it is the world's main producer of cocaine. No one knows how many lives have been lost or destroyed as a result of the drug, but one of the best-known victims may be Elvis Presley, who was hooked on drugs, including cocaine, before his death from an overdose in 1977.

The problem caused by Colombia's economic dependence on cocaine was demonstrated in the gangster movie *Scarface* starring Al Pacino, which showed the extraordinary and brutal lengths to which manufacturers of the drug would go to ensure a steady turnover of their produce. In the film, huge amounts of cocaine are shipped to the USA; however, during the 1980s, the cartels running the industry were so perturbed by the efficiency of the United States Coast Guard that they sought to enlarge other avenues. It was natural that Spain should become one of these. Despite the distance, there was a natural affinity between the countries through their similar cultures and, more importantly, language. It did not take the authorities in Spain long to work out that the increasing number of Colombians arriving there had to have some connection with an escalation in the cocaine trade.

Operation Costa, an investigation carried out in 1988 in which police raided thirty-seven Spanish resorts in a two-day sweep for drugs, unearthed six kilos of cocaine. Experts working with Interpol discovered enough evidence to conclude that 40 per cent of the Colombian cocaine circulating in Europe had come through Spain. A year earlier, a major surveillance operation involving police in South America, France and Spain ended with a raid on an abandoned warehouse in the Basque town of Irún in which a staggering one ton of Charlie was recovered – enough to provide 50 million lines.

It was a situation that worried police in Britain. Detective Superintendent Geoff Wood of the National Drugs Intelligence Unit told reporters, 'The American market is saturated, so the cartels are sneaking into Europe through the back door. We are seriously concerned about this foothold.' There was another factor causing the cartels to organise a marketing campaign in Europe: cocaine was in such demand and there was such a shortage that they were able to triple the price and still sell out. The difficulty was that with so much being channelled into Spain the police there were wise to what was happening and began slowly winning the war. In addition, successfully landing the drug in Spain was only part of the battle; it then had to be transported on to other destinations. Each border crossing, each ferry terminal meant one more search and one more chance of discovery. The answer was to ship directly to the country where the drug was to be sold. This method had worked especially well with cargoes to Rotterdam from where much of central Europe could be supplied. But there still remained the huge, untapped demand in the British market.

While Doran was living in exile in Marbella, he received a visit from one of his Glaswegian friends. The men had made regular rounds of bars in the resort, where Whacko had introduced the friend to a Colombian. The South American had been interested in the Happy Dust Gang and wondered how they had managed to get hold of cocaine in Scotland, hardly regarded as one of the world's hotbeds of drug abuse at the time. The visitor, who had from time to time bought Charlie from Andy Tait, explained the ruse dreamed up by George Duncan to fool Customs checks.

'So, your man buys gear in Amsterdam, hides it in a car, drives it over the sea and then someone else brings it to you?' he asked.

'Something like that, only it was slightly more complicated.'

'How so?'

'Well, he used one man to drive the car, but another courier to bring the stuff to Scotland.'

'So how many people altogether?'

'The man in Holland who sold it, the guy who put the Parachutist—'

'The Parachutist?' the Colombian interrupted.

'He was called the Parachutist because he seemed to float in from nowhere.'

'I see.'

'The guy who put the Parachutist in touch with the supplier, the car driver, the courier and the Parachutist himself.'

'Five people. And getting it from Holland?'

'It depended on which ferry they used. But they would go through frontier and Customs checks.'

'And they were never caught at any of these?'

'Never.'

'Why not use a bigger car. Or a lorry and bring in more?'

'It was safer this way. Using a lorry would have meant having to trust a driver and pay him. There would be dozens of cars on each ferry and Customs would hardly want to take each one to pieces. There would have been a riot. As it was, he brought gear over as often as he could.'

'And how much did you pay?'

'I paid between £55 and £60 a gramme, but I gather they were giving it to the Parachutist for about £45.'

'£45 a gramme. That was good business for him.'

'We were happy with it. If it had been necessary to go to London to buy, we would have paid nearly £100 a gramme.'

'Did Brian and the others ever think of buying direct themselves?'

'From the man in Holland?'

'No, the people in Colombia.'

'Well, I suppose they must have thought about it but for the amounts involved it would hardly have been a worthwhile proposition.'

'And the Happy Dust Gang, it had the only cocaine in Scotland?'

'It had the only large quantity of cocaine in Scotland. Others had very tiny amounts, but cocaine only began coming into the country big-style once the gang started.'

'And now?'

'There is cocaine coming through now, but not in large amounts. The police seem to think that having caught the gang they've stopped large-scale smuggling.'

'And is there a demand?'

'Is there a demand? You could sell every gramme of cocaine you managed to get into Scotland ten times over.

They are crying out for it, travelling down to London and Manchester to try buying it.'

'So if someone in Scotland had a very large supply of cocaine, they would make lots of money?'

'A fortune. But where would anyone get a large amount? People are frightened by the risks. There are so many checks the odds are that someone will be caught and then it's prison for a very long time.'

'But what if there were no checks?'

'How do you mean, no checks? There are checks everywhere. At every port, every ferry landing and even the occasional roadside check by the police.'

'What if you took a load of cocaine from Colombia, or Ecuador, or somewhere in that region, put it on a yacht and sailed it directly to Scotland?'

'Where would you land?'

'Anywhere. Take your pick. Aren't there quiet bays in Scotland where a boat can anchor and not attract suspicion.'

'Sure. It could be done. But aren't you forgetting something?'

'What's that?'

'Where does the money come from to buy the yacht and the load?'

'My friend, all things are possible. You heard of buy now, pay later?'

'Of course, but this is out of my league. I'm only a user.'

'Don't worry. It is Brian I was thinking of.'

'You mentioned this to him?'

'Once or twice, but only in passing, he has too many other worries for now. For him it is too risky to go back to Scotland but perhaps in the future.'

'You get on well with Brian?'

'Brian is a good guy, one of the best. He is very well liked and very much trusted. He speaks our language.'

When Doran rejoined his friends, he asked what they had been chatting about.

'Sailing,' said the Colombian.

Later, his Glaswegian visitor recounted the conversation to Doran.

'It's a good idea,' said Whacko. 'But you'd be talking about putting up millions of pounds. You could probably lose a yacht in the English Channel but getting away with sailing one up the coast of Scotland is another matter. It would be sure to be picked up by the coastguards and then you'd have a lot of explaining to do.'

'So take one into somewhere along the south coast of England.'

'That's all very well, but you can't just walk into the territory of guys there, especially in London where you'd need to do most of the business, and start operating. It's just not done. You'd need their permission to deal and there would have to be something in it for them.'

The two did not discuss the matter again, but Doran had built up many contacts in the Costa underworld, including men suspected of stashing away fortunes from crime, and the idea of a direct drugs project nagged and nagged at him. It was still in his mind when he was extradited and jailed. Trying to go straight had left him angry, mainly because he was unable to lavish the good things in life on his family and friends as he had once done in the past, and it was at this time that the idea dragged itself from the back of his memory.

A routine feature of police work is, from time to time, the targeting of men, and very occasionally women, suspected of being behind major crimes. Highly trained teams will monitor targets around the clock, their every movement watched, every meeting shadowed, everyone they meet photographed and identified, their pasts checked out and associates investigated with the intention of discovering a motive for the get-together. Vehicles will be tracked and telephone records subjected to intense scrutiny. Who has been called at what hour? Did something significant take place at that moment, or shortly before or after? Informants

313

will be asked to sniff out the latest gossip concerning a target. What has he been talking about? Have connections come into money? Has he discussed going on holiday and, if so, where? More often than not, nothing out of the ordinary concerning the suspect will come to light, in which case the scrutiny will move to another career criminal. But when a man widely regarded as being in the premiere crime league is suddenly no longer around, then police want to know why. Has he fallen foul of a rival and been wasted, or has he chosen to disappear from the face of the earth? So it was in 1992 when Whacko vanished into thin air after his court appearance in Stirling. Where was he?

The police guessed, with some logic, that Doran had returned to Spain. Maybe he had been attracted back to Marbella by the many friends and contacts he had made there while on the run and by the lure of the cocaine pumping into the country. Perhaps there was a girlfriend waiting for him there.

An intelligence operative who had studied Whacko's file flew to the Costa del Sol and began asking questions, but he was soon to send back a blank report to his superiors and was recalled. As a gesture of thanks for his efforts, his bosses decided, in a moment of black humour, that he was to fill an opening that had come up for an officer to train with counterparts in Colombia, learning how the cocaine cartels operated, their methods of smuggling and how they established connections in Europe. He flew to South America in 1993.

Two weeks after arriving, he telephoned one of his gaffers. 'Doran. I know where he is.'

'Spain?'

'No, the fucker's here.'

'In Colombia? You must be kidding.'

'No way, he's been over here for months.'

'You sure?'

'Positive.'

'How can you be so certain?'

'The police here have been talking about a guy they call El Jock. Nobody could understand his accent until somebody who'd had a drink with him found he was from Scotland.'

'And?'

'They don't know his name, but I got them to describe him. Balding, wears glasses, between 45 and 50.'

'Fucking hell, that's him.'

'Even better.'

'How do you mean? They didn't say he was from the Happy Dust Gang did they?'

'Not quite, but close; one of the guys I'm doing liaison with said he looked like Groucho Marx without the stoop.'

'Hell, the chances of you, of all people, coming across him must be a million to one. What's our friend up to?'

'I don't know nor do the people here, but it must be to do with cocaine, and lots of it. The cartels wouldn't be interested in somebody looking for 100 grammes. Apparently, they've been laying out the red carpet for him.'

'Who has he been seeing?'

'They think the Ochoa people and that would fit. He got to know one of the crowd when he was on the run. And he speaks the lingo.'

'Where is he now?'

'He was somewhere around Bogotá.'

'For fuck sake, don't lose him.'

'Stop worrying, just keep watching the flights.'

'OK.'

'And something else.'

'Yes?'

'He's apparently mentioned somebody called Kenny a few times in company.'

'Who's Kenny?'

'I reckon it is Kenneth Togher, the guy he was in court with.'

'Is he there?'

'Don't think so. Might be an idea for you to track him down.'

315

Discovering the whereabouts of Doran was the most incredible stroke of luck and it was one the authorities were determined to milk dry. Investigations by the Colombian authorities, officially at odds with the cartels, revealed he was not merely in the country on a flying visit but had been there for some months and appeared to have no intention of leaving. They were convinced he was there for a specific purpose, perhaps to set up a major cocaine coup, and in the mean time act as an adviser to the producers on the situation in Europe. But was he alone or had a new version of the Happy Dust Gang been born?

30

PEEPING TOMS

Like a schoolboy not wishing to attract the attention of his headmaster, Doran kept his head down in Colombia. And the more he did so, the more police in Britain became worried. Was he on the payroll of one of the cartels, or had he teamed up with others to set up a one-off deal that would hit the jackpot? No one seemed to know. Until another remarkable fluke provided the likely answer.

In March 1993, a new nightclub, Rhapsody, was opened in Glasgow. Nothing unusual about that until a police informant spotted one of the guests, Kenneth Togher, with a beautiful girl on his arm, the pair looking like a couple fresh from millionaires' row. Again, nothing out of the ordinary. Or was there? The informant knew Togher and remembered that when he last saw him, just a few months earlier, he had been struggling to break even running a car sales business. Now here he was, wearing a Versace shirt and designer clothes that made heads turn, sporting expensive jewellery and with a stunner for company. Sudden apparent wealth is a trigger for suspicion.

The informant rang his handler in the Scottish Crime Squad.

'Kenneth Togher,' he told him.

'Who?'

'Kenny Togher. Remember a few weeks ago he and Brian Doran were nicked over some credit-card bother?'

'I remember Doran, why, what's happened?'

'Kenny's suddenly rich.'

'Tell me.'

And the snout did.

Suddenly, the jigsaw began falling into place. The natural guess would be that if Togher, or anyone else for that matter, had suddenly become wealthy with no evident sign of where the money was coming from, then the source was probably drugs. Togher had evidently teamed up with Doran. He was in Colombia, or at least he was the last time police sounded out the Bogotá authorities, believed to be either setting up a drugs deal or working with one of the cocaine cartels, almost certainly that headed by the notorious Ochoa family. And 'Kenny' was one of the names that had cropped up in his conversations. It was enough for police to decide they needed to know more about Doran's new associate and his beautiful brunette girlfriend who had moved in with him within weeks of their first date. One of their priorities was to photograph Togher – and he was discreetly snapped during a visit to a Glasgow club with the girl. The second was to pass on the information to the National Drug Intelligence Unit.

Czech-born Madeleine Mullin had moved to Scotland as a child with her parents, who spared no expense in trying to give their daughter the best possible start to life. She was privately educated at Wellington School for Girls in Ayr where she left to attend the Royal Scottish Academy of Music and Drama in Glasgow. Shortly after enrolling, she was on a night out with friends in Glasgow's Tunnel club where Togher introduced himself. She was 21 and immediately attracted by this smooth-talker who appeared wealthy and popular. He soon made it clear he was not just besotted by her but desperate to put his money where his thoughts lay.

From the first moment of their meeting, he made it plain he adored her and she, in turn, worshipped him. Madeleine confided to a friend, 'He's wonderful and outrageous at the same time, totally charismatic. I can't believe he would look twice at someone like me.'

When her mother, Libuse, a doctor, asked what he did for a living, she told her he was a car dealer who also owned property, which he rented out. 'He'll end up hurting you,' her mother warned. But the lovers became inseparable and she moved into his home on the banks of Loch Lomond, with his favourite red Porsche parked outside and a fortune in cash stored inside. He spent endlessly, treating her to shopping expeditions. She would return to a five-star hotel her arms heavy with bags labelled with Bond Street addresses and filled with new clothing and jewellery.

She also discovered he had a voracious appetite for sex, encouraging her to dress in revealing outfits and even buying her a £10,000 Harley Davidson motorcycle on which they made love. Madeleine was not to know it but soon others would be taking a keen interest in her.

As lady luck had played her part for the Scottish police, she had yet one more ace to deal for another arm of the forces of law and order. Like the police, Customs and Excise take a keen interest in lawbreakers. As a branch of the Treasury, one of their many roles is the collection of various taxes and to ensure the government is not cheated of its dues from Mr and Mrs Public. Officers are keen, for example, to make sure that UK citizens returning from holidays abroad do not try robbing the Chancellor, who gives what he sees as generous concessions in the amounts and values of various goods that can be brought home free of the duty. Hence random pounces by Customs men, which often expose those attempting to sneak in an extra bottle of Scotch or packet of filter-tipped cigarettes. Those miffed by having their bank balance cleared or family car confiscated as a result of this zeal will be reminded that they are smugglers – on a tiny scale perhaps, but smugglers nevertheless. And the game revenue men track with the greatest enthusiasm is smuggling. Like the police, the organisation will sporadically mount a campaign to unveil what the suspected smugglers-in-chief are up to.

So it was that in July 1993, the Customs and Excise National Investigation Service began Operation Stealer to monitor major players in the drugs trade. One of the targets was to be Anthony White, a near legend among underworld figures in south London. He had been acquitted of involvement ten years earlier in an infamous bullion robbery from the Brinks-Mat warehouse at Heathrow airport in which a reputed £26 million was stolen. White, quiet-spoken, pleasant to neighbours and a good dad to his two children, lived modestly, evidently from the profits of his Catford pub appropriately named Blanco's. He always denied being one of the Brinks-Mat gang but as the money never turned up, when he was sued by the company insuring the victims, despite the court finding him innocent, he was ordered to pay up the full sum. There were those who wondered what a man might do with his share of £26 million tucked away. It could not be banked without bringing down a heap of official trouble, but it might be invested and give the sort of return for which a dealer in equities would cheerfully sell his soul to the devil. Buying and selling drugs involved risks but offered astronomical profits.

Within a month of the Operation Stealer file being opened, the rapidly expanding team of investigators had its first break. All known associates of White came under the umbrella of scrutiny, among them armed robber John Short and Robert Parsons, who assisted in the running of Blanco's. In August 1993, Parsons had dinner with a stranger in a Kent restaurant. The two men might have wondered why those around them were so silent, evidently more interested in listening than chatting, but then their fellow diners were Customs officers intently trying to pick up every scrap of conversation. Among the mundane and predictable, they overheard a name: Brian Doran. Back in their offices, checks on Whacko soon led back to Togher and the photograph taken earlier while out with Madeleine confirmed he was the man in the restaurant with Parsons.

What was going on? Logic dictated that Doran, still out in Colombia, had access to huge amounts of cocaine. White, suspected of having access to more than enough money to fund a major deal, had connections to a criminal network that could easily distribute and market the drug. Had the two chiefs left it to their right-hand men to sort out the detail? There were further get-togethers between Togher and Parsons. The two strolled through the Tate Gallery, visited London Zoo, shared drinks and meals, sometimes with Madeleine joining them, in exclusive hotels and backstreet pubs.

At this stage, it was time to introduce the cloak-and-dagger brigade. Financial checks on banks and financial institutions, who were reminded in no uncertain terms of the draconian powers of the Revenue and the penalties for what might be interpreted as obstruction, had revealed vast amounts of money being exchanged between Togher and Doran.

In September 1993, Togher and Madeleine arrived at Edinburgh airport for a flight to Gatwick. After checking in their luggage, they went off to enjoy a drink while waiting for their flight to be called, not bothering to watch their luggage as it headed along a little conveyor belt running behind the check-in desks before vanishing through rubber curtains. They expected it to be immediately met by loaders, who would heave it onto a trailer prior to being taken out to their aircraft. Of course, the bags did eventually arrive at their destination, but on the way were diverted into an office and carefully opened; inside £250,000 in cash was discovered. The haul was photographed and the luggage closed and locked, and when the couple arrived at Gatwick there it was in the baggage reclaim section.

Careful though the team had been, they would wonder if they had missed some safeguard placed by Togher in the luggage to detect its being searched because the following month they monitored him as he bought sophisticated scanning equipment that would tell him if his telephones were being tapped, and his car, hotel rooms or home bugged. It was a sensible precaution, but it could not tell him if meetings were observed, conversations overheard, guests and their backgrounds investigated. Had it been able to do so, it would have warned him that in December the participants at a crucial meeting had been photographed – he and the others involved were well and truly in the spider's web.

Midway through the month, Doran flew back to London to spend Christmas with Mary and the children in Glasgow. He had been looking forward for months to the reunion, but it needed to be placed on hold for another week. Togher met him at Heathrow, the two looking simply like old business pals reunited after a long absence and with lots to discuss. Much as they might have wished to be alone, they were not at any time. The surveillance team was never more than a few yards away. The Scots had booked into a Swallow hotel in south-west London and it was there the Customs team found out for certain what they had until then suspected. Proof that whatever Doran was planning involved White came when the Londoner, accompanied by Parsons, turned up for a meeting with Doran and Togher. It was clear the two chiefs were no strangers, giving weight to the theory that what was being planned had been proposed many moons earlier before Doran vanished to Colombia. It was a moment of triumph for the Operation Stealer squad, many of whom were booked into the same hotel to keep an eye on the targets.

But just when it appeared all the months of planning and personal sacrifice had paid off, the key investigators running the operation made what would turn out to be a fatal bungle. While Togher and Madeleine were out, Customs officers used a set of master keys to secretly enter their room. They made an intimate search but could find nothing incriminating. This was only an incidental part of the exercise, however, because before they left they had installed a hidden camera and a series of listening devices that would relay to a receiver in an adjoining room every word and every sigh made by the couple. If they listened to television, talked about the day's events or even made love, every sound, every inflection, intonation and modulation would be recorded. Bugging is a common enough practice among the security services, though written permission is required, sometimes at ministerial level depending upon the nature of the invasion into the sanctity of privacy. As the specialists quietly tested their equipment with a colleague operating the receiving device, they congratulated themselves on a job well done. It would be a costly piece of work.

Meanwhile another team unlocked the door to Whacko's room, hoping to find evidence to provide concrete links to White. They would later claim to have discovered £10,000 in cash, a Cartier watch and details of bank transfers to Colombia.

That Christmas was a happy one for the Dorans, although there was not much cheer for the team of shadows. A group had to follow Brian to Glasgow, where they monitored the family during a round of church services and visits to relatives and friends, and then tag along as he flew back to London in January 1994. It soon became evident that whatever he had been working to set up in Colombia had been achieved for instead of heading back to South America, Doran went house-hunting in London along with Togher, both ultimately settling for flats in the Chelsea area and then leasing part of a BMW showroom to use as an office.

Just as over a decade earlier, the police in Glasgow had been convinced large amounts of cocaine were coming into the city but had been unable to track the route used; now, the Customs team was again certain a huge shipment of drugs was about the enter the UK any day: the problem was where and how. The monitoring of Togher and Doran was intensified. Togher and Madeleine were spotted meeting a man who would later be identified as Joseph Tanner. He too joined the band being watched. Checks with airlines showed Tanner was booked on a flight to Madrid, so a female officer was detailed to travel with him with orders not to let him out of her sight. Her brief was to see if he collected drugs and to find out how they would be brought back to Britain. The signs were that a smuggling route was about to be tested. Was it to enable cocaine shipped to Spain to then cross the Channel and be sold on to addicts in the south of England? The Customs controllers, out of courtesy and because they might need their help at any time, rang detectives in the Spanish capital to tell them what was happening and were promised members of the Madrid drug squad would keep a discreet eye on what happened. They warned though that if there seemed any likelihood of Tanner vanishing with drugs then they would have to arrest him. It was a stance with which the UK officers could not argue.

So far, all had gone smoothly. Unaware of how much he was interesting a woman he had never met or heard of, Tanner arrived in Madrid and headed to the city railway station, where he waited for a train from Málaga. Out stepped a Colombian couple, who handed him a suitcase. Tanner headed into the city centre and booked into a hotel. The female operative was in an impossible position – Tanner might remain in the hotel for days and there was no way she could, on her own, keep round-the-clock checks on his movements – so she called her bosses in London, who decided the Spanish police should take over. They did and in his room discovered 35 kilos of cocaine and 100 kilos of cannabis hidden in an air-conditioning duct. It was an expensive blow to the smugglers.

In an episode filled with coincidences, one more highlighted the fine line between the rich rewards success brings smugglers and the bleak price of failure. At the time the Colombian pair were boarding the train for the fateful journey from Málaga, a VW Golf was leaving the resort behind a Ford Escort. Both cars were packed with hashish, the Golf carrying more than 100 kilos. There were two Glaswegians in each car. They drove north, but at the border with France the Escort was pulled over and searched. When nothing was found, the two men were allowed to continue. Both cars were destined for Disneyland in Paris, where, under the cover of night in a car park at the Davy Crockett Ranch complex, the illicit cargoes were transferred into a waiting hired bus while its youthful passengers, teenagers from the Glasgow area, slept soundly. Had it ended there, the journey would have been a success, but the cars had fetched only half the waiting load. More hashish was waiting in Málaga.

The passenger in the Escort got cold feet after the stop and search scare, and refused to return, so his place was taken by a young Glaswegian woman. Both vehicles made it back to Málaga, where they were again loaded up but at the French border their luck was out. Both were stopped and seized, and all four occupants arrested. The three men were each jailed for three and a half years. The girl walked off from a hostel where she had been ordered to remain, her passport confiscated, and caught a train to Charles de Gaulle airport outside Paris, where a friend met her and handed her a passport belonging to a lookalike friend. That night, she was back home in Glasgow in time to read about a huge drugs haul in a Madrid hotel room.

If Tanner's arrest was a blow to the gang, there would at least be some good news soon with which to soften it. In March, Madeleine told Togher he would be a father at the end of the year. She would tell friends, 'Kenny is ecstatic. He can't wait.'

A month later there were shades of the earlier confrontation between Duncan, Tait and Doran on Byres Road. As he had waited for his friend George that day, Robert Bruce had been photographed eating an ice cream. This time it was an undercover Customs investigator who now came into the picture licking a cornet as a rendezvous was recorded. As he sat on the steps of the Tate Gallery enjoying the ice cream in the spring sunshine, Togher and Doran were spotted meeting a group of men that included convicted armed robber George Caccavale, a hard-case Londoner, and Terence Reeves, one of his associates. Reeves had joined the growing list of criminals under surveillance. He was later spotted in a pie shop in Kent closely examining a map of South America. One of Reeves's friends was Robin Sargent, the skipper of luxury catamaran the *Frugal*. He had served a prison term after being caught with cannabis. And where was the *Frugal* now? A few days after the Tate Gallery meeting, it had sailed from British waters with Sargent in charge. It would eventually turn up in the Caribbean, but it would be nine months before it came home. There was no doubt in the minds of the team of eavesdroppers about what the catamaran would be used for.

Customs already had experience of a near identical plot and so the Stealer team got in touch with colleagues in Scotland who had worked on Operation Klondyke. During 1989 and 1990, Customs investigators were convinced a Scottish-based gang was setting up a huge drugs-smuggling network. The plotters had assembled in Málaga, then set off to South America in a merchant ship, the *Dimar B*, where it hove to off the coast of Colombia and waited while a light aircraft dropped bales of cocaine into the sea around it. With the cache on board, the vessel headed back across the Atlantic. Off the north coast of Scotland, the smugglers took to an inflatable dinghy and in atrocious weather sailed the drugs ashore, landing them in Clashnessie Bay in Sutherland. In January 1991, as the drugs were prepared to begin their trip south to London, a sharp-eyed police sergeant spotted a suspect van near Ullapool. It was stopped and inside were 500 kilos of cocaine, said to have a street value of £100 million. The Scot widely believed to have masterminded the plot is still at large, although his cohorts served long jail sentences. Now another drama was unfolding, this time with a different cast, but the gamekeepers were determined to repeat the earlier success of their colleagues.

In April 1994, Doran and his friends suddenly shifted their operations to the south of France. He paid £37,000 in cash to hire a plush villa on the outskirts of Nice and shortly after arriving John Short became his first visitor. Anthony White was already in the area and Togher joined the group, leasing a villa and paying £240,000 for a yacht berthed in Ibiza on which he and Madeleine would party with friends. It seemed the gang were simply enjoying the sunshine, or at least wanted to give that impression – while for the investigators maintaining the surveillance meant hard, hot work.

In June, they spotted Short as he caught a flight to Bogotá and wondered if he was taking advantage of the contacts set up with the cartels in Colombia by Doran. He stayed just two weeks before flying back to London. Six weeks later in early August, Doran and White climbed into Togher's Mercedes and the three set off, heading north. They were followed for 200 miles to a bank in Geneva, Switzerland, where discreet inquiries showed White had an account in a fake name.

The following month, Customs officers pounced. They seized a lorry at Fleet Services on the M3 motorway near Portsmouth and discovered cannabis worth £250,000 stuffed into a tyre, while on 25 September they first discovered 22 kilos of cocaine under a false floor of a Mini van that was stopped as it drove off the Calais to Dover ferry. In France, officers shadowing the pilot of a light aircraft uncovered 500 kilos of cannabis hidden in a campervan. The aircraft was to have flown the drugs to the UK. White and his closest cohorts were arrested but true to the underworld code, White was saying nothing. Doran and Togher, meanwhile, remained fancy free, although the latter, by choice, decided to tie himself to the lovely Madeleine for life. She was seven months pregnant when, in late October, they flew to Las

Vegas to be married before jetting on to the Caribbean for a honeymoon in Barbados.

There was no sign of the *Frugal*, but the newlyweds met up with Caccavale, who joined them for drinks. And talks. When he flew back to London, he was followed and during a meeting with Doran the Scot was overheard telling him, 'I've got problems with delivery.'

Back home in Chelsea, her new husband would sometimes ask Madeleine to carry bundles of banknotes to a safe-deposit box at Harrods, the world-famous store. She was out shopping in the capital one day in November when she had a scare. Back home, she told Kenny what had upset her. 'The guy was following me. Every time I turned around, he seemed to be there.'

'What did he look like?'

'Untidy, scruffy.'

'Seen him before?'

'No, but I'm sure he was following me.'

'He probably fancied you. Don't worry about it.'

'That's the trouble, Kenny, I do.'

In fact, the writing was on the wall, but Togher couldn't read it. And trouble was brewing, too, for Doran. That month, El Latigo and his troops in Spain announced they had reopened the inquiry into the 1987 hash find in which Whacko and Andy Tait had been among those initially arrested but later freed. Now the police wanted Doran back for further questioning. A judge in Madrid asked Interpol to investigate his whereabouts. But first the British authorities would want to speak to him.

31

QUASHED BUGS

What of the *Frugal?*

Minutes after Doran was spotted using a telephone kiosk on London's Fulham Road, a sign went up saying it was out of order. Back at the main telephone exchange, technicians did a series of complex checks, which showed the number he had been dialling. It was a booking agency, which he had called to arrange a flight to St Lucia in the Windward Islands under the name of Caccavale. Two more names were quickly added to the passenger list: those of male and female Customs officers.

At the beginning of December 1994, all three found themselves at the exclusive Rodney Bay marina in the north of St Lucia, a haven for oceangoing yachts owned by real-estate millionaires from the USA and the finishing point for the internationally renowned 2,700-nautical-mile Atlantic Rally for Cruisers, a prestigious race from Las Palmas de Gran Canaria. The trio arrived amid a hubbub of excitement, as the marina authorities were preparing for the leading boats to dock. This also provided cover for the imminent departure of another vessel, the *Frugal*, which investigators had seen for the first time in eight months.

Days after Caccavale turned up, the catamaran sailed, turning her twin bows into the Atlantic. Those watching guessed her destination was the UK.

On 9 January 1995, the *Frugal* appeared on the radar screen of the Customs ship the *Searcher* as she battled up the English Channel. The Stealer team's objective was to board her before the crew could get rid of the cocaine they were convinced lay below her decks. It was a dangerous task at the best of times, but the notoriously unpredictable weather made the prospect even more daunting. By the following night, the *Frugal* was approaching Pevensey Bay in East Sussex, her navigation lights switched off, intent on berthing near a cottage hired by the smugglers where the cargo would be landed and stashed before being taken by road to London. In torrential rain – so heavy, in fact, visibility was down to a few yards – the *Frugal* signalled to waiting helpers onshore, but missed the point where she ought to have headed inshore and sailed on. The waves were, at times, so high dozens of Customs officers monitoring the shoreline were unable to see the catamaran and had to use mobile radar technology to follow her. As a result, they missed inflatables ferrying the drugs to land. By the time a five-man team on board a Customs raft reached her, the evidence had vanished.

In the early hours, the *Frugal* was escorted to harbour and the entire coastline sealed off, but it was dawn before the drugs were found in six plastic-wrapped bundles dumped on the shore along with wetsuits. A few miles away, a truck was found abandoned after ploughing into a brick wall. Inside was a bag containing false passports. The two men whose job it had been to collect the happy dust, load it and move it to a London warehouse were arrested later, one in the south of England, the other in Spain. Scientists who examined the haul worked out there were 250 kilos of cocaine worth around £37 million. They concluded the venture had been financed by earlier drug runs.

In London, other members of the Stealer squad called at

the BMW showroom where they arrested Doran and Togher. Both vehemently denied having any involvement in the drugs trade. At her Chelsea home that morning, Madeleine was in her dressing gown breastfeeding her 11-day-old daughter, Ivana, when Customs officers and police called and told her she was being arrested on suspicion of being a cocaine trafficker. She spent four months in Holloway prison – Ivana being taken into care – before being freed on bail. After a series of trials at Bristol Crown Court, she was cleared but Doran and Togher were convicted and jailed for 25 years each.

The judge ruled Doran should pay drugs profits of £2,091,084 to the Crown and Togher £2,410,281. El Jock admitted to being involved in the Madrid racket in 1994 and was sentenced for this to nine years.

In 1998, the Court of Appeal in London ruled the judge had misdirected the jury and granted both a retrial. The following year at that hearing, the convictions were quashed and Customs officers severely criticised when it was decided they had not received the necessary authorisation to bug the bedroom of Togher and Madeleine at the Swallow hotel. Additionally, the amount each was ordered to pay in compensation to the Crown was reduced to £800,000. They were told, however, that should they fail to pay up, they would be jailed for an extra four years.

In 2003, both were released after each completing a nine-year sentence. They maintain that the investigations that led to these spells in jail were the result of illicit activity by the Stealer squad.

32

LOVE AND HATE

The Happy Dust Gang set a precedent many have followed.
It is impossible to estimate how many have been successful
– drug smugglers do not advertise their achievements.
Others of course have not been so lucky despite continuing
the tradition of ingenuity.

In September 2002, a shipment of bales of rubber was
intercepted by Customs officers at Felixstowe, Suffolk,
suspicious that the consignment was said to come from
Panama, not known as a rubber exporter. Hidden inside
was cocaine worth £50 million. They replaced it with sand
and pounced on the gang alleged to be behind the racket
when the load reached Kilwinning in Ayrshire. The following
month, a truckload of bananas was used to hide a huge
cocktail of drugs, including 220 lbs of cocaine, as it headed
for a now dead Glasgow drugs baron. Police stopped the
wagon at Abingdon, South Lanarkshire, having tracked it
from Belgium, and later a number of men were jailed.

Cocaine, once confined through financial necessity to
the middle classes, is now so cheaply available that single
mums on government benefits can afford a line. A heavily
cut gramme may change hands for a £20 note. This is

because the motive for smuggling cocaine is no longer pleasure but pure greed.

Those involved with the Happy Dust Gang swear the intention was never to flood Scotland with the drug, rather to satisfy the needs of an elite group. In doing so, they placed Glasgow on a par, if a dubious one, with exotic capital cities around the world where the rich took their pleasures in Charlie. They protest the gang became the victim of a modern-day witch-hunt. There can be no doubt that cocaine dominated and dictated the lives of the gang and its customers, yet at the same time many of those participants would question whether the punishment fitted the crime. It is, of course, fair to argue that the real victims were the families of the Happy Dust Gang, and so it ought to be remembered that the loved ones of those who took the drug for pleasure or through addiction were not allowed a choice in their enforced sacrifices.

The story of the Happy Dust Gang has never before been told and perhaps its most extraordinary feature is the remarkable variation in the fortunes of those involved.

Brian Doran, Whacko, has known five-star-hotel luxury and prison cells, having made and lost a fortune, although the legal authorities believe he has built another through drugs to which they have a right to the lion's share. His devoutly religious wife, Mary, has stuck by him. Associates of the family say she hates the police with a passion, blaming them for the virtual destruction of the marriage. 'If Mary had her way, she would demand justice for the manner in which, as she sees it, the police hounded Brian,' said one. 'She has suffered in the cause of her faith and loyalty to her husband. And she hates the people who supplied him with cocaine. Had it not been for them, he would never have become embroiled in the things he did. He might have gone on making a fortune from the travel business.'

Another wife, Geraldine, who battled and laboured to help her husband, Andy Tait, build up a respected and admired business, has also cast blame, but in her case in the direction of Brian Doran. It is said she constantly warned the baker, 'Be careful of that man; he'll lead you into trouble.' He failed to listen and lost everything.

George Duncan has become highly successful in the food-and-drink business in Utrecht. He and Rosa live in a secluded detached home on the fringe of the city centre. He has worked tirelessly to build up a Glasgow Rangers supporters' base in Holland and speaks fluent Dutch.

Thomas Sim lives modestly in Utrecht and is involved in a demolition company but has little or no contact with his once fellow conspirator.

Robert Bruce also lives and works in Utrecht, occasionally returning to call on his many friends in Glasgow. He too is successful, mainly in the catering trade.

Alan Bartlett now lives in England with his wife, Pamela. He is a director of the extremely successful family firm set up in 1962 and now with a turnover of more than £80 million. His brother and fellow director, Ronnie, still resides in Lanarkshire. Both are well respected and liked.

Ronnie Edgar and Joe Corrigan are retired from the police force and now work in civilian occupations.

The Monkey is dead. Scouse Willie vanished long ago.

Joop and Anna gave up dealing in cocaine after a friend in the same line was shot in the head in a gangland execution the year Brian Doran was extradited from Amsterdam. Scared Joop might be next, they quit their big house and moved to a village on the coast, running a small hotel, knowing thanks to cocaine they would never have to worry or want. Within a year, Anna was pregnant. Now the proud father of three children, he adores his wife and the plump curves she developed during pregnancy and never lost.

On the wall of their sitting room hangs a demure photograph of a young woman in a blue dress. She is pale and drawn. The portrait is one of their friend, Sophie. The French courier, three years after meeting Duncan and Sim, lost her head and her heart to a visiting Frenchman with a heroin habit he passed on to her. When he abandoned her to return home, she tumbled down life's ladder and despite the support and help of Joop and Anna ended up sharing needles with the dregs of Amsterdam. She became HIV positive and after contracting pneumonia died in 1988, with her friends by her bedside, whispering in her native French the name of the long-forgotten mother she said was calling to her.